EGYPT

AND

THE BOOKS OF MOSES,

OR

THE BOOKS OF MOSES ILLUSTRATED BY THE
MONUMENTS OF EGYPT:

WITH AN APPENDIX.

BY

DR E. W. HENGSTENBERG,
PROFESSOR OF THEOL. AT BERLIN.

FROM THE GERMAN
BY R. D. C. ROBBINS,
ABBOT RESIDENT, THEOL. SEM., ANDOVER.

WITH ADDITIONAL NOTES
BY W. COOKE TAYLOR, ESQ., LL.D., M.R.A.S.,
OF TRINITY COLLEGE, DUBLIN.

ISBN: 978-1-63923-638-1

All Rights reserved. No part of this book maybe reproduced without written permission from the publishers, except by a reviewer who may quote brief passages in a review to be printed in a newspaper or magazine.

Printed: January 2023

Published and Distributed By:
Lushena Books
607 Country Club Drive, Unit E
Bensenville, IL 60106
www.lushenabks.com

ISBN: 978-1-63923-638-1

PREFACE.

THE recent interest in the subject of Egyptian antiquities began with the publication of the works of Champollion the younger, about twenty years ago. Since his death, which occurred in 1832, these researches have been prosecuted with much zeal by several of his scholars and other distinguished archaeologists. Two of the learned men of Holland, Professors Reuvens and Leemans, have made important contributions to the subject, derived in part from the treasures of the Leyden Museum. The results of the labours of Rosellini, professor of oriental languages and antiquities at Pisa, are of the highest value. In 1829, he and his brother accompanied Champollion in the scientific expedition to Egypt, which was undertaken under the joint auspices of the governments of France and Tuscany. Champollion, just before his death, committed to him the honourable office of bringing before the world the result of their associated labours and studies. The first part of the great work of Rosellini, which is yet incomplete, appeared in 1832, at Pisa, in folio, entitled, "I monumenti dell' Egitto e della Nubia disegnati della Spedizione scientifico-letteraria toscana in Egitto, distribuiti in ordine di materie, interpretat ed illuistrati." Through the liberality of the Grand Duke of Tuscany, it is brought out in the highest style of typography.

It consists of a series of treatises which embrace the most important results of the investigations into the history and civil institutions of the ancient Pharaoh-dynasties, under the Pagan, Greek, and Roman dominion. The contents of the work are as rich as the plan is comprehensive. It abounds in researches relating to the languages, civil history, and history of the arts in the valley of the Nile. Rosellini published in Rome, in 1837, in quarto, a valuable Egyptian grammar, entitled, "Elementae Linguae Egyptiacae, vulgo Copticae."

In this interesting field of research, several Englishmen have acquired high distinction. Among these are Dr Young, Major Felix, Lord Prudhoe, and Sir Gardner Wilkinson. Dr Young shares with Champollion the honour of having first indicated the right method of deciphering the hieroglyphical language. To Mr Wilkinson justly belongs the encomium which he has himself bestowed on Rosellini. "He is a man of erudition and a gentleman, and one whose enthusiastic endeavours, stimulated by great perseverance, are tempered by judgment, and that modesty which is the characteristic of real merit." Mr Wilkinson's principal works on Egypt are contained in nine volumes, namely, "A general View of Egypt, and Topography of Thebes," in two vols. (a new edition was published in 1843), and "Manners and Customs of the ancient Egyptians, including their private life, government, laws, arts, manufactures, religion, and early history," in two series of three volumes in each. A second edition of the first series was published in 1842. These works are full of most valuable materials, accompanied with many fine illustrations. They everywhere exhibit that caution, sound judgment, modesty, and enthusiasm, which greatly delight the reader. At the same time, the arrangement is susceptible of improvement, while the style is somewhat heavy, and wanting in precision and scholarlike finish. It is delightful to observe the reverence with which the author regards the sacred volume, and the gratification which every undoubted illustration of its authenticity affords him. He has now, for the fourth time, we believe, taken up his abode in Egypt.

Another distinguished investigator in these fascinating studies is Dr Richard Lepsius, a native of Naumburg, in Prussia. He published, in 1834, a prize dissertation, entitled "Palaeographie als Mittel für die Sprachforschung zunächst am Sanscrit nachgewiesen." His studies led him to Turin and then to Rome, where he was appointed one of the two corresponding secretaries of the Archaeological Institute there. In 1842, Dr Lepsius was sent to Egypt by the Prussian government, in connection with a number of other learned men. He is reaping "a rich harvest on this earliest scene of the history of mankind." If the results of the expedition correspond to the promises of the commencement, much new light will be thrown on the ancient condition of Egypt.

These researches derive special importance from the light which they cast upon the Old Testament records, especially upon the Mosaic history. An incidental, undesigned, but most valuable proof is thus drawn from witnesses that cannot lie, in favour of the trustworthiness of those records. "Paintings, numerous and beautiful beyond conception, as fresh and perfect as if finished only yesterday," exhibit before our eyes the truth of what the Hebrew lawgiver wrote, almost five thousand years ago. The authenticity of the documents of our faith thus rests, not on manuscripts and written records alone, but the hardest and most enduring substances in nature have added their unsuspecting testimony.

"Egyptian history and the manners of the most ancient nations," Mr Wilkinson remarks, "cannot but be interesting to every one; and so intimately connected are they with the scriptural accounts of the Israelites and the events of succeeding ages relative to Judea, that the name of Egypt need only to be mentioned to recal the early impressions we have received from the study of the Bible."

It is the object of the present volume to collect and apply the results obtained by these and numerous other authors, as far as they relate to the Books of Moses. This had not been done before the appearance of this work in 1840. Even the most recent German commentators are sadly deficient in this respect. They have scarcely made any advance upon the works of Spencer and Le Clerc, who wrote more than a century ago. Some of the other works of the author of this volume, Dr E. W. Hengstenberg, are too well known in this country to render a statement of his general qualifications for the work which he has here undertaken necessary. It may, however, be proper to say, that he has made the Pentateuch a subject of special study, and probably no one in Germany or elsewhere has devoted more attention to that interesting, but too much neglected portion of the sacred volume. His situation as Professor at Berlin also gave him access to the rich collection of Egyptian antiquities in the Berlin Museum, and the reader is left to judge whether he has not made good use of his advantages.

The form of the work has been somewhat changed in the translation. The references to authorities, which in the original volume were in the text, are thrown to the bottom of the page. Nearly all of the italic headings have been inserted. In a very few cases, notes, which it was thought would add more to the size than value of the volume to an English reader, have been omitted or abridged. In one instance, a long note from another untranslated work of the author, has been inserted in the text. The very few notes at the end have been added by the translator. It was his intention to insert many more, but they have been unavoidably omitted.

The translator is under great obligations to Prof. H. B. Hackett, of Newton Theological Seminary, who consented to listen to a large part of the manuscript before it was printed, and make such corrections as his accurate knowledge of the German language suggested. Much valuable advice and assistance has also been received from Professor B. B. Edwards, of Andover Theological Seminary.

ANDOVER, *September*, 1843.

ADDENDUM BY THE ENGLISH EDITOR.

A NEW field of Biblical Criticism has been opened by the recent discoveries in the tombs and temples of Egypt; the memorials of their manners, customs, and institutions, which the people of the Pharaohs depicted on the walls of their sepulchres, afford a decisive, because an unsuspicious, test of the historical veracity of the Old Testament, and they have furnished confirmations of its minute accuracy, which must silence where they do not convince the most sceptical. Dr Hengstenberg has ably employed these new sources of evidence to overthrow the rash theory of Bohlen, that the sacred books of the Jews were written at a period posterior to the Babylonish captivity; it is to be regretted, that while exposing the groundless theories of others, he should himself have shown some tendency to adopt a scarcely less dangerous error, by throwing doubts on the originality, and consequently on the inspired character of the Mosaic legislation. In republishing his work in England, the Editor has deemed it advisable to examine the nature of the doubts which Dr Hengstenberg raised, and to take advantage of the most recent researches as tests of their validity. He has found, that the more closely the subject is investigated, the more clearly does it appear that the code of Jewish law was derived from no previously existing institutions, and that, on the contrary, it is in all its parts marked by a peculiar individuality such as no other Theocracy ever possessed.

The proofs of this will be found in the notes appended to the English edition. Some other notes have been added, more fully illustrative of the connection between the pictorial records of Egypt, and the written records of Moses, than Hengstenberg's plan admitted.

A supplemental Chapter has been added, for the purpose of examining Dr Hengstenberg's theory respecting the Hycsos; though this is but an incidental topic, it has a very important bearing on the main argument, and the discussion involves many points of great interest to all students of general history.

W. C. T.

CAMDEN TOWN, *November* 9, 1844.

CONTENTS.

NEGATIVE PART.

	Page
Material used for Building in Egypt,	1
The Animals of Egypt and the Pentateuch,	3
Use of Animal Food in Egypt,	8
Winds of Egypt,	9
Cultivation of the Vine in Egypt,	13
Origin of Civilization in Egypt,	18
Use of Iron in Egypt,	19

POSITIVE PART.

CHAPTER I.

THE HISTORY OF JOSEPH. GEN. CHAPS. XXXVII—XL.

Joseph carried to Egypt and sold to Potiphar,	21
Joseph's Exaltation,	24
Joseph's Temptation and the Morals of the Egyptians,	25
The Dream of the Chief Baker of Pharaoh,	27
Pharaoh's Dream and the Magicians of Egypt,	27
The Hair and Beard—how worn in Egypt,	30
Dress and Ornaments of the Egyptians,	30
The Marriage of Joseph,	32
Joseph collects the Produce of the Seven Years of Plenty,	36
Famine in Egypt and the adjoining Countries,	37
Joseph, his Brethren, and the Egyptians, *sit* at an Entertainment,	38
The Practice of Divining by Cups,	39
The Arrival of Jacob and his Family in Egypt, and their Settlement in Goshen,	40

CONTENTS.

REFERENCES OF THE PENTATEUCH TO THE GEOGRAPHICAL FEATURES OF EGYPT.

The Land of Goshen,	42
Location of Pharaoh's Treasure-Cities—Pithom and Raamses,	47
The March of the Israelites from Raamses to the Red Sea,	55
"Between Migdol and the Sea,"	58

HISTORY OF JOSEPH—*continued.*

Kings and Priests, the Possessors of the Land in Egypt,	60
Embalming, Lamentation for the Dead, &c.,	66
APPENDIX TO CHAPTER I. by the Editor,	73

CHAPTER II.

EXODUS, CHAPTERS I—VII.

The Fears of Pharaoh and his Severity to the Israelites,	78
Use of the Papyrus and Bitumen in Egypt,	85
The Daughter of Pharaoh finds the Child, Moses,	86
The Israelites directed to borrow of the Egyptians Ornaments, &c.,	86
Moses's Rod,	87
Writing, much practised in Egypt,	88
Preparation of Stone for Inscriptions,	90
The Bastinado,	90
The Shoterim of the Israelites, the same as the modern Sheikh el-Beled,	91
The Duties of the Shoterim,	92
The Arrogance of the Pharaohs,	92

CHAPTER III.

THE SIGNS AND WONDERS IN EGYPT.

The Connection of the Supernatural with the Natural in the Plagues of Egypt,	95
Moses's Rod changed to a Serpent,	98
The First Plague—the Water of Egypt changed to Blood,	103
The Second Plague—the Frogs,	111
The Third Plague—the כִּנִּם, Gnats,	112
The Fourth Plague—the Flies,	112
The Fifth Plague—the Destruction of the Animals in Egypt,	115
The Sixth Plague—the Boils,	115
The Seventh Plague—the Tempest,	116

CONTENTS.   xi

The Eighth Plague—the Locusts,   -   -   -   -   -   119
The Ninth Plague—The Darkness,   -   -   -   -   -   120
The Tenth Plague—The Death of the First-born of the Egyptians,   123

CHAPTER IV.

EXODUS, CHAPTERS XIV. AND XV.

The Military force of the Egyptians,   -   -   -   -   -   126
Musical Instruments among the Egyptians,   -   -   -   -   129

CHAPTER V.

THE MATERIALS AND ARTS EMPLOYED IN THE CONSTRUCTION OF THE
TABERNACLE AND PRIESTS' GARMENTS.

Cultivation of the Arts among the Egyptians and Israelites,   -   133
The Art of Cutting and Setting precious Stones,   -   -   -   134
The Art of Purifying and Working Metals,   -   -   -   -   135
Skill in Carving Wood,   -   -   -   -   -   -   -   138
Use of Leather,   -   -   -   -   -   -   -   -   138
Spinning, Weaving, and Embroidery,   -   -   -   -   -   139
Preparation and Use of Unguents,   -   -   -   -   -   - 142

CHAPTER VI.

EGYPTIAN REFERENCES IN THE RELIGIOUS INSTITUTIONS OF THE BOOKS OF
MOSES.

Law among the Egyptians and Israelites,   -   -   -   -   144
The Stuff and Colour of the Priests' Garments,   -   -   -   145
Urim and Thummim,   -   -   -   -   -   -   -   -   149
The Cherubim and the Sphinxes,   -   -   -   -   -   -   153
The Figure and Significance of the Sphinxes,   -   -   -   - 153
The Cherubim—their Form and Import,   -   -   -   -   -   156
Leviticus, chap. xvi. Azazel,   -   -   -   -   -   -   159
Numbers, chap. xix.   -   -   -   -   -   -   -   - 173
Laws with Reference to Food,   -   -   -   -   -   -   180
The Institution of the Holy Women,   -   -   -   -   -   184
The Nazarites,   -   -   -   -   -   -   -   -   - 190

CHAPTER VII.

MISCELLANEOUS PASSAGES.

The Genealogical Table in Gen. x.,	195
Abraham and Sarah in Egypt—Gen. xii.,	199
Genesis xiii. 10,	201
Exodus xx. 25,	202
The Festival of the Golden Calf, &c., Ex. xxxii. and Lev. xvii. 7.,	202
Prohibition of Marriage between near Relatives, Lev. xviii.,	205
Defilement with Animals, Lev. xviii. 23; Exod. xxii. 18, &c.,	206
Leviticus xxiv. 10—12,	207
Numbers xi. 4,	208
The Grass (helbeh), חָצִיר,	208
The Fish,	210
The Cucumber,	212
Melons, אֲבַטִּיחִים,	213
Onions,	213
The Garlic,	214
Numbers xvii. 2,	214
Deuteronomy vi. 9, and xi. 20,	215
The Diseases of Egypt severe. Deut. vii. 15.; xxviii. 27, 35, 60. Exod. xv. 26,	215
Cultivation of the Land in Egypt and Palestine. Deut. xi. 10, 11,	217
Deuteronomy xvii. 16.	222
Kind Treatment of the Israelites by individual Egyptians, Deut. xxiii. 8, (7),	222
Deuteronomy xxiii. 12, 13,	223
Threshing with Oxen. Deut. xxv. 4.	223
Deuteronomy xxviii. 56,	224
Deuteronomy v. 15; iv. 20; vi. 20 seq.; vii. 8. &c.,	225

APPENDIX.

MANETHO AND THE HYCSOS.

I. Manetho,	227
II. The Hycsos of Manetho,	245

EGYPT AND THE BOOKS OF MOSES.

NEGATIVE PART.

It is incumbent on us, first, in the negative part of our inquiry, to disprove the pretended "mistakes and inaccuracies" of the author of the Pentateuch, in relation to Egypt. By these, as has lately been asserted, he has betrayed, that he lived out of Egypt, and long after the time of Moses.

MATERIAL USED FOR BUILDING IN EGYPT.

The author, says *von Bohlen*,[1] comes under strong suspicion of having transferred to the valley of the Nile, many things from Upper Asia; as the Egyptians were accustomed to build with hewn stone, and the great buildings of brick, Ex. i. 14, instead of being Egyptian, seem rather to have been borrowed from Babylonia.

[1] Einleitung zur Genesis, S. LV. Von Bohlen (Peter) was born at Wäppels in 1796, of poor parents, and was left an orphan in 1811. In 1817 he was received into the Gymnasium at Hamburg, where he turned his attention to oriental studies. He was the pupil of Gesenius, Roediger and Hoffmann, in the University at Halle, in 1821; and in 1822 he went to Bonn and attended upon the instructions of Freytag and Schlegel. In 1825 he was elected Professor extraordinary of Oriental Languages at Königsberg, and regular Professor at the same place in 1830. He has since removed to Berlin. His work, so often referred to in this volume, is entitled, "Die Genesis historischcritisch erläutert," Königsberg, 1835. It was answered by Drechsler, at Leipsic, in 1837. The neological sentiments of the author may be easily inferred from the quotations and references made by *Hengstenberg*. Allusion is also made in this volume, in one or two cases, to his book on India: "Das alte Indien mit besonderer Rücksicht auf Aegypten." He has published several other works which are somewhat known in Germany.

We can scarcely trust our own eyes, when we read such things. Is it possible that any one who undertakes to comment upon the Pentateuch, and even ventures to accuse its author of ignorance in relation to Egyptian affairs, can show himself grossly uninformed in these same things, and make assertions whose incorrectness is conclusively shown by the first good compendium!

In a case like the one before us, any one would first of all have recourse to *O. Müller's* Archæologia.[1] There we read: "Building with brick was very common in Egypt. Private edifices were indeed generally of this material."

If we examine further, *Herodotus*[2] mentions a pyramid of brick,[3] which is probably still standing.[4]

But we are literally overwhelmed with proofs of the abundant use of brick in Egypt, when we turn to those who, during the present century, have explored the Egyptian monuments. *Champollion*,[5] for example, speaks of a tomb built of crude brick at Sais, and a temple of brick at Wady Halfa.[6] *Rosellini*[7] says: "Ruins of great brick buildings are found in all parts of Egypt. Walls of astonishing height and thickness are preserved to the present time, as, for example, the circumvallation of Sais; also whole pyramids, as those of Dashoor, and a great number of the ruins of monuments, both great and small." *Wilkinson*[8] says: "The use of crude brick, baked in the sun, was universal in Upper and Lower Egypt, both for public and private buildings. Enclosures of gardens and granaries, sacred circuits encompassing the courts of temples, walls of fortifications and towns, dwelling-houses and tombs, in short, *all* but the temples themselves, were of crude brick." The same author shows that building with brick was practised even in very early times, since the bricks themselves,

---

[1] § 226. [2] 2. 136.

[3] Four built of brick are still in existence in Lower Egypt, two at Dashoor and two at the entrance of the Fyoom. Several of smaller size are also found in Thebes. See *Wilkinson*, Vol. I. 131, and III. 317.

[4] See Bähr upon the passage. Mannert Geog. 10. 1. S. 444, 67. Macrizi, in his description of the condition of Egypt under the Mameluke Sultans, mentions a pyramid of brick in Lower Egypt, which is probably the same as that noticed by Herodotus.   T.

[5] In den Briefen aus Aeg. S. 14 der. Deutsch. Uehers.   [6] S. 83.

[7] I monumenti dell' Egitto e della Nubia, II. 2, p. 249.

[8] Manners and Customs of the Ancient Egyptians. London, 1842, Vol. II. p. 96.

both in Thebes and the neighbourhood of Memphis, often bear the names of the monarchs who ruled Egypt in that early age.[1]

THE ANIMALS OF EGPYT AND THE PENTATEUCH.

The author, remarks *v. Bohlen* further in the passage referred to, supposes the existence of camels and asses in Egypt. The allegation, as fully stated by him, with his reasons,[2] is as follows : " The narrator mentions the animals of his own native land, a part of which Abraham could not receive in Egypt. Gen. xlv. 23. xlvii. 17. Ex. ix. 3. He ascribes to him no *horses* which were native to Egypt, as the relator indeed is aware, Gen. xli. 43, xlvii. 17 ; but, on the other hand, he mentions *sheep,* which are found in the marsh lands of Egypt as seldom as *camels* (hence these last are denied to the country by the ancient writers) and *asses,* which were especially odious to the Egyptians on account of their colour."

It is said in the passage designated : " And he [Pharaoh] entreated Abraham well for her sake ; and he had sheep, and oxen, and he-asses, and men servants, and maid servants, and she-asses, and camels."

We inquire, first, why the *horse* is not also among the presents. Even *v. Bohlen* dares not assert that this circumstance is accounted for, by supposing that the author did not know how abundant horses were in Egypt. In the enumeration of the animals of the Egyptians, in Gen. xlvii. 17, horses stand first, also in Ex. ix. 3. The rearing of horses is considered in the Pentateuch as so peculiar to Egypt, that in Deut. xvii. 16, it is represented as possible, that an Israelitish king, merely from love to the horse, might wish to lead back the people to Egypt. If now the reason why horses are not mentioned cannot be found on the part of the giver, it must be found with the receiver. It appears

[1] As *Hengstenberg* has not given the precise dates here, it may be proper to add, that arches were constructed of brick at least as early as 1540, B. C. in the reign of Amunoph I., and probably in the time of the first Osirtasen, who is supposed by *Wilkinson* to have been contemporary with Joseph. " It is worthy of remark," says the same author, " that more bricks bearing the name of Thothmes III. (whom I suppose to have been king of Egypt at the time of the Exodus,) have been discovered, than of any other period."

[2] S. 163, upon Gen. xii. 16.

that horses were not yet in use among the Israelites, either in peace or war, at the time of Joshua and the Judges.[1] They were first commonly used in the time of the kings. But if the horse was not yet used by the Israelites, at the time of Joshua and the Judges, much less was it surely in the age of the Pentateuch, when the main object, which the keeping of horses subserved in Egypt, did not exist.[2] If now this is the reason why the horse does not appear in the enumeration of the presents, it is entirely in favour of the true historical character and Mosaic origin of the narration. If it owed its origin to the poetic tradition of the time of the kings, horses would certainly have been mentioned, since we cannot suppose that the time of the introduction of them was accurately known, and still less that the fiction was so carefully managed for the sake of maintaining historical consistency. But we need not stop with merely the present passage. The Pentateuch in other places continually implies that in the ancient times with which it is concerned, there were no horses among the patriarchs and their descendants. "Moses," says *Michaelis*, "repeatedly describes to us the riches of the patriarchs, as consisting of their herds, among which, while oxen, sheep, goats, camels and asses are enumerated, we never once find horses mentioned."[3] The tabernacle was drawn by oxen in the desert, Num. vii. 3. That a great number of horses could not be conveniently kept in Egypt, is implied in Deut. xvii. 16. These facts, according to modern views respecting the Pentateuch, are entirely inexplicable. They compel us at least to the assumption, that the composition of the narration precedes the time of the commencement of the kingdom, while at the same time the attempts to refer the substance of the history in the books of Joshua and Judges to later

---

[1] See J. D. Michaelis, Mosaic Laws, Eng. Trans. Vol. II. p. 434.

[2] From the monuments we learn that horses were used chiefly in war, especially for drawing chariots, in which the most distinguished Egyptian warriors rode to battle. Solomon was the first ruler of the Hebrews who formed an efficient corps of cavalry, and he obtained most of his horses from Egypt. As Abraham was a peaceful patriarch, who avoided war even under circumstances of great provocation, a gift of animals rarely used at the period would have been every way unsuitable. The omission of the horse then, instead of being an objection, is one of the strongest possible of undesigned confirmations of the truth of the narrative. T.

[3] Mich. Mos. Laws, Eng. Trans. Vol. II. p. 436. Compare Gen. xx. 14, xxiv. 35, xxvi. 14, xxx. 41, xxxii. 6, 8, 15, 16.

times, have also a formidable obstacle in the apparently trivial circumstance, that in them the horse is not represented as in use. Let it be borne in mind here, that we find nowhere a historical notice of the time of the introduction of horses, that they were in all probability introduced gradually, and that the Israelites did not probably know that which a scholar of the last century, by a laborious comparison of many scattered passages, has made entirely certain.

It has occurred to no one before *v. Bohlen* to deny, that there were *asses* in Egypt. All of the authors who speak of the hatred of the Egyptians to this animal, imply that it existed there.[1] How, also, could they otherwise have been sacrificed to Typhon. Swine too were considered unclean in Egypt, yet they were kept.[2] He and she-asses appear in great numbers on the monuments. The former were commonly used for riding—we find them represented with rich trappings,—the latter as beasts of burden.[3] A single individual is represented on the monuments, as having 760 of them, which makes it evident that they were very numerous.[4]

The assertion that *sheep*[5] were not found in Egypt, every me-

[1] Compare the passage in Schmidt, de sacerd. et sacrif. Aeg. p. 283.
[2] Herod. 2. 47, 48. Schmidt, p. 269.
[3] Taylor, pp. 6, 7. This distinction is noticed in the account of the presents sent by Joseph to Jacob, when he invited the patriarch to Egypt: "And to his father he sent after this manner; ten asses laden with the good things of Egypt, and ten she-asses laden with corn and bread and meat for his father by the way," Gen. xlv. 23.   T.
[4] Wilkinson, Vol. III. p. 34.
[5] *Wilkinson*, in his "Manners and Customs of the Ancient Egyptians," second series, Vol. I. pp. 130, 131, &c. gives the representation of a scene from a tomb hewn in the rock near the pyramids of Geezeh, which is of special interest as illustrating several points in Egyptian antiquity. The tomb bears the name of the king Suphis or Cheops, which shows it, at least, to be the work of an age before the 18th dynasty, and in all probability it was made about 2090 or 2050 B. C., more than a century before the arrival of Abraham in Egypt. The head shepherd presents himself to give an account of the flocks committed to his charge which follow after him. "First come the oxen, over which is the number 834, cows 220, goats 3234, asses 760, and sheep 974. Behind follows a man carrying the young lambs in baskets slung upon a pole. The steward, leaning on his staff and accompanied by his dog, stands on the left of the picture; and in another part of the tomb, the scribes are represented making out the statements presented to them by the different persons employed on the estate." The bearing of this painting upon several

dern manual of Geography confutes. *Ukert*[1] says, "Sheep are found in great numbers in Egypt. Their wool is an important article of trade, and their flesh is the most common which comes upon the table."[2] Ancient authors often mention the sheep of Egypt. According to *Herodotus*,[3] rams were considered sacred by the Thebans, and sheep were sacrificed by the inhabitants of the Mendesian nome[4] in the Delta. *Plutarch* says, the Lycopolites ate the flesh of sheep, and according to *Diodorus*,[5] the sheep produced their young twice in a year, and were twice shorn. Sheep appear on the monuments often and in great numbers. Large herds of them were kept, especially in the neighbourhood of Memphis. Sometimes the flocks consisted of more than two thousand.[6]

That the *camel* existed in ancient Egypt is indeed probable from the analogy of the present time.[7] It is acknowledged that they have not yet been found delineated on the monuments,[8]

quent parts of this volume should not be unnoticed; compare especially pp. 25, 87.

[1] Nordhälfte von Afrika, S. 169.

[2] Compare, on rearing sheep in Egypt, Girard in the Description, t. 17, p. 129 seq. The assertion that sheep were unknown in Egypt, where the ram (Ammon) was notoriously an object of religious worship, is as extraordinary an instance of theoretic rashness as Neology has ever produced. T.

[3] 2. 41. and 2. 42.

[4] *Nome, province*, from the Greek νομός, is the name given to each of the 36 parts into which Sesostris divided Egypt.

[5] 1. 36. and 87.

[6] See Wilk. Vol. II. p. 368. Champollion, Briefe, S. 51, according to whom the treading down of the ground by rams is represented in the grottoes of Beni Hassan, 53.

[7] Ukeri, S. 169. Girard in the Description, t. 17, p. 128, says: "The camels which are used in Saïd for the transportation of all kinds of freight, unless it is sent by water upon the Nile or upon the canals, are inferior in size and strength to those in Lower Egypt. The raising of these animals is one of the chief employments of the Arabs who dwell upon the borders of the valley of Egypt. They furnish the markets of different provinces with them. The camels which are used for the transportation of the harvest, do not always belong to the husbandman. He hires them as he needs them. During the remainder of the year, he makes use of the ass. There is no land-owner who does not possess several asses," &c. According to t. 15, p. 215 of the Descr., the camels of the Delta are less valued than those of the provinces which border upon the desert.

[8] Wilk. I. p. 351.

except those scattered traces which *Minutoli*[1] thinks that he discovered on the obelisks of Luxor. But this circumstance, at most, only proves that camels were not very abundant in Egypt, and even that not with entire certainty.[2] The Pentateuch itself also intimates the same thing, since in the passage under consideration, camels are mentioned last, and in chap. xlv. 23, not at all. A multitude of objects, which can be demonstrated to have existed among the ancient Egyptians are wanting in their paintings. In the numerous hunting scenes, for example, the wild boar is not seen, although it is a native of Egypt. The wild ass, which is common in the deserts of Thebaid, is also not met with.[3] Even fowls and pigeons, which Egypt had in so great abundance, do not appear, while "geese are repeatedly introduced."[4] Of others objects, which, although they certainly existed, are not found upon the monuments, the same author speaks on page 254, Vol. III., with which compare too what is said on page 344 of the same volume, concerning the great deficiency of the monuments.

---

[1] Reise, S. 293. Minutoli, Henry, Baron Menu Von, born at Geneva, of a Savoyard family, in 1772, is best known by his antiquarian researches in Egypt. He went to that country in 1820, and returned in 1822. A part of his collection of antiquities was lost by a shipwreck. The remainder, purchased by the king of Prussia for about 15000 fr., were deposited in the new museum at Berlin. His most distinguished work is the "Journey to the Temple of Jupiter Ammon in the desert of Lybia," Berlin, 1824. He published "Additions to his Journey," &c. in 1827.

[2] The absence of any particular animal from the monuments, is by no means a proof that it was unknown in the country; especially when we have decisive evidence of the converse of the case—the appearance of an animal on the monuments, not mentioned by any ancient writer in connection with Egypt. I allude to the giraffe or camelopard, which appears more than once among the articles of tribute brought down from southern Africa to the Pharaohs. It is no difficult matter to account for the omission of camels on the monuments: the great object of Egyptian policy, so long as the country was subject to native princes, was to train a settled agricultural people; but the camel, or "ship of the desert," as it is poetically named by the Bedouins, was, as it still continues to be, peculiarly the animal of nomade life. Even at the present day, camels are chiefly bred by the Arabs on the borders of Egypt, and are only hired by the agriculturists for transport as they are needed.   T.

[3] Wilk. III. p. 21.

[4] Wilk. p. 35. In an Egyptian fresco preserved in the British museum, representing a garden and pleasure-ground, geese and ducks are depicted swimming in the ponds.   T.

USE OF ANIMAL FOOD IN EGYPT.

"The author," says *v. Bohlen*,[1] "represents Joseph, Gen. xliii. 16, in most manifest opposition to the sacredness of beasts to prepare flesh for food." In his commentary[2] it is said: "The Egyptians partake, at most, of consecrated flesh-offerings, and the higher castes, especially the priests with whom Joseph was connected by marriage, abstain entirely from animal food." Further:[3] "The hatred of this people to foreign shepherds is founded on the inviolableness of animals, especially of neat cattle, goats and *sheep*, (the author forgets he has denied the existence of these animals in Egypt), which were killed by the shepherds, but accounted sacred by the Egyptians."

Our astonishment at the condition of our great critic's knowledge of Egypt is here again not a little increased, and the credulity with which so many use such an author's work on India as good authority, becomes, after the successive developments of his ignorance, unaccountable to us. No one before *v. Bohlen* has ever thought of asserting that the Egyptians abstain from all animal food. The contrary is found in all works of acknowledged authority. *Heeren*,[4] for example, says: "Oxen are commonly used for food and offerings." And *Beck*:[5] "The Egyptians abstain from the flesh of several animals, some of them sacred, as the cow, and some of them otherwise, as from swine's flesh." How also can any one doubt that the Egyptians ate flesh, when *Herodotus* alone furnishes abundant proof of the fact? According to 2. 18, cows only, not oxen, were sacred among the Egyptians; in 2. 168, the quantity of the flesh of oxen received daily, by each Egyptian warrior, is mentioned. According to 2. 69, even crocodile's flesh was eaten by the inhabitants of Elephantine; but the most important passage is 2. 37, where it is said that the Egyptian *priests* receive each day a large portion of flesh.[6] Even *Porphyry*[7] himself merely says, that at *certain times* the Egyptian priests ab-

[1] S. LV. [2] S. 399. [3] S. 397, upon Gen. xliii. 16.
[4] In den Ideen, Aegypten, S. 170.
[5] In der Weltgeschichte, 1, 1. S. 763.
[6] Καὶ κρεῶν βοίων καὶ χηνίων πλῆθός τι ἑκάστῳ γίνεται μολλὸν ἡμέρις ἑκάστης.
[7] In Schmidt, p. 62.

stain from animal food. In this state of things we scarcely need to take the trouble to mention, that upon the monuments, in kitchen scenes and the delineation of feasts, animal food appears in abundance.[1]

THE WINDS OF EGYPT.

"The author," we read further in *v. Bohlen*,[2] "mistakes so materially with regard to the natural phenomena of the country, that he transfers there the scorching east wind of Palestine," Gen. xli. 6, and represents the ebb in the Red Sea as produced by this same wind. In his commentary[3] on the passage above referred to, it is said, When there is a cool and refreshing east wind along the Arabian Gulf in Egypt, it is cut off from the Nile by the eastern mountain range, the Mokattam, and cannot even press in, much less then scorch the ears of corn.[4] On the contrary, it is the south which is the hot wind in Egypt.[5] A similar error is found in Ex. xvi. 13, where the locusts should be represented as coming with the south wind out of Nubia.

We will first examine Gen. xli. 6,[6] where the seven thin ears, and "blasted with the east wind," are mentioned.

The quotation from *Abdollatiph*, by which it is said to be proved, that there is no east wind in Egypt, is not conclusive. That author himself shows[7] that he does not intend to be understood as speaking of all of Egypt, and particularly not of the part with which we are here concerned, the Delta: "For this reason without doubt the ancient Egyptians chose for the residence of their kings, Memphis and the places which like Memphis are most remote from the eastern mountains."

---

[1] Wilk. Vol. II. p. 368. There is in the Egyptian room of the British Museum, a stand on which are the remains of some of the animals cooked for an Egyptian feast, in a wonderful state of preservation. Rosellini has given a representation of an Egyptian kitchen, which was probably attached to a palace; the servants are represented as slaughtering and cutting up a great variety of animals, under the superintendence of the head-cook, who appears, even in the age of the Pharaohs, to have been a person of importance. T.

[2] S. LVI. [3] S. 381.
[4] Abdollatiph, p. 16. Hasselquist, 254. [5] Abdollatiph, p. 19.
[6] Compare verses 23, 27 of the same chap. [7] P. 5. De Sacy.

It is conceded, that there is seldom a wind directly from the east or west in Egypt.[1] But there is oftentimes a south-east wind, which is precisely the one to produce the effects which are here ascribed to the east wind; and besides, it blows commonly at the time in which these things are understood to have taken place, before the corn harvest, which in Egypt is in March and April.[2]

Ukert[3] thus sums up the accounts of modern travellers with regard to the east wind: "In the spring the south wind oftentimes springs up towards the south-east, increasing to a whirlwind, &c. The heat then seems insupportable, although the thermometer does not always rise very high. The south wind is called Merisi, the south-east, Asiab or Chamsin. As long as the south-east wind continues, doors and windows are closed, but the fine dust penetrates everywhere; every thing dries up; wooden vessels warp and crack. The thermometer rises suddenly from 16—20 degrees up to 30, 36, and even 38 degrees of Reaumur. This wind works destruction upon every thing. The grass withers so that it entirely perishes, if this wind blows long."

Volney[4] says: "The south and south-east wind produce no dew, since they come from the African and Arabian deserts. But the north and west winds bring the evaporations of the Mediterranean to Egypt. In March the *south-east*, the due south, and the south-west winds, prevail. Then they become sometimes westerly, and sometimes northerly and easterly."

That this south-east wind[5] is here designated by the word

---

[1] Rüppell in Ukert, S. 113.
[2] Nordmeier calend. Aeg. oecon. p. 29. From the unpublished journal of a traveller at present in Egypt, the following extract may be taken, in confirmation of what Hengstenberg has stated: "I thought that the south wind was intolerable, but it has veered round several points to the east this morning, and every change it makes in that direction renders its effects more and more oppressive." T.
[3] S. 111. [4] Voyage En Syrie et in Egypte, t. 1, pp. 54, 55.
[5] Numerous books of travels might be referred to, in which easterly winds in Egypt are mentioned. But it is unnecessary. *Russell*, in his Ancient and Modern Egypt, says: "About the autumnal equinox they (the winds) veer round to the east, where they remain nearly six weeks, with only slight deviations." Although this declaration may not be *strictly* correct, yet it is an additional testimony to the fact, that they have easterly winds in Egypt, which is all that is needed here; for it is uni-

קָדִים, which commonly signifies, east wind, is not surprising, since the Hebrews had terms only for the four principal winds; and besides, if a more accurate designation had been possible, it would still have been entirely unsuitable here in relating a dream. But we can even quote a traveller who does not scruple to designate the south-east as merely the east. *Wansleb*[1] says: "From Easter to Pentecost is the most stormy part of the year; for the wind commonly blows, during this time, from the Red Sea, from the east."

So much upon Gen. xli. 6. We do not trouble ourselves with Ex. xiv., since the assertion, that the east wind is not the appropriate one, depends upon the arbitrary supposition, that the passage of the Red Sea took place at the time of the ebb tide. There is therefore now remaining to us only Ex. x. 13.

V. Bohlen is not the first who has thought the mentioning of the east wind here a suspicious circumstance. *Bochart*,[2] as long ago as his time, supposed that קָדִים must in this place signify the south wind, since the east wind could bring locusts hither only out of Arabia, while the south wind would bring them from Ethiopia, which produces them in far greater numbers. *Eckhorn*[3] says: "Since the locusts, from blind instinct, always move from south to north, without ever turning to the east or west, their swarms never come out of Arabia to Egypt, but always from Ethiopia."

---

versally acknowledged by Hebrew scholars, that any wind from the eastern quarter of the heavens would be designated by a Hebrew as east wind. The following extract from Prof. *Robinson's* Biblical Researches is introduced, not only from its appropriateness in this connection, but as furnishing a similar style of reasoning to that employed by *Hengstenberg*, in treating of the plagues in Egypt, in chapter iii. of this volume: "The Lord, it is said, caused the sea to go (or flow out) *by a strong east wind*. The miracle, therefore, is represented as mediate; not a direct suspension of, or interference with the laws of nature, but a miraculous adaptation of those laws to produce a required result. It was wrought by natural means supernaturally applied. For this reason we are here entitled to look only for the natural effects arising from the operation of such a cause. In the somewhat indefinite phraseology of the Hebrew, an east wind means any wind from the eastern quarter; and would include the northeast wind, which often prevails in this region."—Vol. I. pp. 82, 3.

[1] In Paulus Reisen Th. III. p. 18.   [2] Hieroz. 3. p. 287.
[3] De Aeg. anno mirabili, p. 26.

It is certain, without argument, that the author has here neither used קָדִים with the signification of south wind, nor inadvertently named the east where the south should be; but that, on the contrary, with clear knowledge of the natural relations of Egypt, he meant to say, that the locusts came hither from the east, from the Arabian Gulf. This is clear from verse 19 : " And the Lord turned a mighty strong west wind, which took away the locusts, and cast them into the Red Sea." *The west wind*, which is expressly represented as the opposite of קָדִים, carries the locusts directly back to the region whence they came.

It cannot therefore be asserted that the author betrays himself, and incautiously transfers a condition which belongs to Palestine to Egypt. But it is yet asked, Can the locusts possibly come to Egypt from the east, from beyond the Arabian Gulf?

The argument which *Eichhorn* urges against this, that the locusts always travel from south to north, is not tenable. *Credner*,[1] who in his commentary on Joel decidedly substantiates the correctness of the statement in our passage, has shown that they come with *every* wind. It also can be no objection to this opinion, that the swarm coming from the east must pass the Arabian Gulf. For *Credner*[2] has shown, that the flight of the locusts is successfully made, not merely over smaller channels, as the Straits of Gibraltar, the Red Sea,[3] &c., but over larger bodies of water, as the Mediterranean Sea, in case they are favoured by the wind. As soon as this fails them, changing to a storm, or when a calm succeeds, the whole numberless swarm is precipitated into the sea, just as it here occurred after the locusts had accomplished the work of the Lord upon the Egyptians.

If it is true, that the locusts come from the east not less than from the south, and that the sea is no hindrance to them, and if it is further settled that Arabia is one of the principal places where the locusts are found, it is also certain that they come from there to Egypt not less than from Nubia. A single case of this kind, a plague of locusts of peculiar severity, which came from the east upon Egypt, is described by a Syrian writer, the continuator

---

[1] S. 286. [2] S. 288.
[3] Niebuhr remarks, that the wind drives the swarms of the locusts over the Arabian Gulph in its broadest part. Beschr. S. 169.

of *Barhebræus*:[1] "In the year 1774,[2] (1463, A. D.) many locusts came from the east. They advanced even to Egypt, destroyed the crops," &c.

THE CULTIVATION OF THE VINE IN EGYPT.

Ignorance of the condition of Egypt is also said to appear in the dream of the chief butler of Pharaoh.[3] In reference to this, *v. Bohlen*[4] remarks : " An important specification of time for the late origin of the narrative, is contained here in the dream of the butler, in which the existence of the *vine* in Egypt is implied. For after Psamaticus, consequently just about the time of Josiah, had its cultivation first been commenced, in a small degree, and could, in a low country, which at the time of the ripening of the grape is overflowed, find entrance only at some few points. The Egyptians used for drink a kind of beer, in speaking of which *Herodotus* explicitly adds that no vines grow in the land. Among the orthodox Egyptians it is considered as the blood of Typhon. They did not drink it, says Plutarch, before the time of Psamaticus, and they also did not offer it in sacrifice."

Tuch[5] shares with *v. Bohlen* unbounded regard for every disconnected saying of Plutarch, which, if we take into view the whole character of this writer, appears to have very poor foundation. He also, as well as the author before mentioned, has no regard to the information which the monuments have furnished, since the beginning of this century, upon the question concerning the cultivation of the vine in Egypt. He does not even seem to have noticed that which *Heeren* has adduced from the Description of the French scholars.[6] In vindication of the author of the book

---

[1] In dem neuen Repert. von Paulus, Th. I. S. 67. Mirkhond, in his account of the Saracenic wars, says that the Arabs were contemptuously called "locust-eaters" by the Greeks and Persians; a clear proof that locusts are abundant in the Arabian peninsula. The Egyptian agriculturists at the present day believe that the most destructive locusts come from Arabia, which is in some degree confirmed by Dr Bowring in his Report on Syia. T.

[2] This refers to the Grecian era, or era of the Seleucidae, which dates from the reign of Seleucus Nicator 311 B. C.

[3] Gen. xl. 10, seq. [4] S. 373. [5] In dem Comm. zur Genesis, S. 513.

[6] Ideen, Aegypt. S. 362. The full title of this Work, which is so often quoted by *Hengstenberg* as the Description, is, " Description de l'Egypte, ou Recueil des Observations et des Recherches pendant l'Expédition de

of Genesis, he assumes that there is no mention made of wine in the passage, but of drinking the newly expressed, unfermented, unintoxicating juice of the grape. The procedure described in the chapter supposes an evasion, consequently the continued existence of the prohibition of wine, and an observance of this prohibition; and it is an escape from a difficulty which, besides him, *Rosenmueller* has also borrowed from *J. D. Michaelis*,[1] for whom it was exceedingly convenient, but yet it is nothing more than an escape from difficulty. It rests upon the fact, that one does not pay attention to what passes in dreaming, and it does not take into account that the words, "I took the grapes and pressed them into Pharaoh's cup," if they are separated from their connection with the dream, show a procedure in the preparation of the royal drink, which has nowhere else any analogy. Besides, the employment of cup-bearer, as a distinguished office at court, could scarcely exist, where the drink and its preparation are so extraordinarily simple —the latter such as is elsewhere practised only by *children*. Still further, if the passage in Plutarch be allowed to have any force, we cannot even by this explanation free ourselves from difficulty. For, according to Plutarch, wine was considered by the Egyptians as the blood of Typhon, inasmuch as it was the product of the vine, and not in consequence of its having previously undergone a fermentation.

Even the accounts of ancient authors permit us not to doubt, that from the most ancient times, the vine was cultivated in Egypt. *Herodotus* in many ways contributes to this proof. Thus, according to him, dried grapes appear among the things which are placed in the body of the bullock offered to Isis, together with bread, honey, &c.[2] The grapes can only have reference to the domestic culture of the vine. Also the identification of Osiris with Bacchus in *Herodotus*,[3] is an argument for the origin of the cultivation of the vine in Egypt. Bacchus and wine stood, at least

---

l'Armée Française." It consists of 25 volumes, with more than 900 engravings and 3000 sketches. The last number appeared in 1826. It is composed of the documents prepared by the eminent *savans* and artists who accompanied Bonaparte in his expedition to Egypt. It was printed at the expense of the French Government, and " corresponds in the grandeur of its proportions," says a writer in the Am. En., " to the edifices which it describes."

[1] Mos. Laws, Vol. III. p. 120.

[2] " Quae pertinent," remarks Creuzer, Comm. 1. p. 115, " ad frumenta inventa vitesque cultas," &c. [3] 2. 42 and 144.

according to the popular idea, which is all that is here important, in indissoluble union. *Diodorus*,[1] in like manner, not only asserts the identity of Osiris and Bacchus, but also expressly attributes to Osiris the discovery of the art of cultivating the vine.[2] " But it is said that he first discovered the vine near Nysa, and after having acquired skill in the management of its fruit, first made use of wine himself, and taught other men the planting of the vine-stock, the gathering of the grapes, the drinking of wine, and its preservation." But the authority of *Diodorus* is of itself sufficient to outweigh that of *Plutarch*. Further, according to *Hellanicus* in *Athenaeus*, the cultivation of the vine was first discovered in the Egyptian city Plinthinus.[3] But these passages of ancient authors have no longer much interest for us, since we have upon the monuments a testimony for the origin of the culture of the vine in Egypt, far more sure and sufficient in itself. How little that assertion of *Herodotus*[4] agrees with these, was first remarked in the Description.[5] Since then, the proofs from the monuments for the cultivation of the vine have very much multiplied, and the fact may now, since the appearance of *Champollion's* Letters and the Works of *Rosellini* and *Wilkinson*, be considered as fully settled. According to *Champollion* there are found in the grottoes of Beni Hassan, " representations of the culture of the vine, the vintage, the bearing away and the stripping off of the grapes, two kinds of presses, the one moved merely by the strength of the arms, the other by mechanical power, the putting up of the wine in bottles or jars, the transportation into the cellar, the preparation of boiled wine,"[6] &c. *Rosellini*[7] has a separate section on *grape gathering and the art of making wine.*

" Numerous," says he, "are the representations in the tombs, which relate to the cultivation of the vine, and these are found,

---

[1] In Book I. chap. 11.   [2] 1. 15.
[3] Compare this and other passages quoted in Jablonski, Opusc. II. p. 119, seq. 1. 432, 72.
[4] 2. 77.
[5] T. 6, p. 124, ed. Pancret. It is there said : " Among the numerous details given by Herodotus concerning the diet of the Egyptians, this is found : As they have not the vine, they drink beer, (2. 77). Our paintings prove, conclusively, that the Egyptians cultivated the vine, and also made wine. Many critics have previously remarked, that this observation of Herodotus wants accuracy."
[6] S. 51.   [7] Vol. II. 1. p. 365 et seq.

not merely in the tombs of the time of the 18th and some later dynasties, but also in those which belong to the time of the most ancient dynasties." " The described pictures,"[1] it is said, "show more decidedly than any ancient written testimony, that in Egypt, even in the most ancient times, the vine was cultivated and wine made." In the inscriptions of the time of the Pharaohs, at least seven different kinds of wine are represented, among which is the wine of Lower Egypt, and the wine of Upper Egypt.[2] *Wilkinson*[3] gives the engraving and description of an Egyptian vineyard, and the different kinds of labour bestowed on it. In a painting[4] from Thebes, boys are seen frightening away the birds from the grape clusters. In one from Beni Hassan, the kids appear which are allowed to browse upon the vines after the vintage. The substance of what is communicated by *Rosellini* and *Wilkinson*, with the necessary plates, can be found in *Taylor*.[5]

The assertion of *Herodotus*, that there is in Egypt no vine, must be considered as an entire mistake. The attempt made first by *Dupuy*[6] and *Larcher*,[7] finally also by *Bähr*, to rescue his authority, without disparaging the witnesses who attest the existence of the cultivation of the vine in ancient Egypt, by saying that *Herodotus* speaks only of a *part* of Egypt, the cultivated part, has been already set aside as inadmissible by *Rosellini*. " Certainly,"[8] says he, " *Herodotus* speaks only of fertile Egypt, but

---

[1] Page 373.   [2] Page 377.   [3] Vol. II. p. 143 et seq.   [4] Page 149.
[5] Page 48 et seq. In the passage to which the author refers, I have given representations of a vineyard, and of various kinds of wine-presses. Here I may add, that grapes do not appear to have been very abundant in the valley of the Nile; for the crushed pulp which remained after the grapes were trodden in the press, instead of being thrown away, as is usual in most wine-growing countries, was carefully collected by the Egyptians, and placed in a bag, made of flags or rushes, in which the pulp was compressed, by twisting the end of the bag with staves or handspikes. Even after it had undergone this process, the pulp was deemed too valuable to be thrown away, and the pressure on the bag was increased, by some of the workmen throwing their whole weight on it, until every drop of the precious fluid was squeezed out. Mirhaud (Con. d'Orient) says, that the clusters and grapes are very small in Egypt; and this explains the surprise of the spies at the enormous produce of the vines in southern Palestine.   T.
[6] In the Mem. de l'Acad. d. Inscr. t. 31, Hist. p. 20.
[7] Upon Herod. 2. p. 333.   [8] Page 374.

only there could the vine be cultivated, and most certainly was cultivated. The remainder was either desert or swamp."[1]

The many representations on the monuments of wine-offerings, which the kings present to the gods, show how little reliance is to be placed on the assertion of *Plutarch*, that, before the time of Psamaticus, wine was neither offered nor made use of as drink.[2] This is one of those numerous fabrications, by which the Egyptians attempt to give astonished foreigners an idea of the nobility and piety of their ancestors. Even *Herodotus* does not think of anything at all like this. If wine had been considered as the blood of Typhon, how could it be explained, that even in his time, the priests received a regular allowance of wine?[3] Their practice would surely have corresponded to their theology, if indeed the kings and the people had been led astray by Grecian customs.

When *v. Bohlen* asserts, that the vine could not have found entrance into Egypt, except at some few points, on account of the inundation, we can against this refer to *Michaud* among others, who says, vines flourish in Egypt in the water like water-plants.[4] And when *J. D. Michaelis* alleges, that the Delta is in August and September, the months of the wine-harvest, entirely overflowed,[5] we, in opposition to him, refer to *Hartmann*,[6] according to whom the grape-gathering takes place in part even in July, and is finished in August, while the inundation, as a general thing, does not begin until the end of August, and never before the middle of that month.[7]

[1] Even Bähr says, in remarking upon the words, οἱ μὲν περὶ τὴν σπειρομένην Αἴγυπτον οἰκέουσι, in the beginning of C. 77, B. II.: " Est enim Aegyptus ad Nili utramque ripam sita per aliquot dierum itinera fertilis frugibusque colendis apta, quam rustici incolae habitant; quae sequuntur regiones pastorum potius sunt atque nomadum neque frugum capaces." See also Heeren, S. 146 ff.

[2] Comp. Ros. S. 376. Wilk. II. p. 164 et seq. According to Wilkinson, p. 168, men are seen in the sculptures who, unable to walk from excess in drinking, are carried home from a feast by servants. For proof, that the prohibition of wine and other intoxicating drinks to the priests who were to perform the service of the sanctuary, in Lev. x. 8, seq. was not inappropriate among a people who had come from Egypt, where both wine and other intoxicating drinks were much loved, see Wilk. Vol. III. p. 172 seq.

[3] Comp. 2. 37.

[4] T. 7, Correspondence d'Orient. Compare also concerning the cultivation of the vine in the Delta, Hartmann, Aegypten, S. 187.

[5] See passage above referred to.   [6] Page 214—15.   [7] Page 118.

We add here, in conclusion, an explanation from Egyptian antiquity, of some objections, which, although they have not yet been, easily might be made to the credibility of the Pentateuch.

THE ORIGIN OF CIVILIZATION IN EGYPT.

It has often been confidently affirmed in modern times, that colonization and civilization descended from Ethiopia down the Nile to Egypt. From this view one can hardly avoid a certain suspicion of the notices respecting Egypt in the Pentateuch. Already, in Abraham's time, we find the seat, not of *a*, but of *the* flourishing Egyptian kingdom in Lower Egypt, whither colonization and civilization could scarcely, at that time, have been carried. Zoan or Tanis in the Delta appears in Numbers xiii. 22, as one of the oldest cities in Egypt.

But this position is entirely hypothetical, and its inadmissibility, as is now more and more acknowledged, appears, even when we for the present leave the Pentateuch out of the account. From antiquity arises a distinguished witness, *Herodotus*, who[1] derives the civilization of Ethiopia from the deserters from the army of Psamaticus. Among the moderns, *Jomard*[2] has most thoroughly confuted this position. " Nubia," he remarks, " consists almost entirely of barren rocks. Such a land, where the most urgent wants of man can only be supplied with the utmost exertion, is not the cradle of the fine arts. Accordingly the majority of French travellers have not embraced the opinion, that the arts have descended further and further from the mountains of Ethiopia." " So soon as I received information of the true character of the antiquities of Nubia, when I in the pictures and sculptures saw the same objects which are represented on the monuments of Thebes, it was clear to me, that most of the monuments of Nubia are far later than those of Thebes, and by no means served as models for them. The climate is different in the two lands, the productions of the vegetable kingdom are not the same, the most distinguished plants which the Egyptian artists have so often represented,—the lotus, the papyrus, the vine, &c. are not found in this high region, and the reed and the date

---

[1] 2. 30.

[2] In the Descript. of the Scholars who accompanied the French Expedition into Egypt, t. 9, p. 163 et seq.

tree but seldom. The arts, already cultivated and perfected, could have been brought to these shores, but their inhabitants could not have transplanted the arts, for which their country offered no natural type, to the shores of the lower Nile." *Wilkinson*[1] represents the hypothesis of the origin of culture in Ethiopia as entirely exploded by modern investigations. The specimens of art which remain in Ethiopia are not merely inferior in conception to those of Egypt, but bear far less the stamp of originality. He thinks it probable, though not demonstrable, that civilization was carried from Thebes to Lower Egypt. He declines, however, the task of defending this hypothesis with those who oppose him. It seems almost as if this asserted probability were founded entirely upon a misconception, namely, upon the circumstance that the monuments of Upper Egypt, in consequence of their situation, are in a far better state of preservation than those of Lower Egypt, where even the traces of them are for the most part obliterated. We are much too readily disposed to consider that a thing, which now appears noble in the ruins, was originally the most noble and ancient.[2]

THE USE OF IRON IN EGYPT.

One further difficulty ; according to Gen. iv. 22, Tubalcain was the father of all forgers of brass and iron. Against the working of iron so early, it might be argued, that among the ancient Egyptians, all implements in common use, weapons, household furniture, instruments, were made of copper hardened by an alloy of tin. But, on the other hand, *Wilkinson*[3] remarks: "The constant employment of bronze arms and implements is not a sufficient argument against their knowledge of iron, since we find the Greeks and Romans made the same things of bronze long after the period when iron was universally known." From the great proficiency in metallurgy in Egypt, it cannot be supposed, that

---

[1] Vol. I. p. 4.
[2] The best account of the Ethiopian monuments is given by Hawkins: from the representations he has given of the principal remains, it cannot be doubted that the civilization of the Thebaid reached a higher degree of perfection than that of Nubia, and that the best of the Nubian edifices were of later construction than the best of the Egyptian. T.
[3] Vol. III. 245. Compare also 246.

the art of working iron was unknown. The extensive use of brass (it is not to be overlooked that also, in our passage, *brass* occupies the first place) must be first, on account of the greater ease of procuring and working it. The same author [1] says, that it is scarcely supposable, that without tempered iron the hieroglyphics could have been cut deep into hard granite and basaltic rocks. But there is a yet stronger argument for the use of iron in ancient Egypt from *Herodotus*,[2] who, after relating how great an expense the support of the labourers on the Pyramids of Cheops occasioned, remarks: " How immense, therefore, must have been the sum which was expended on the iron with which they worked," unquestionably implying that the Egyptians, even in this early age, made use of iron as they did in his own time. Upon the sculptures in Thebes, *Wilkinson*[3] also found battle-axes, which, if we may judge from their colour, were of steel. By these remarks, the other passages[4] of the Pentateuch, in which iron implements are mentioned, are vindicated at the same time with those which have been noticed.

The problem of our negative part is solved.[5] We have, we hope, conclusively proved, that Egyptian antiquity furnishes no evidence against the Books of Moses. By this, much is already gained. Were the Pentateuch really what, according to the views of modern criticism it must be, such evidence would necessarily appear against it, since the events narrated, so many of them, transpired on Egyptian ground. The negative part, therefore, acquires no inconsiderable positive importance. It now belongs to us, in the positive part, to inquire what evidence Egyptian antiquity furnishes in favour of the Books of Moses.

[1] Vol. I. p. 60.   [2] Book 2. 124.
[3] Vol. I. p. 324. Compare, concerning other probable indications of the existence of iron on the sculptures of the early Pharaohs, Vol. III. p. 247, (241—55); and concerning the use of iron generally in ancient Egypt, Rosellini, II. 2. p. 301 seq.
[4] Num. xxxv. 16. Deut. iii. 10. xxvii. 5.
[5] We have reserved the consideration of some objections which might seem appropriate here, for the positive portion of our work, because, in the cases referred to, the positive element predominated over the negative.

POSITIVE PART.

CHAPTER I.

THE HISTORY OF JOSEPH.—Gen. Chaps. xxxvii—xl.

JOSEPH CARRIED TO EGYPT AND SOLD TO POTIPHAR.

ACCORDING to chap. xxxvii., Joseph is sold by his brothers to an Arabian caravan who are going to Egypt with merchandize, and they sell him in Egypt. An argument for the early commencement of trade by caravans with Egypt is furnished by the fact, that the king Amun-m-gori II., of the 16th dynasty,[1] erected a station in the Wady Jasoos, to command the wells which furnish water

---

[1] The first king of Egypt was Menes, who, according to *Wilkinson*, ascended the throne about 2320 B.C. The kings from him to the invasion of Cambyses are divided by *Manetho* into twenty-six dynasties. But very little is known of any of those who precede Osirtasen I., who belongs to the sixteenth dynasty. The names of most of the succeeding monarchs of the sixteenth, and those of the seventeenth and eighteenth dynasties, often occur on the monuments, and are so often mentioned in this volume, that it was thought it might be well to insert here, with some slight changes, the table found in *Wilkinson*. Thus, when the name of a king, as Amun-m-gori or Osirtasen occurs, by turning to this table, the date of his reign may be seen, and in some cases an important event which occurred during it. The eighteenth dynasty is of special interest in several respects. It was the period of conquest. In it most of the events recorded in the Books of Moses occurred. And a large part of the monuments were constructed about this time. Four hieroglyphical lists of the kings of this dynasty exist, in addition to the list of *Manetho*: "The Tablet of Abydos, the Procession of the Ramesseion, the Procession of Medeenet Haboo, and the Tomb of Gurnah." The chronology of *Wilkinson* has been followed here, as generally in this volume. Those who are desirous

for those passing through the desert.[1] The same author shows that slaves were procured by the Egyptians, not only in war, but also by purchase.[2]

of comparing that of *Rosellini*, will find it for substance in Mr Gliddon's "Ancient Egypt."

Name from ancient Authors.	Name from the Monuments.	Events.	Ascended the Throne.
16th Dynasty, of Tanites ?			B. C.
Misartesen . .	Osirtasen I. . .	Arrival of Joseph, 1706. . .	1740
	Amun-m-gori? I. .	. . . . . .	1696
	Amun-m-gori? II. .	. . . . . .	1686
17th Dynasty, of Memphites ?			
(Uncertain.) . .	Osirtasen II. . .	. . . . . .	1651
	Nofri-Ftep, or Osirtasen III.	} Joseph died 1635. . .	1636
	Amun-m-gori? III. .		1621
	(Unknown.) . .	. . . . . .	1580
18th Dynasty, of Theban or Diospolitan Kings.			
Amosis (Chebron)	(Chebron) Ames .	{ "There arose a new (dynasty, or) king, who knew not Joseph." Exodus i. 8. Moses born 1751.	} 1575
Amenoph . .	Amunoph I. . .		1550
Amesses, or Amenses, his sister . .	} Amense, his sister .	{ Included in the reign of Thothmes I. . .	
Mephres, Mesphris, or Mesphra-Tuthmosis	} Thothmes I. . .	{ His 14th year found on the monuments. . .	} 1532
Misphra-Tummosis or Tothmosis . .	} Thothmes II. . .	{ The reign of Amunneit-gori included in this. . .	} 1505
Thummosis, or Tothmosis . .	} Thothmes III. . .	{ Exod. of the Israelites, 1491, 430 years after the arrival of Abraham. . .	} 1495
Amenophis . .	Amunoph II. . .	Moses died 1451. . . .	1456
Horus . . .	Thothmes IV. . .	. . . . . .	1446
Achenchres, (a queen)	{ Maut-m-Shoi (Regency) . .	{ Included in the reign of her son, Amunoph III.	
Rathotis . .	Amunoph III. .	{ The supposed Memnon of the vocal statue. . .	} 1430
Achencheres, or Chebres . .	} Amum-men ?	. . . . . .	1408
Achencheres, or Acherres . .	{ Remesso, or Remeses I.	}	1395
Armais . . .	Osirei ? I.	. . . . . .	1385
Remeses Maimun	{ Amun-mai Remeses, Remeses II., or the Great	{ The supposed Sesostris of the Greeks. The date of his 44th and 62d year found on the monuments. Manetho allows him 66.	1355
Amenophis . .	{ Pthahmen-Thmeioftep? his son	. . . . . .	1289

[1] Wilkinson, Vol. I. pp. 45 and 46.
[2] Herod. 8. 105 : παρὰ τοῖσι βαρβάροισι τιμιώτεροί εἰσι οἱ εὐνοῦχοι, πίστιος εἵνεκα τῆς πάσης, τῶν ενορχίων.

The master of Joseph, chap. xxxvii. 36, is designated as Potiphar, the eunuch of Pharaoh, chief of the body-guard (literally, the executioners). A eunuch in the literal sense cannot be meant. The term in this place is equivalent to court-officer. But the transferred signification rests upon the employments in which real eunuchs engaged,[1] and thus it follows from this designation of Potiphar, that there were, in the opinion of the author, eunuchs, even in Egypt. Now *v. Bohlen* asserts, that it cannot be proved that there were eunuchs in Egypt, and that the author is justly suspected of transferring that, which belonged to the Hebrew court, to Egypt. But this suspicion is removed by what *Rosellini*[2] says of the existence of eunuchs in Egypt. Men are sometimes represented, he remarks, on the Egyptian monuments with evident marks of fulness, especially of the chest and stomach, which is unusual among the Egyptians in this hot climate. Their complexion is almost a medium between the brown and yellow, by which men and women are generally distinguished from one another. These marks are characteristic of eunuchs. The employments of these men are also in favour of this opinion. They are repeatedly represented as attendants of the women, then as musicians, and finally as servants, who are entrusted with the important duties of household management. It is evident from *Herodotus*,[3] that the kings of Egypt had a *guard* who, in addition to the regular income of the soldier, also received a separate salary. In the paintings of marches and battles on the monuments, these royal guards are commonly seen to be employed in protecting the person of the king, and are distinguished by a peculiar dress and weapons.[4] During the reign of the Ptolemies, who in general adhered to the usages of the ancient Egyptians, the office of the commander of the bodyguard[5] was a very important one. They possessed the confidence of the king, and were often employed in the most important business transactions.[6] Finally, the superintendence of executions belonged to the most distinguished of the military cast.[7]

[1] Vol. I. pp. 403 and 4.   [2] Vol. II. 3. p. 132 seq.   [3] 2. 168.
[4] Ros. II. 3. p. 201.   [5] ἀρχισωματοφύλαξ.   [6] Comp. Rosellini, p. 202.
[7] P. 273. Before quitting this subject, it is necessary to say a word respecting Hengstenberg's strange acquiescence in Bohlen's assertion that Potiphar is described as a Eunuch. The word סריס *Seris,* correctly rendered "officer" in our version, like the Greek word "eunuch," originally signified a "chamberlain," or "attendant of state;" the root (סרס) is still

JOSEPH'S EXALTATION.

According to chap. xxxix. 4 and 5, Potiphar placed Joseph over his house and over all his substance, and the Lord blessed him for the sake of Joseph, in all which he had in the house and in the field. Joseph had also, after his exaltation, a man who was over his house.[1] A peculiar and characteristic Egyptian trait! "Among the objects of tillage and husbandry," says *Rosellini*, "which are portrayed in the Egyptian tombs, we often see a steward, who takes account and makes a registry of the harvest before it is deposited in the store-house." "In a tomb at Kum el Ahmar, the office of a steward with all its apparatus is represented; two scribes appear with all their preparations for writing, and there are three rows of volumes, the account and household books of the steward," &c.[2] The same author remarks, in reference to a painting in a tomb at Beni Hassan: "In this scene, as also in many others which exhibit the internal economy of a house, a man carrying implements for writing,—the pen over his ear, the tablet or paper in his hand, and the writing-table under his arm,—either follows or goes before the servants."[3] According to the inscription, this is the overseer of the slaves or the steward. Compare also the representation in *Wilkinson*, of an Egyptian steward in his employment, "overlooking the tillage of the lands."[4]

preserved in the Aramaic, and designates a higher degree of servitude than the ordinary verb of submission (עבד). The instances of secondary meanings obliterating primary significations, are sufficiently common in every language; and Bohlen's error, in which he is strangely followed by Hengstenberg, arises from mistaking the secondary and prevalent signification of the word for its original and primary.   T.

[1] Gen. xliii. 16, 19. xliv. 1.   [2] II. 1. p. 329.   [3] II. p. 403, 4.
[4] II. p. 136. The favour which the Hebrew captive found with his master is not to be taken as a fair example of the conduct of the Egyptian slave-owners: "the Lord was with Joseph;" and to this, rather than to the clemency of Potiphar, the mildness of his servitude must be attributed. Most of the Egyptian slaves were captives taken in war. They were dragged to the market bound and fettered; and, with a disgraceful refinement of cruelty, they were bound in the most painful posture. Women and children shared the fate of their husbands and fathers. Melancholy processions of the unhappy beings frequently occur on the monuments; and the artists have, sometimes, depicted the joyous and thoughtless ignorance of infancy, contrasted with the anguish of an unhappy mother, too

JOSEPH'S TEMPTATION AND THE MORALS OF THE EGYPTIANS.

With impudent shamelessness Potiphar's wife seeks to seduce Joseph.[1] How great the corruption of manners with reference to the marriage relation was among the Egyptians, appears from *Herodotus*,[2] whose account *Larcher* has compared with the one under consideration. The wife of one of the oldest kings was untrue to him. It was a long time before a woman could be found who was faithful to her husband. And when one was, at last, found, the king took her without hesitation for himself. From such a state of morals, the Biblical narrative can easily be conceived to be natural. The evidence of the monuments is also not very favourabl to the Egyptian women. Thus, they are represented as addicted to excess in drinking wine, as even becoming so much intoxicated as to be unable to stand or walk alone, or "to carry their liquor discreetly."[3]

Potiphar's wife avails herself of the opportunity when her husband and the rest of the men of the house were gone out, and Joseph had come in to perform some duty.[4] It has lately been affirmed, that an error against Egyptian customs is here detected. *V. Bohlen* says: "Since eunuchs are supposed to exist, Joseph well acquainted with the miseries of her future lot. Here it may be remarked, that this representation explains a passage in the Lamentations of Jeremiah, which has given needless perplexity to many commentators; it forms part of his description of the woes inflicted on the vanquished by the Babylonian conquerors of Jerusalem: "The yoke of my transgressions is bound by his hand: they are wreathed, and come up upon my neck: he hath made my strength to fall, the Lord hath delivered me into their hands, from whom I am not able to rise up." (Lam. i. 14.) The "binding on of the yoke"—the "wreathing of the penal bonds around the neck," are frequently represented on the monuments; and it requires no great stretch of imagination to conceive, that if the march be of long duration the "strength" of the captives must "fall, and render them unable to rise up." The treatment of Joseph himself, on the false accusation of Potiphar's wife, (the Zuleikha of Eastern tradition,) is a sufficient proof of the inhumanity exhibited to slaves. "His feet they set in the stocks, the iron entered into his soul;" and if any faith is to be placed in Rabbinical legends, he was frequently brought out to be tortured for the amusement of the infamous Zuleikha. T.

[1] Chap. xxxix.
[2] 2. 111.
[3] Compare Wilkinson, Vol. II. p. 167.
[4] Comp. v. 11.

could not so much as come into the presence of the women, still less into the harem ;" and *Tuch* remarks : " The narrator abandons the representation of a distinguished Egyptian, in whose house the women live separately, and descends to a common domestic establishment," &c. The error, however, lies here, not on the side of the author, but on that of his critics. They are guilty of inadvertently transferring that which universally prevails in the East to Egypt, which the author avoids, and thereby exhibits his knowledge of the condition of the Egyptians. According to the monuments, the women in Egypt lived under far less restraint than in the East, or even in *Greece*.[1]

The delineations of Egyptian social intercourse are especially appropriate here. *Taylor*,[2] collecting in few words the results as they are, without reference to our passage, says : " In some entertainments, we find the ladies and gentlemen of a party in different rooms ; but in others, we find them in the same apartment, mingling together with all the social freedom of modern Europeans. The children were allowed the same liberty as the women ; instead of being shut up in the harem, as is now usual in the East, they were introduced into company, and were permitted to sit by the mother or on the father's knee."[3]

---

[1] See the proof in Wilk. Vol. II. p. 389. Some of the Egyptian artists have represented ladies sitting unveiled at banquets, and indulging in large libations of wine, and in some instances they exhibit the consequences of such excesses.   T.

[2] P. 171.

[3] Several captious objections have been made to the history of Joseph's imprisonment : it is said that prisons were not likely to be used in the age of the early Pharaohs, and that, if used, it is improbable that the prisoners would be allowed any opportunities of communication. It is, indeed, very doubtful, whether simple incarceration was ever employed as a punishment under the Pharaohs ; criminals and captives were always employed in public works, and it is remarkable that the Samaritan text, instead of בית הסהר *Beth Hasahar*, " the house of confinement," reads בית הסחר *Beth Hasachar*, " the house of employment" or " emolument ;" and when Pharaoh sent for Joseph, a different word is used for the place of his confinement, viz. בור *Bor*, " an excavated dungeon." The superintendence over the other captives granted to Joseph, still further proves, that he was confined in a kind of workhouse.   T.

THE DREAM OF THE CHIEF BAKER OF PHARAOH.

According to chap. xl. 16, the chief baker,[1] in his dream, carries the wicker baskets with various choice baker's commodities on his head. Similar woven baskets, flat (which the circumstance that the three are placed one upon another here implies) and open, for carrying grapes and other fruits, are found represented on the monuments.[2] The art of baking was carried to a high degree of perfection among the Egyptians. *Rosellini* says, after describing the kitchen scenes upon the tomb of Remeses IV. at Biban el Moluk: "From all these representations, it is clear, that the Egyptians were accustomed to prepare many kinds of pastry for the table, as we see the very same kinds spread out upon the altars and tables which are represented in the tombs. They made even bread in many and various forms. These articles are found in the tombs kneaded from barley or wheat, in the form of a star, a triangle, a disk, and other such like things."[3] But the custom of *carrying on the head* is most peculiar and characteristic of Egypt, and it is so much the more to be remarked, as it is mentioned incidentally, and the author does not characterize it as a custom peculiar to the Egyptians. *Herodotus*[4] mentions the habit of bearing burdens on the head by the men, as one by which the Egyptians are distinguished from all other people: "Men bear burdens on their heads, and women on their shoulders." Examples of this custom are frequently found upon the monuments.[5] To be sure, the monuments also show, what is evident without argument, that the custom was not universal.[6]

PHARAOH'S DREAM AND THE MAGICIANS OF EGYPT.

In the account of Pharaoh's dream, chap. xli. 1, seq. we are first struck with the use of the word אָחוּ (*Achú*,) Nile-grass,[7]

---

[1] As most of the Egyptian meats were baked, this officer must have been also the head-cook of the palace.   T.

[2] Wilk. II. 151—2.

[3] Vol. II. 2. p. 464. Compare the representation of these different kinds of pastry, &c. in Wilkinson, Vol. II. p. 385.

[4] 2. 35.

[5] Compare drawings in Wilkinson, Vol. II. p. 151—2 and Vol. III. p. 385, where a man is carrying bread or cakes to the oven upon a long board.

[6] Costaz in the Descr. t. 6, p. 138. Wilk. as above. Rosellini, II. p. 453.

[7] Our translators have inaccurately rendered it "meadow,"

—an Egyptian word for an Egyptian thing. In the next place, the seven poor and the seven fat kine attract our attention. The symbol of the cow is very peculiar and exclusively Egyptian. Upon the signification of this symbol we have two important passages, one from *Plutarch*[1]: "They consider the cow as the image of Isis and the earth," i. e. the symbol of them.[2] The other is found in *Clemens*[3]: "The cow is the symbol of the earth itself and its cultivation, and of food." Now, therefore, since the cow is the symbol of fruitfulness, it appears entirely natural, that the difference of the year in respect to fruitfulness was represented by the different condition of the kine—that unfruitful years were denoted by lean kine. It is scarcely conceivable that a foreign inventor should have confined himself so closely to the peculiar Egyptian symbols. The circumstance that the kine come up out of the Nile, the fat and also the lean, has reference to the fact that Egypt owes all its fertility to this stream, and that famine succeeds as soon as it fails.

According to chap. xli. 8, Pharaoh calls "all the magicians of Egypt and all the wise men thereof," that they may interpret his dream, by which he is troubled. These same magicians appear also in Ex. vii. 11: "Then Pharaoh called the wise men and the sorcerers; and they also, the magicians of Egypt, did in like manner by their enchantments;" and they are also represented in Ex. viii. 3, 14, 15—(7, 18, 19,) ix. 11, as the wise men of the nation, the possessors of secret arts.

Now we find in Egyptian antiquity, an order of persons, to whom this is entirely appropriate, which is here ascribed to the magicians. The priests had a double office, the practical worship of the gods, and the pursuit of that which in Egypt was accounted

---

tic plants of the Nile, particularly those of the Iitus-kind, were so valuable in Egypt that they were reaped in as regular a harvest as the flax and corn. It is to be regretted that the slight inaccuracy of the authorized version obscures the force of this proof of the sacred writer's familiarity with the minute peculiarities of Egypt: the most captious objector—even Bohlen himself—must confess, that the history of Joseph could only have been written by a person well acquainted with the land and the natural productions of the Valley of the Nile.   T.

[1] In Bähr upon Herod. 2. 41.
[2] Βοῦν γάρ Ἴσιδος εἰκόνα καὶ λῆν νομίζουσι, upon which Bähr: Manet vacca Isidis signum procreatricisque naturae symbolum.
[3] Strom. B. V. p. 671, Potter.

as wisdom. The first belonged to the so-called prophets, the second to the holy scribes, ἱερογραμματεῖς. These last were the learned men of the nation; as in the Pentateuch, they are called *wise men*, so the classical writers named them *sages*.¹ These men were applied to for explanation and aid in all things which lay beyond the circle of common knowledge and action. Thus, in severe cases of sickness for example, along with the physician a holy scribe was called, who, from a book, and astrological signs, determined whether recovery was possible.² The interpretation of dreams, and also divination, belonged to the order of the holy scribes.³ In times of pestilence, they applied themselves to magic arts to avert the disease.⁴ A passage in *Lucian*⁵ furnishes a peculiarly interesting parallel to the accounts of the Pentateuch concerning the practice of magic arts: " There was with us in the vessel, a man of Memphis, one of the holy scribes, wonderful in wisdom and skilled in all sorts of Egyptian knowledge. It was said of him, that he had lived twenty-three years in subterranean sanctuaries, and that he had been there instructed in magic by Isis."⁶

---

¹ Compare Jablonski, Panth. Proll. p. 31 seq. Drumann, Inschrift von Rosette, S. 122, ff. Pharaoh is represented as consulting two different classes of persons for the interpretation of his dream, the חרטמים *Charetummim* (magicians), and the חכמים *Chakamim* (wise men). If the first be a Semitic name, which we see no reason to doubt, it is one of the few examples of Hebrew compounds, and must come from חרט *Cheret* " a pen," and חרם *Charam* " to be sacred:" we thus identify the *Charetummim* with the ιερογραμματεις or " holy scribes" mentioned as a distinct order of the Egyptian priesthood by Josephus and several other authors. This class appears to have been independent of caste; among the Hindús learning was allowed to redeem lowness of caste, a circumstance on which many of their traditional legends turn. There is reason to believe, that both Joseph and Moses were raised to this order, for Joseph asks his brethren, " Wot ye not that such a man as I can certainly *divine?*" and Moses is described as " learned in all the wisdom of the Egyptians." T.
² Drumann, S. 129. ³ S. 130. ⁴ S. 130. ⁵ In Jablonski, p. 95.
⁶ Ἔτυχεν ἡμῖν συμπλέων Μεμφίτης ἀνήρ, τῶν ἱερῶν γραμματέων, θαυμάσιος τὴν σοφίαν καὶ τὴν παιδείαν πᾶσαν εἰδὼς τὴν Αἰγυπτίον ἐλέγετο δὲ τρία καὶ εἴκοσιν ἔτη ἐν τοῖς ἀδύτοις ὑπολέλοις ᾠκηκέναι, μαγεύειν παιδευόμενος ὑπὸ τῆς Ἴσιδος.

THE HAIR AND BEARD—HOW WORN IN EGYPT.

When Joseph is called before Pharaoh he *shaves* himself, chap. xli. 14. Even the most prejudiced, as for example, *v. Bohlen*, must, in this incidental notice, recognise a purely Egyptian custom. Even *Herodotus*[1] mentions it among the distinguishing peculiarities of the Egyptians, that they commonly were shaved, but in mourning they allowed the beard to grow.[2] The sculptures also agree with this representation. "So particular," says *Wilkinson*,[3] "were they on this point, that to have neglected it was a subject of reproach and ridicule; and whenever they intended to convey the idea of a man of low condition, or a slovenly person, the artists represented him with a beard." "Although foreigners," says the same author,[4] "who were brought to Egypt as slaves had beards on their arrival in the country, we find that as soon as they were employed in the service of this civilized people, they were obliged to conform to the cleanly habits of their masters; their beards and head were shaved; and they adopted a close cap." According to *Rosellini*,[5] the priest shaved not the beard only, but also the head; and others, if they did not shave it with a razor, were accustomed to wear the hair very short; the abundant and long hair which often covers the head of the figures on the monuments was probably false, like our wigs. The same author remarks, that this was considered by the neighbouring nations, and especially by the Asiatics, as a peculiar and distinguishing characteristic of the Egyptians.[6]

DRESS AND ORNAMENTS OF THE EGYPTIANS.

According to chap. xli. 42, Pharaoh put upon Joseph, at the time of his advancement, his signet-ring, and arrayed him in garments of byssus, and put *the* gold chain (the article shows that it was done in reference to a custom common in such a case) about his neck. As the gift of the seal-ring is not peculiar to Egypt, but common in the East, we do not delay upon it.[7] But the gar-

---

[1] Chap. 2. 35.
[2] See Bähr upon this passage, S. 558.
[3] Vol. III. p. 357.
[4] III. p. 358.
[5] Vol. I. 2. p. 486 seq.
[6] Vol. II. 2, p. 395.

[7] "Pharaoh said unto Joseph, See, I have set thee over all the land of Egypt. And Pharaoh took off his ring from his hand, and put it upon

ments of byssus belong necessarily to the naturalizing of Joseph. Garments of cloth from the vegetable kingdom, linen and cotton, were considered by the Egyptians as pure and holy, and were in high estimation among them; the priests wore these only, according to *Herodotus*, 2, 37, where the term linen, in opposition to woollen, includes also cotton.[1] And even among the rest of the Egyptians, these were the most valued garments. *Herodotus* says, "They wear woollen garments, which are ever newly washed,"[2] and the woollen garments which they commonly wore for outer garments were thrown off as soon as they entered the temple.[3] In reference to the third mark of distinction, the putting on of the necklace, the monuments furnish abundant explanation. In the tombs of Beni Hassan,[4] many slaves are represented, each of whom has in his hand something which belongs to the dress or ornaments of his master. The first carries one of the necklaces, with which the neck and breast of persons of high rank are generally adorned. Over it stands: *Necklace of Gold*. At Beni Hassan there is also a similar representation in another tomb of a noble Egyptian.[5] By the *form* of the necklace, it is remarked,[6] the distinction of individuals in regard to rank and dignity was probably denoted. Men of the common order seldom wear such

Joseph's hand, and arrayed him in vestures of fine linen, and put a gold chain about his neck; and he made him to ride in the second chariot which he had; and they cried before him, Bow the knee: and he made him ruler over all the land of Egypt." (Gen. xli. 41—43.) Investiture of office is here given by the signet-ring, the K'heldt, or dress of honour, the necklace, and the privilege of riding in the second chariot. At the present day, public documents in the East are more frequently authenticated by the royal signet than by the sign manual: the seal, however, is a stamp giving an impression with ink, similar to those made for Henry the Eighth and George the Fourth, when disease rendered those monarchs incapable of writing, and is rarely used to give an impression on wax, or any similar substance. It would lead us too far from our immediate subject, to elucidate many passages in Holy Writ which are commonly misunderstood from ignorance of the Oriental use of the seal; it is sufficient to say, that the bestowing of it on Joseph was equivalent to intrusting him with the charge of the administration; because its impression attached to any document gave it as much authority as if it had been signed by the king's own hand. T.

[1] Heeren, p. 133. [2] Herod. ii. 37.
[3] Herod. 2. 81, and Heeren in the passage above referred to.
[4] Rosellini, II. 2, p. 404. [5] Ros. II. 2, p. 412. [6] Ros. II. 2, 420.

ornaments, while the pictures of the kings and the great are always adorned with them.[1]

The remark of *v. Bohlen* upon Gen. xli. 42: "It is, however, scarcely necessary to mention, that these objects of luxury, especially polished stones, belong to a later time," has interest only as it shows how far the investigations of the rationalists, in reference to the Pentateuch, fall short of the present advanced state of knowledge respecting Egyptian antiquity. It is now far too late for such remarks.

THE MARRIAGE OF JOSEPH.

According to chap. xli. 45, Pharaoh gives to Joseph, Asenath, the daughter of Potiphera the priest of On, in marriage. The name Potiphera, Petephra, he who belongs to the sun, is very common on the Egyptian monuments.[2] This name is especially appropriate for the priest of On or Heliopolis. Since Pharaoh evidently intended by this act to establish the power bestowed on Joseph upon a firm basis, it is implied in this account ; first, that the Egyptian high-priests occupied a very important position, and secondly, that among them the high-priest of On was the most distinguished. Both these points are confirmed by history. The following words of *Heeren*[3] will show how conspicuous the station

---

[1] See concerning the necklaces of the Egyptians, which in like manner also pertained to the costume of the gods, Wilkinson, Vol. II. p. 215 and Vol. III. p. 375—6, with the plate, 409 M. The " vesture of fine linen " was a dress peculiarly Egyptian ; Herodotus informs us that the priests wore no others, which however must be limited to the supreme hierarchy. From the example of the horizontal loom, we find that the Egyptians were acquainted with the art of weaving colours in chequers like the Scottish plaids, but that the process, from the simplicity of their machinery, must have been both tedious and expensive. It was probably such a garment which Jacob bestowed upon Joseph, (" a coat of many colours," Gen. xxxvii. 3) ; and the envy of the other brothers was excited, not merely by the beauty of the dress, but by the fact that such a dress was a symbol of power and authority. The necklace appears on the monuments as a regular ensign of rank ; and Bohlen's objection that such ornaments were not used in the time of the Pharaohs, is refuted, not merely by the pictorial representations, but by the actual discovery of the necklaces themselves in the Egyptian tombs : there are some beautiful specimens of them in the British Museum.   T.

[2] Rosellini, I. 1, p. 117.   [3] S. 128.

of the high-priests in general was: ".The priesthood belonging to each temple were again organized among themselves with the greatest exactness. They had an high-priest, whose office was also hereditary. It is scarcely necessary to mention, that the stations of the high-priests in the principal cities in Egypt were first and highest. They were in a manner hereditary princes, who stood by the side of the kings, and enjoyed almost the same prerogatives. Their Egyptian title, Piromis,[1] was, according to the explanation of *Herodotus*,[2] equivalent to the noble and good, (καλὸς κȣγαϑός); which, however, does not refer perhaps to moral character, but to nobility of descent. Their statues were placed in the temples. When they are introduced into history, they appear as the first persons of the state." The passage of *Bähr* [3] on *Herodotus* 2, 3, (where the priests of Heliopolis are described as the most learned among all the Egyptians,) shows that among the Egyptian colleges of priests, the one at On or Heliopolis took the precedence; consequently the high-priest of On was the most distinguished. The great antiquity of religious worship at On is also attested by the monuments. *Wilkinson* says: "During the reign of Osirtasen (whom he makes contemporary with Moses), the temple of Heliopolis was either founded or received additions, and one of the obelisks bearing his name attests the skill to which they had attained in the difficult art of sculpturing granite." [4]

V. Bohlen has attempted to make out a contradiction in this account, which accords in so remarkable a manner with the state of affairs in Egypt. "An alliance of intolerant priests," says he, " with a foreign shepherd, is entirely opposed to the character of the Egyptians." [5] But the connection took place in obedience to

---

[1] *Herodotus* undoubtedly is mistaken in regard to the meaning of this word. It signifies *the man*, and is composed of the Egyptian article prefixed to 'romi,' man. See *Wilkinson*, Man. and Cus., second series, Vol. I. p. 170.

[2] 2. 143.

[3] Videntur fuisse tria omnino potiora Aeg. sacerdotum collegia Memphiticum, Thebaicum et Heliopolitanum, in quibus Heliopolitae primum locum obtinuerunt, si quidem vera retulit Strabo, l. 17. p. 1158 D., solis templum una cum aedibus sacerdotum accurate describens et pluribus de illorum doctrina et disciplina disserens.

[4] Vol. I. p. 44.

[5] P. 388. The chief difficulties in the history of Joseph will be removed, if we can show that there was an order of "prophets," "magicians,"

the command of the king, and the high-priest of On the less dared to disobey the king, since, according to the result of modern investigations, the Pharaohs themselves at all times were invested

or "sacred scribes" distinct from the priestly caste, inferior indeed to the *Chakamím*, or chief priests, but not so far removed from them in dignity as to be excluded from their alliance. To avoid anything like a parade of learning, we shall state the evidence for the existence of a "sacred order" distinct from a "sacred caste," as briefly as possible. In the fourth and fifth lines of the Greek inscription on the Rosetta Stone, in the British Museum, we find Grecian ladies—and, among others, Irene, the daughter of Ptolemy—recorded as "priestesses ;" a conclusive proof that strangers were admitted into some kind of sacerdotal order under the Macedonian kings of Egypt; though it is notorious that the chief policy of the Ptolemies was to restore the religious institutions of the Pharaohs. Diodorus Siculus describes Athyrtis, the daughter of King Sesoosis, as remarkably skilful in divination (μαντικη χρωμενην), and taking her omens from sacrifices and visions in the temple itself. The sixth line of the Rosetta Stone thus enumerates the members of the Egyptian hierarchy: "The chief priests and prophets, and those who have access to the shrines to clothe the gods, and the *pterophoræ*, and the sacred scribes, and all the other sacred persons." Now the *pterophoræ* ("wing-bearers") appear to have been a higher order of the "sacred scribes." Diodorus Siculus expressly mentions the wearing of wings on the head as an attribute of this class, (i. 87); and Clemens Alexandrinus uses εχων πτερα επι της κεφαλης (having wings over the head) as an equivalent to ιερογραμματευς ("sacred scribe.") Now, it appears exceedingly improbable that any ceremony similar to ordination should be requisite in the case of a hereditary priesthood; but we find, from the monuments, that such a form was used in Egypt, and the smaller size of the person thus initiated, intimates his inferiority to the officiating priests. The "winged sun," under which the ceremony is performed, was the well-known symbol of "a protecting and superintending Providence';" and hence the beautiful allusion of the prophet Malachi: " Unto you that fear my name shall the Sun of righteousness arise with healing in his wings ; and ye shall go forth, and grow up as calves of the stall." (Mal. iv. 2.) The wings ascribed to the sacred scribes have probably a reference to this symbol ; for, as the learned Drunann justly observes, Hesychius gives πτερον (a wing) as an equivalent to σκηνη (any overshadowing); and hence, instead of actually wearing wings on their heads, the *pterophoræ* may merely have displayed this symbol above it. Lucian speaks of the "sacred scribes" as a body distinct from the priesthood ; and we find Moses making a similar distinction between the priests and the professors of magical arts. (Deut. xiii. 10). We have been rather minute in our examination of this point, because one of the greatest objections brought against this part of the Sacred Writings is the improbability of a foreigner like Joseph being allowed to exercise sacerdotal functions, and form a priestly connection.

with the highest sacerdotal dignity,[1] and consequently possessed not an external authority merely, over the priesthood. The transaction assumes an entirely different aspect when we consider that Joseph did not by any means marry the daughter of the high-priest while a foreign shepherd, but after he had been fully naturalized by the king, had assumed the Egyptian dress, taken an Egyptian name, &c. Chap. xliii. 32 shows, that Joseph had formally withdrawn from the community of his own people, and connected himself with the Egyptians.[2] In the circumstance that this is represented as necessary, as well as in the fact that Pharaoh believed it important to give a firm basis to the position of Joseph by a union with the daughter of the high-priest of On, we plainly recognise the traces of that Egyptian intolerance, which *v. Bohlen* fails to perceive here, and which in later times certainly appears to have very much increased. To this we shall have occasion hereafter to advert.

But this improbability is removed when we find a sacerdotal order into which distinguished persons were admitted, without any reference to their descent ; and we may add, that Pythagoras, according to Plutarch, was similarly admitted to the privileges of the Egyptian priesthood, though a foreigner, by command of King Amasis. T.

[1] Leemans, lettre to Mr Salvolini, p. 14.

[2] It is quite clear from the narrative, that Joseph had taken extraordinary pains to naturalize himself in Egypt. As a stranger is said to have been recognised in Athens from the superior purity of his Attic dialect, so the chief means by which Joseph could be recognised as a foreigner, was his greater strictness in adhering to purely Egyptian usages. This strictness had nearly led to his detection, when he caused his brethren to be marshalled at the banquet in the order of their age. "And they sat before him, the first-born according to his birthright, and the youngest according to his youth : and the men marvelled one at another." (Gen. xlii. 33.) The mention of the posture used at table, proves that the writer of the history was well acquainted with Egyptian customs, for the patriarchal usage was to recline at meals. (Gen. xviii. 4.) There are indeed frequent instances of couches on the Egyptian monuments, but these were only used for sleeping ; in all the representations of entertainments the ladies and gentlemen are depicted sitting on stools or chairs. It is also mentioned that Joseph sat apart from the rest, and we find from the monuments that a separate table was usually placed before each of the distinguished guests present. The number and variety of dishes set on each table were proportioned to the rank of each guest, or to the estimation in which he was held by the person who gave the entertainment. To this custom allusion is distinctly made by the sacred writer. (Gen. xliii. 34.) T.

JOSEPH COLLECTS THE PRODUCE OF THE SEVEN YEARS OF PLENTY.

The labours of Joseph described in chap. xli. 48, 49, in building store-houses, are placed vividly before us in the paintings upon the monuments, which show how common the store-house was in ancient Egypt. In a tomb at Elethya, a man is represented whose business it evidently was to take account of the number of bushels which another man acting under him measures. The inscription is as follows: The writer or registrar of bushels, *Thutnofre.* Then follows the transportation of the grain. From the measurer others take it in sacks and carry it to the store-houses. In the tomb of Amenemhe at Beni Hassan, there is the painting of a great store-house, before whose door lies a large heap of grain, already winnowed. The measurer fills a bushel, in order to pour it into the uniform sacks of those who carry the grain to the corn magazine. The carriers go to the door of the store-house and lay down the sacks before an officer who stands ready to receive the corn. This is the overseer of the store-house. Near by stands the bushel with which it is measured and the registrar who takes the account. At the side of the windows there are characters which indicate the quantity of the mass which is deposited in the magazine. Compare with this the clause,[1] " Until he left numbering," in verse 49. By these paintings, light is also thrown upon the remark in Ex. i. 11 : " And they [the Israelites] built for Pharaoh treasure-cities."[2]

---

[1] Rosellini, II. p. 324 seq.

[2] According to Champollion, Briefe, S. 228, the wide halls of the great palace at Thebes, which are surrounded by large colonnades, all have the name *Manosk,* according to the Egyptian inscription, i. e. the place of the harvest, and hence is derived, the place where corn is measured. Is this Manosk probably the same as the Hebrew, מִסְכְּנוֹת ? Here we may remark, that the Egyptians paid great attention to the storing of their corn ; the granaries appear to have been public buildings ; they are represented on the monuments as of vast extent, and it deserves to be remarked, that the roofs are generally arched. They were probably excavated, and this may serve as a confirmation of the theory, that the first notion of the arch was suggested by caves. When we see the vast extent of these stores, as represented on the monuments, we cannot doubt that they would contain sufficient corn to supply not only the wants of Egypt, but also of the neighbouring nations, during the seven years of famine.   T.

FAMINE IN EGYPT AND THE ADJOINING COUNTRIES.

The declaration that famine seized at the same time upon Egypt and the adjoining country, appears at first view suspicious, and indeed with reference to this also, *v. Bohlen*[1] has very confidently charged the author with ignorance of the natural condition of Egypt. The climate and tillage of Egypt do not stand in even the most remote connection with Palestine. In Egypt fertility depends, not as in Palestine, on the rains, but entirely on the overflowing of the Nile. But on a closer examination the suspicion changes into its direct opposite. The account of the author is shown to be entirely in accordance with natural phenomena, and the reproach of "ignorance respecting the country of Egypt" comes back upon him who made the accusation. Had the author known Egypt only by hearsay, he would probably have written in the manner that *v. Bohlen* demands of him. The fruitfulness of Egypt depends, it is true, upon the inundations of the Nile. But these are occasioned, as even *Herodotus* knew, by the tropical rains which fall upon the Abyssinian mountains.[2] These rains have the same origin with those in Palestine. "It is now decided," says *Le Père*,[3] "that the Nile owes its increase to the violent rains which proceed from the clouds that are formed upon the Mediterranean Sea, and carried so far by the winds, which annually at nearly the same time blow from the north. There are not wanting also other examples of years of dearth, which were common to Egypt with the adjoining countries. Thus *Macrizi*[4] describes a famine which took place in Egypt, on account of a deficiency in the increase of the Nile, in the year of the Hejra 444, which at the same time extended over Syria and even to Bagdad.

But *v. Bohlen* goes so far as even to impute it to the author's "ignorance of the natural condition of Egypt," that he represents a famine as coming upon this country at all. The overflowing of the Nile never fails to take place altogether, or for several years in succession, and the Delta is fruitful even without it, &c. And yet there is scarcely a land on the earth in which famine has raged, so often and so terribly as in this same Egypt, or a land that so very much needs the measures which Joseph adopted for

---

[1] S. 421.   [2] Ritter Erdk. 1. S. 835.   [3] Descr. t. 7. p. 576.
[4] In Quatremère, Mem, s. l' Eg. t. 2. p. 313.

the preservation of the people. *Macrizi* could write a whole volume on the famines in Egypt! The swelling of the Nile a few feet above or below what is necessary, proves alike destructive.[1] Particular instances of famine which history has handed down to us, are truly horrible, and the accounts of them are worthy of notice also, inasmuch as they present the services of Joseph in behalf of Egypt in their true light. *Abdollatiph*[2] relates thus: "In the year 569 Hejra, (1199) the height of the flood was small almost without example. The consequence was a terrible famine, accompanied by indescribable enormities. Parents consumed their children, human flesh was in fact a very common article of food; they contrived various ways of preparing it. They spoke of it and heard it spoken of as an indifferent affair. Man-catching became a regular business. The greater part of the population were swept away by death. In the following year also, the inundation did not reach the proper height, and only the low lands were overflowed. Also much of that which was inundated could not be sown for want of labourers and seed, much was destroyed by worms, which devoured the seed corn; also of the seed which escaped this destruction, a great part produced only meagre shoots which perished." Compare with this account the "thin ears and blasted with the east wind," in chap. xli. 6. *Macrizi*[3] has given an account of the famine in 457, which was not at all less severe than that of 596 (Hejra). The calif himself nearly perished with hunger.

JOSEPH, HIS BRETHREN AND THE EGYPTIANS *SIT* AT AN ENTERTAINMENT.

According to chap. xliii. 32, at the entertainment to which Joseph invited his brethren, they sat apart from the Egyptians, while Joseph was again separated from both. The author shows the reason of this in the remark: "Because the Egyptians might not eat bread with the Hebrews, for that is an abomination to the Egyptians." *Herodotus*[4] also remarks, that the Egyptians abstained from all familiar intercourse with foreigners, since these were unclean to them, especially because they slew and ate the animals which were sacred among the Egyptians. "Therefore

---

[1] Le Père, Descr. 18. p. 573.
[2] Page 332 seq. De Sacy.
[3] In Quatremère, t. 2. p. 401 seq.
[4] 2. 41.

(since the Egyptians honour much the cow) no Egyptian man or woman will kiss a Greek upon the mouth, they also use no knife or fork or kettle of a Greek, and will not even eat any flesh of a clean beast,[1] if it has been cut up with a Grecian knife." The circumstance that Joseph eats separately from the other Egyptians, is strictly in accordance with the great difference of rank, and the spirit of caste[2] which prevailed among the Egyptians.

It appears from chap. xliii. 33, that the brothers of Joseph *sat* before him at the table, while, according to patriarchal practice, they were accustomed to recline.[3] It appears from the sculptures, that the Egyptians also were in the habit of sitting at table, although they had couches.[4] Sofas were used for sleeping. In a painting in *Rosellini*,[5] "each one of the guests sits upon a stool, which, in accordance with their custom, took the place of the couch."

THE PRACTICE OF DIVINING BY CUPS.

The steward of Joseph, chap. xliv. 5, in order to magnify the value of the cup which his brothers were said to have stolen, designates it as that out of which he *divineth*. *Jamblichus*, in his book on Egyptian mysteries, mentions the practice of divining by cups.[6] That this superstition, as well as many others, has conti-

---

[1] From this passage it may be inferred with how much propriety v. Bohlen has asserted, that the Egyptians abstained from all animal food.

[2] The people in Egypt were divided into four great classes, and each of these were again subdivided. The first was the sacerdotal caste, consisting of priests of various grades, scribes, embalmers, &c. The second was the agricultural class, including the military order, farmers, gardeners, and persons of similar occupations. The third class were the townsmen, composed of artificers, tradesmen, &c. The fourth class, the common people, included factors, labourers, and various others. The military order seems to have been much more honoured than the rest of the second class, if indeed they did not compose a separate caste. The king could be chosen only from among them or the sacerdotal order. If chosen from the military caste, he was immediately admitted to the order of priests, and instructed in all their secret learning. The subject of caste is discussed at large in *Wilkinson*, Vol. I. p. 236 seq., and Vol. II. p. 1 seq., to whom the reader is referred.

[3] See chap. xviii. 4, "rest yourselves."

[4] Wilk. 2. p. 201.   [5] Ros. II. 2. p. 439, T. 79.

[6] 3 Part, § 14. p. 68. Divination by the cup is one of the most ancient forms of superstition, and traces of it are still to be found in the rural districts of England.   T.

nued even to modern times, is shown by a remarkable passage in *Norden's* Travels.[1] When the author with his companions had arrived at Derri, the most remote extremity of Egypt, or rather in Nubia, where they were able to deliver themselves from a perilous condition only through great presence of mind, they sent one of their company to a malicious and powerful Arab, to threaten him. He answered them: "I know what sort of people you are. I have consulted my cup, and found in it that you are from a people of whom one of our prophets has said: There will come Franks under every kind of pretence to spy out the land. They will bring hither with them a great multitude of their countrymen, to conquer the country, and to destroy all of the people."

THE ARRIVAL OF JACOB AND HIS FAMILY IN EGYPT, AND THEIR SETTLEMENT IN GOSHEN.

A remarkable parallel to the description of the arrival of Jacob's family in Egypt, chap. xlvi. is furnished by a scene in a tomb at Beni Hassan: "strangers" who arrive in Egypt.[2] They carry their goods with them upon asses. The number 37 is written over them in hieroglyphics. The first figure is an Egyptian scribe, who presents an account of their arrival to a person in a sitting posture, the owner of the tomb, and one of the principal officers of the reigning Pharaoh.[3] The next, likewise an Egyptian, ushers them into his presence, and two of the strangers advance, bringing presents, the wild goat and the gazelle, probably as productions of their country. Four men with bows and clubs follow leading an ass, on which there are two children in panniers, accompanied by a boy and four women. Last, another ass laden and two men, one of whom carries a bow and club, and the other a lyre, which he plays with the plectrum. "All the men have beards, contrary to the custom of the Egyptians, although very general in the east at that period, and represented in their sculptures as a peculiarity of foreign uncivilized nations." Some believe that this painting has a direct reference to the arrival of Jacob with his family in

---

[1] Vol. III. p. 68. Edit. Langlés, quoted from Burder in Rosenm. Alt. u. Neu. Morgenl. Th. I. S. 212.

[2] Wilkinson, Vol. II. p. 296 and 7, and plate.

[3] Comp. the phrase, "Princes of Pharaoh," in chap. xii. 15.

Egypt. On the contrary, *Wilkinson*[1] remarks, the expression "captives," which appears in the inscription, makes it probable that they are of the number of prisoners so frequently occurring, who were taken captive by the Egyptians during their wars in Asia. But in his more recent work, he considers this circumstance as no longer decisive. "The contemptuous expressions," he says, "common among the Egyptians in speaking of foreigners, might account for the use of this word." In fact, it speaks very decidedly against the idea of their being prisoners, that they are armed.[2] Whether this painting has a direct reference to the Israelites will of course ever remain problematical, but it is at any rate very noticeable, as it furnishes proof that emigration with women and children into the Egyptian state, and formal admission, took place even in very ancient times, or more correctly *yet*, in these times.

Joseph charges his brothers, chap. xlvi. 34, that they shall say to Pharaoh, that they are shepherds, in order that they may obtain a residence apart from the Egyptians, in the land of Goshen. "For," adds the author, "every shepherd is an abomination to the Egyptians." The monuments even now furnish abundant evidence of this hatred of the Egyptians to shepherds. The artists of Upper and Lower Egypt vie with each other in caricaturing them.[3] In proportion as the cultivation of the land was the more unconditionally the foundation of the Egyptian State, the

---

[1] Egypt and Thebes, p. 26.

[2] Rosellini, who speaks at length on this representation, in a separate section, Vol. III. 1. p. 48 seq., "concerning a picture of the tombs of Beni Hassan, representing some foreign slaves which are sent by King Osirtasen II. as a present to a military chieftain," considers it certain that these individuals are captives, since they are so designated in the inscription. But even the inscription, when it is allowed to have its just and certain significance, gives no support to this opinion, since the epithet, captives, as Wilkinson supposes, may be adequately accounted for by the pompous style of the Egyptians, and their disdainful arrogance, which would not allow them to speak of foreigners except in connection with victory and captivity. At any rate, the picture is more to be relied on than the inscription, and in this, in addition to the fact that they are armed, which has already been mentioned, the circumstance, that the persons delineated bring gifts and play on musical instruments, things which captives are not and cannot be found represented as doing on the Egyptian monuments, is decisive.

[3] Wilk. II. p. 16.

idea of coarseness and barbarism was united with the idea of a shepherd among the Egyptians.[1]

The region in which the Israelites received their residence, the land of Goshen, is designated, Gen. xlvii. 6, 11, as the *best* of the land. This statement has occasioned interpreters some perplexity, but it is justified by what *Wilkinson*, without reference to this passage, says of the nature of this eastern district: "It may not be irrelevant to observe, that no soil is better suited to many kinds of produce than the irrigated edge of the desert, (it is generally composed of lime mingled with sand,) even before it is covered by the fertilizing deposit of the inundation."[2]

Since the reference of the Pentateuch to the geographical relations of Egypt are most numerous in the chapters now under consideration, it will appear proper that we make them the subject of a connected examination in this place. The bearing and importance of these separate notices can be correctly understood only when thus seen in connection.

REFERENCES OF THE PENTATEUCH TO THE GEOGRAPHICAL FEATURES OF EGYPT.

THE LAND OF GOSHEN.

The references of the Pentateuch to the geographical features of Egypt, as we should naturally expect in a book of sacred history, are neither numerous nor particular; yet enough of these references exist to show that its author possessed an accurate knowledge of the topography of the country to which he alludes. And the more scattered, incidental, and undesigned these notices are, the more certain is the proof which they afford, that the author's knowledge was of no secondary character, was not laboriously produced for the occasion, but, on the contrary, natural, acquired from his own personal observation, and was such as to preserve him from every mistake, without the necessity of his being constantly on his guard.

---

[1] Concerning the causes of this hatred of the Egyptians, see especially Rosellini, I. 1. p. 178 seq. also Heeren, S. 149.
[2] Wilk. I. p. 222.

Let us direct our attention, first, to what the author says of *the land of Goshen*. He nowhere gives a direct and minute account of the situation of this land. But it is evident that this must be referred to some other cause than his ignorance, since he communicates, in reference to it, a great number of separate circumstances, which, although some of them appear at first view to be entirely at variance with each other, are yet found to be entirely consistent when applied to a particular district.

The land of Goshen appears, *on the one hand*, as the eastern border-land of Egypt. Thus it is said, Gen. xlvi. 28: "And he [Jacob] sent Judah before him unto Joseph, to direct his face unto Goshen." That Jacob should send Judah before him, to receive from Joseph the necessary orders for the reception of those entering the country, is entirely in accordance with the regulations of a well-organized kingdom, whose borders a wandering tribe is not permitted to pass unceremoniously. This account also agrees accurately with the information furnished on this point by the Egyptian monuments.[1] That Jacob did not obtain the orders of Joseph until he was at Goshen, shows that this was the border-land. We come to the same result also from chap. xlvii. 1 : "And Joseph came and told Pharaoh, and said, My father and my brethren are come out of the land of Canaan, and behold they are in the land of Goshen." It is most natural that they should remain in the border-province until the matter was laid before the king. This is also confirmed by Gen. xlvi. 34: "And ye shall say, Thy servants' trade hath been about cattle—from our youth even until now—that ye may dwell in the land of Goshen ; for every shepherd is an abomination unto the Egyptians ;" for this passage can only be explained on the supposition that Goshen is a frontier province, which could be assigned to the Israelites without placing them in close contact with the Egyptians, who hated their manner of life.[2] Finally, the circumstance, that the Israelites under Moses, after they had assembled at the principal town of the land, had reached in two days the confines of the Arabian desert, points to Goshen as the eastern boundary.

On the *other hand*, Goshen appears again as lying in the neigh-

---

[1] See remarks upon Gen. xlvi. p. 39 seq.
[2] The Israelites received the land of Goshen in military tenure, being bound to guard the exposed north-eastern frontier.

bourhood of the chief city of Egypt. Thus in Gen. xlv. 10 : " And thou shalt dwell in the land of Goshen, and thou shalt be near to me," (to Joseph who dwelt in the principal city of Egypt).[1] The Pentateuch nowhere expressly mentions which was this chief city of Egypt, just as the surname of no one of the reigning Pharaohs is mentioned by Moses, and for the same reason. Yet the necessary data for designating this city are found. It must at any rate have been situated in Lower Egypt, for this appears in the Pentateuch generally as the seat of the Egyptian king. But the remarkable passage, Num. xiii. 23 : " And Hebron was built seven years before Zoan of Egypt," points us directly to Zoan or Tanis, and at the same time plainly shows that the reason why the author did not mention the chief city by name, can be sought in anything rather than in his ignorance concerning it. That Zoan is here directly named by way of comparison, implies, first, that it was one of the oldest cities in Egypt.[2] Secondly, that it held the first rank among the Egyptian cities, and stood in the most important connection with the Israelites. Hebron, the city of the patriarchs, could be made more conspicuous only by a comparison with the chief city of Egypt, arrogant and proud of its antiquity, and there was no motive for such a comparison, except with a city which by its arrogance had excited the jealousy of the Israelites. The designation, Zoan of Egypt, which means no more than that the city lay in Egypt, also indicates that this was the chief city. What is here only intimated is expressly affirmed in Ps. lxxviii. 12, 43 ; where it is said, Moses performed his wonders " in the field of Zoan." In accordance with the foregoing intimations, which bring us into the neighbourhood of the chief city, Moses is exposed on the bank of the Nile, Ex. ii. 3, and at the place where the king's daughter was accustomed to bathe, v. 5, and the mother of the child lived in the immediate vicinity, v. 8. They had fish in abundance, Num. xi. 5 ; they watered their land as a garden of herbs, Deut. xi. 10.

Further, the land of Goshen, on the one hand, is described as a *pasture*-ground. So in the passage above referred to, Gen. xlvi. 34, and also in chap. xlvii. 4 : " They said, moreover, unto Pha-

[1] So also in chap. xlvi. 28, 29.

[2] That Tanis already existed in the time of Remeses the Great, appears from the monuments yet existing among its ruins. Wilk. Vol. I. p. 6. Rosellini, I. 2. p. 68.

raoh, To sojourn in the land are we come; for thy servants have no pasture for their flocks; for the famine is sore in the land of Canaan; now therefore, we pray thee, let thy servants dwell in the land of Goshen."

On the other hand, the land of Goshen appears as one of the most *fruitful* regions of Egypt, chap. xlvii. 6: " In the best of the land make thy father and brethren to dwell." Also in verse 11 of the same chap.: " And he gave them a possession in the land of Egypt, in the best of the land, in the land of Rameses." The Israelites employed themselves in agriculture, Deut. xi. 10, and obtained in rich abundance, Num. xi. 5, the products which Egypt, fertilized by the Nile, afforded its inhabitants.

All these circumstances harmonize, and the different points, discrepant as they may seem, find their application, when we fix upon the land of Goshen as the region east of the Tanitic arm of the Nile[1] as far as the Isthmus of Suez or the border of the Arabian desert, Ex. xiii. 20. Goshen then comprised a tract of country very various in its nature. A great part of it was a barren land, suitable only for the pasturage of cattle. Yet it also had very fruitful districts, so that it combined in itself the peculiarities of Arabia and Egypt. To it belonged a part of the land on the eastern shore of the Tanitic branch of the Nile;[2] also the whole of the Pelusiac branch with both its banks, which as late as in the time of Alexander the Great was navigable—through it his fleet pressed into Egypt,—but is now almost entirely filled up with the sand of the desert, while the Tanitic arm, being further removed from the desert, has sustained itself better.[3] Between two branches of the Pelusiac canal lies the island Mycephoris, which in ancient times was inhabited by the Calasiries, or a part of the military caste.

---

[1] The view of our author with regard to the position of the land of Goshen agrees, substantially, with that of Dr Robinson and other scholars of the present day. " This tract," it is said, in the Biblical Researches, Vol. I. p. 76, " is comprehended in the modern province esh-Shŭrkīyeh, which extends from the neighbourhood of Abu Za'bel to the sea, and from the desert to the former Tanaitic branch of the Nile; thus including also the valley of the ancient canal."

[2] On which see Ritter also, Afrika, S. 827.

[3] See Malus, Memoire sur l' état ancien et moderne des provinces Orientales de la basse Egypte, Descr. 18. 2. p. 18.

Of this island *Ritter*[1] says: "At this present time it is a well cultivated plain, full of great palm-groves and opulent villages." "Generally," continues the same author, "the country here is by no means barren; the water of the canal diffuses its blessings everywhere. Thus there lies upon the canal, about fifteen miles below Bustah, the little modern village Heyeh, surrounded by rich palm-groves, which is almost entirely unknown to recent Geographers, but in its vicinity is a luxuriance of vegetation which makes the country appear like a European garden."[2] So is it even now with this region, notwithstanding the great bogs and sand heaps which have been here formed in the course of a hundred years.[3] Even in the interior of the ancient land of Goshen, there is still a large tract of land good for tillage, and fruitful. There is, for example, a valley which stretches through the whole breadth of this province from west to east, and in which, as we shall hereafter see, the ancient chief city of this province lay. This tract of land, from the ancient Babastis on the Pelusiac arm of the Nile even to the entrance of the Wady Tumilat, is, according to *Le Père*,[4] even now under full cultivation, and is annually overflowed by the Nile. Also a great part of Wady Tumilat is susceptible of cultivation,[5] and likewise the eastern part of the valley, which is very accurately delineated upon the chart of Lower Egypt in the Atlas of *Ritter's* Geography, the tract from Ras el Wady to Serapeum,

---

[1] S. 824.
[2] Comp. Deut. xi. 10, "as a garden of herbs."
[3] Ritter, S. 834. Prokesch, (In den Erinnerungen aus Aegypten und Kleinasien, Th. 2. S. 130,) says: "There is no country that cannot better dispense with the arts of civilized life, than Egypt. By them it can be made a paradise, and without them a desert. During the century of modern Greek, Arabian, Mameluke and Turkish dominion, when, with the exception of some short intervals, nothing was done for the country, the inhabitants lived upon the inheritance which descended from the flourishing century under the Pharaohs, Ptolemies, and Romans. It is no merit to them that desert and morass have not swallowed up all of their arable land. The canals and dykes existed and still exist on such a foundation, and in so great numbers, that a thousand years would not be sufficient to make of Egypt what the country between the cataracts is at this day. The tillable land of Egypt has by degrees decreased in quantity, as the public works of the ancients have gradually crumbled, until half its extent has gone, but the remainder is yet sufficient to furnish sustenance for a people proportionally less than formerly."
[4] Memoire sur le canal des deux mers, in the Descr. t. 11. p. 116.
[5] Le Père, p. 117.

furnishes not merely pasture grounds, but also laud suitable for cultivation.[1]

It is certain, that the Pentateuch in the intimations, evidently undesigned, which it gives of the position and nature of the land of Goshen in the most disconnected passages, is always consistent with itself, as, for example, in one whole series of passages, it alludes to the fact, that the Israelites dwelt upon the Nile, and in another, that they dwelt in a border-land in the direction of Arabia. This fact, as also the circumstance that all its allusions to the position and nature of the land are substantiated by actual geography without the most distant reference to an imaginary land, are not explicable, if the author was dependent on uncertain reports for his information. On the contrary, the whole serves to impress us with the conviction, that he, as would be the case with Moses, wrote from personal observation, with the freedom and confidence of one to whom the information communicated comes naturally and of its own accord, and from one who has not obtained it for a proposed object.

THE LOCATION OF PHARAOH'S TREASURE-CITIES, PITHOM AND RAAMSES.

We go further. In Ex. i. 11, it is said: "And they built for Pharaoh treasure-cities, Pithom and Raamses." There can be no doubt that in the view of the author, these cities, upon whose fortifications the Israelites were compelled to labour, were situated in the land of Goshen. It is most natural to suppose that the Israelites built where, according to the foregoing account, they dwelt; moreover, all doubt is precluded, since one of these cities, Raamses, is afterwards represented as the place of rendezvous from which the Israelites commenced their departure from the land. The question now is, whether these cities really lay in the land of Goshen, or did the author probably, out of the number of the names of Egyptian cities known to him, take two at random?

Before we answer these questions, we remark, that even the circumstance that the author represents the king of Egypt as building treasure-cities in the land of Goshen, is in favour of his knowledge of Egypt, or rather of his credibility as a historian. Nowhere are the treasure-cities more in place than precisely there.

[1] Le Père, p. 121.

That they were *fortified*, even the Seventy understood, for they translate the Hebrew word here directly, *walled cities.* The same thing is evident from 2 Chron. viii. 3—6, according to which they were placed in the particularly insecure border land (Hamath), and are designated as "fenced cities, with walls and gates and bars." Compare xi. 12, where the store-cities are spoken of in connection with castles. But that such walled cities, provided with stores of provisions, were nowhere more needed than on the eastern boundary of Egypt, is indeed evident from the circumstance, that according to the accounts of profane writers, just upon this border, the most exposed of all, the military power of the Egyptians was concentrated. "It is clear from *Herodotus*," says *Heeren*,[1] "that almost the whole military force of Egypt was stationed in Lower Egypt; four and a half districts within the Delta were possessed by the Hermotybies, and twelve others by the Calasiries. On the contrary, only one district was possessed by each of these in all Middle and Upper Egypt, namely the district of Chemmis and Thebes." Of the land on the east side of the Tanitic arm of the Nile, *Ritter*[2] says: "This is believed to be the land of the ancient Calasiries, who were here to guard the ancient ports of Egypt against eruptions from Asia."[3]

We will now endeavour to determine the position of the two cities named. With regard to the first, this can be determined without difficulty. It will be denied by no one, that it lay within the land of Goshen. Pithom is incontestably, and by universal admission, identical with the Patumos of *Herodotus*.[4] Speaking of the canal which connected the Nile with the Red Sea, this author says: "The water was admitted into it from the Nile. It

---

[1] S. 37.   [2] S. 829.

[3] The declarations of ancient writers with regard to the chief stations of the military caste in Egypt, are of no small importance respecting another passage of the Pentateuch. They show how appropriate it is, when the author, in Ex. xiv., represents the Egyptian host as ready forthwith to pursue after the Israelites, and as able to overtake them in a short time. "In Mosaic times," says Heeren, S. 37, "the military caste first make their appearance in Lower Egypt. The suddenness with which the Pharaoh who then ruled could assemble the army with which he pursued the Israelites in their Exodus, shows distinctly enough, that the Egyptian military caste must have had their head-quarters in just the same region in which Herodotus places them."

[4] Book 2. c. 158.

began a little above the city Bubastis, near the Arabian city Patumos, but it discharged itself into the Red Sea."[1] According to this, Patumos was situated on the east side of the Pelusiac arm of the Nile, not far from the entrance of the canal which unites the Nile with the Red Sea,[2] in the Arabian part of Egypt.[3] The Itinerarium *Antonini* furnishes a further limitation. It can scarcely be doubted that the Thum which is mentioned is identical with Patumos and Pithom. The Π is merely the Egyptian article.[4] Now this Thum was twelve Roman miles distant from Heroöpolis,[5] whose ruins are found in the region of the present Abu Keisheid. All these designations are appropriate, if with the scholars who accompanied the French Expedition we place Pithom on the site of the present Abbaseh, at the entrance of the Wady Tumilat, where there was at all times a strong military post.

Let us now seek to determine the location of Raamses. That the author supposed it lay in Goshen we have, in addition to the general reasons already referred to, a particular one. It is said in Gen. xlvii. 11, "And Joseph gave them a possession in the

---

[1] Ἥκται δὲ ἀπὸ τοῦ Νείλου τὸ ὕδωρ ἐς αὐτήν· ἦκται δὲ κατύπερθε ὀλίγον Βουβάστιος πόλιος, παρὰ Πάτουμον τὴν Ἀραβίην πόλιν· ἐσίχει δὲ ἐς τὴν ἐρυθρὴν θάλασσαν. Larcher wishes arbitrarily to place a point after πόλιος, and reject the δὲ after ἐσίχει. Lange follows his example. Bähr, on the contrary, says: Quidni enim Herodoto dicere licuit: ductum esse canalem paulo supra Bubastin urbem, juxta Patumon, Arabiae urbem (quam sc. urbem praeterfluat), ab ea autem haud procui in mare exire. But Bähr has not been able to entirely free himself from the error of Larcher. From his inclination towards it, comes the entirely arbitrary addition of, ab ea haud procui. Herodotus gives no such information as this: Patumos is situated near the place where the canal discharges itself into the Red Sea. According to him, Patumos lay rather, near the commencement of the canal: it began above Bubastis and *near* Patumos, and ended in the Red Sea.

[2] If the passage from Herodotus is correctly understood, Patumos, situated near the beginning of the canal, cannot be identical with Heroöpolis, as is erroneously asserted by some.

[3] Compare Bähr upon the passage: Arabiae dicitur urbs, quod omnes Aegypti urbes a Nilo Arabiam versus sitae hoc nomine vulgo afficiuntur. The Seventy translate גֹּשֶׁן in Gen. xlv. 10., by Γεσὲμ Ἀραβίας, just as Herodotus calls Patumos an Arabian city.

[4] Champollion l'Egypte sous les Pharaons, t. 2. p. 58.

[5] Itin. Ant.

land of Egypt, in the best of the land,[1] in the land of Rameses." The same land which is everywhere in the preceding and succeeding context called the land of Goshen, is here designated as the land of Rameses, or the land whose chief city is Rameses;[2] and

---

[1] "The land of Goshen," says *Dr Robinson*, "was the best of the land; and such, too, the province esh-Shŭrkîyeh has ever been, down to the present time. In the remarkable Arabic document translated by *De Sacy*, containing a valuation of all the provinces and villages of Egypt in the year 1376, the province of the Shŭrkîyeh comprises 383 towns and villages, and is valued at 1,411,875 *Dinars*,—a larger sum than is put upon any other province, with one exception. During my stay in Cairo, I made many inquiries respecting this district; to which the uniform reply was, that it was considered the best province in Egypt.—This (its fertility) arises from the fact that it is intersected by canals, while the surface of the land is less elevated above the level of the Nile, than in other parts of Egypt; so that it is more easily irrigated. There are here more flocks and herds than anywhere else in Egypt; and also more fishermen." Compare, with this last expression, p. 224 supra.

[2] According to the common opinion, the so called *land* Rameses in this passage is not the same as the city Raamses in Ex. i. 11. But the reason which is relied upon in favour of this difference, (see for example Michaelis Supplem. p. 2256,) the dissimilarity of punctuation, (which is however very trifling,) is of little force. The Raamses in Ex. i. 11., is evidently only the fuller sounding pause-form. But that also in Gen. xlvii, 11., the *city* Raamses is spoken of, is favoured by the following argument. In three passages of the Pentateuch besides Ex. i., in Ex. xii. 37., and Num. xxxiii. 3 and 5., Raamses is undeniably the name of a city. (It is true that some have wished to make it even in these last two passages the name of a province; so has even v. Raumer, in the Exodus of the Israelites, S. 11. But it is perfectly clear that this cannot be. Let us look at the passages a little more minutely: "And the children of Israel removed from Rameses and pitched in Succoth, and they departed from Succoth and pitched in Etham." If Succoth and Etham are names of a single district, not of an entire province, so must Rameses also be.) On the contrary, Rameses is found in no other passage as the name of a province. Accordingly then, the presumption is, that Rameses in Gen. xlvii. 11., is the name of a city. If the author did not intend to be so understood, he ought to have explained himself more minutely. But Rameses cannot properly be the name of the province in Gen. xlvii., since this before and after is called Goshen. Rosellini is also of the opinion, I. 1. p. 300, that the Rameses in Gen. xlvii. is identical with the one in Exodus i. The author of the book of Genesis, he supposes, intends to say that Joseph placed his father and his family in the region in which the city Raamses was afterwards built. It is improbable, even when we leave Ex. i. 11. out of the account, (that this passage is not in favour of the previous non-existence of Raamses, Michaelis has already remarked, Suppl. p. 2256,)

this is entirely in accordance with Ex. xii. 37, and Num. xxxiii. 3, 5, where Rameses, since the departure of the Israelites commences there, is clearly designated as a central point in the land of Goshen.

Now, with reference to the inquiry whether Raamses was really situated where the author of the Pentateuch places it, the proof which alone is sure, is furnished by the Alexandrian translation of Gen. xlvi. 28, 29. While the original text names simply Goshen, the translator has in verse 28: "But Judah he sent before him to Joseph, that he might come to meet him at Heroöpolis in the land of Rameses," (συναντῆσαι αὐτῷ καθ' Ἡρώων πόλιν εἰς γῆν Ῥαμεσσῆ,) and in verse 29: "And Joseph prepared his chariot, and went up to meet Israel his father, at Heroöpolis," (καθ' ἡρώων πόλιν.) It is certain that "at Heroöpolis in the land Rameses" is no arbitrary conceit of the Seventy. They took the designation "land Rameses" instead of Goshen from Gen. xlvii. 11, where the author himself substitutes, for Goshen, the land of Rameses. In the phrase "at Heroöpolis," for the name Rameses, which had gone out of use, Heroöpolis, the current name in their time, was substituted. The city Raamses was to them the same as Heroöpolis, the land of Rameses therefore was situated in the vicinity of Heroöpolis.

This, which is as good as a direct declaration of the Seventy that Raamses is identical with Heroöpolis, seems of no small importance when we consider that the Greek name Heroöpolis, cannot be older than the time of the Greek dominion over Egypt, while the Alexandrian translation of the Pentateuch was made as early as the first period of this dominion; so that the earlier name of the city could scarcely be unknown to the translator. According to *Mannert*,[1] indeed, the city is not supposed to have existed before the time of the Greek dominion, and accordingly had no earlier name. "It was," he says very confidently, "a new Gre-

that this city was already in existence in the time of Joseph. The name furnishes an argument against it. Raamses means: consecrated to the sun (see I. 1. p. 117,) and it is very common among the Egyptian kings, especially those of the Mosaic period. The city evidently derived its name from one of these kings. But according to ancient authors, and the monuments, the name Rameses was given to no one before the eleventh Pharaoh of the eighteenth dynasty, whose reign was considerably subsequent to the time of Joseph.

[1] S. 576 der alten Geographie von Aegypten.

clan city, built merely on account of the canal, and for the sake of trade. Neither *Herodotus* nor any writer before the age of the Ptolemies was acquainted with it, hence its Greek name." But even the name itself, as will directly appear, carries us back to remote antiquity; and what is most important, if it was entirely new, how could the Seventy have identified it with Heroöpolis?

The agreement of the two names indicates also that the Seventy have justly identified the Heroöpolis of their time with the ancient Raamses, just as in chap. xli. 45, they have placed for the On of the original text, Heliopolis, the Greek name. That the city Raamses borrowed its appellation from one of the honoured rulers of that name, is not surely now doubted by any one; the etymology proposed by *Jablonski*, which entirely leaves out of the account the connection between the city and the rulers of the same name, is wholly unworthy of notice. When we now see from the monuments how much the Egyptians employed the name Rameses, and what associations they connected with it, the Greek name Heroöpolis, city of Heroes, seems a very suitable translation of the ancient Egyptian name.

Now it is admitted by all the authorities respecting the location of Heroöpolis, that it was situated in the ancient land of Goshen. For our immediate object, therefore, we need not enter upon a more accurate determination of its position. Yet it is of so much importance for the geographical investigation concerning the Exodus of the Israelites, to which we shall next direct our attention, that, as a preparation for that, we must endeavour to settle more accurately its position.

The ancient geographers until the time of the French expedition, following the [inaccurate] statements of several ancient writers, looked for Heroöpolis directly on the Arabian Gulf.[1]

---

[1] Mannert, S. 514, adhering to this view, still looks for Heroöpolis at the end of the canal which united the Nile with the Red Sea, between the Bitter Lakes and the northern point of the Arabian Gulf, since, he remarks, "all ancient writers who speak of this city, place it in the interior angle of the Arabian Gulf, not far from the city Arsinoe." But Mannert is obliged to remark, first, S. 514, in reference to the considerable ruin of Saba Biyar: "I cannot give an explanation of it." Secondly, S. 515, he concedes that the ruins of *his* Heroöpolis cannot be found. Thirdly, he remarks, S. 516, in reference to the passage of the Seventy, which we shall examine farther in the text: "Now it certainly is the most improbable explanation of all, which makes the city to have been

Against the admission of this opinion, the following reasons are especially important. First, Heroöpolis, as we have already seen, is identical with the ancient Raamses. But this could not lie on the Arabian Gulf, since the Israelites did not arrive in the neighbourhood of the Arabian Gulf until the end of the second day's march, which they commenced at Raamses. Secondly, The passage, Gen. xlvi. 28, 29, according to the Alexandrian version, is entirely inexplicable on the supposition that Heroöpolis was on the Red Sea. How could the Seventy then represent Joseph as going out to meet his father Jacob, in the neighbourhood of this city, which lay so far out of his course in coming from Canaan into Egypt? This reason is of great importance. The Alexandrian translator must necessarily have known the position of Heroöpolis. His authority exceeds in importance that of the most accurate of the Greek Geographers. Thirdly, The statement in the Itinerarium *Antonini*, according to which Hero=Heroöpolis lay between Thum=Patumos and Serapium, about twelve Roman miles distant from each, is also entirely at variance with the older hypothesis.

The correct position of Heroöpolis was first determined by the scholars of the French Expedition, and the view in which the majority of them have united, has obtained almost universal assent. "The researches of the members of the Egyptian Commission," says *Champollion*,[1] "have furnished the certain and acknowledged result that Heroöpolis lies between the Pelusiac arm of the Nile and the Bitter Lakes to the northwest of these lakes, at a place which is now called Abu Keisheid, from the Arab tribe which roves about on the Isthmus."

The most accurate and vivid description of the situation of Heroöpolis is given by *Du-Bois-Aymé*, in his treatise "upon the ancient bounds of the Red Sea."[2] "The valley Seba-Biyar, called by the Arabs Wady, begins about two *myriametres* from Belbeis,

situated, not far to the south, but on the direct road which passes through Abu Keisheid. But the whole statement is a mere error of the translator; the Hebrew text knows nothing of Heroöpolis; Joseph came to *Goshen* to meet his father." As if anything were accomplished by this! Whether the Seventy translated correctly or not, is just the same. It is sufficient that they mention the city Heroöpolis in a connection in which a city on the Arabian Gulf cannot properly be placed.

[1] L'Egypte sous les Pharaons, t. 2. p. 89.
[2] Descr. t. 11. p. 376.

It runs from east to west. The Nile in its greatest rise sometimes reaches even to this place. Sweet water is always found here by digging from twelve to fifteen *decimetres* deep. The soil is of the same nature and appearance with that directly on the Nile. But since the land is seldom overflowed, it has less depth of fertile soil deposited by the flood. It is not more than two decimetres deep. Under this lies a light clay, mingled with sand. The canal which conveys the water of the Nile thither runs to a distance of about one and a half myriametres to the declivity which incloses the valley on the north. This makes the conveyance of the water necessary for culture very easy for the inhabitants. But sometimes the Nile does not reach a height for several years sufficient to supply water for the canal : and then they make use of wells for irrigation. At the entrance of the valley lies the village Abbaseh,[1] near which is a lake called by the Arabs Birket el-Fergeh, or Birket el-Haj el-Kadem. This last name, which signify the ancient Pilgrim's pool, leads to the conjecture that in the earliest term of pilgrimage to Mecca, the great caravan which now passes by Adsherad, went through the valley Seba Biyar, in order to turn to the head of the gulf.—At two *myriametres* from Abbaseh the canal is interrupted. There ends the Wady Tumilat. It takes this name from the Arab tribe Tumilat, who occupy this region. The valley Seba Biyar stretches yet two *myriametres* further to the east ; and in about the middle of this part of the valley there is an extensive heap of ruins which indicate the position of an ancient city ; the Arabs name this place Abu Keisheid. Upon the point of a little hill which is formed by these ruins, there lies a great granite block, upon which in relievo are hewn out three Egyptian deities," &c.[2] Compare also upon the site of Heroöpolis at the place where are now the ruins of Abu Keisheid,

---

[1] The same, on whose site, as has been previously shown, the ancient Pithom or Patumos lay. The two fortified cities, named in connection with one another in Ex. i. 11, were situated therefore in the same valley, and the fortifications which Pharaoh commanded to be built around both had probably the common object of obstructing the entrance into Egypt, which this valley furnished to the enemy from Asia. Pharaoh had so much the more occasion for the construction of these fortifications, since he believed that he had reason to fear, that the Israelites would readily make common cause with the enemies pressing in from this quarter. See Ex. i. 10.

[2] In the Description, t. 11. p. 376.

upon the canal which connects the Nile with the Arabian Gulf, in the middle of the Wady, *Le Père*, in his treatise on the canal of the two Seas.[1]

THE MARCH OF THE ISRAELITES FROM RAAMSES TO THE RED SEA.

Through the just determination of the position of Heroöpolis, and consequently of Raamses, the narrative of the departure of the Israelites has received an unexpected light, and the credibility of the Pentateuch a wonderful confirmation.

On the second day after their departure, the Israelites came into the region about the northern point of the Arabian Gulf. Their first station was Succoth, the second Etham, whose position is designated in Ex. xiii. 20, and in Num. xxxiii. 6, by the words, "which lies at the end of the desert." That by "the desert" here, no other than the Arabian desert, beginning at the northern point of the Red Sea,[2] can be meant, is evident from the following reasons : 1. Although the phrase "the desert" is sometimes used with a more unrestricted reference, as for instance in chap. xiv. 3, where Pharaoh says, "They are entangled in the land, the desert hath shut them in," and in verses 11 and 12 of the same chapter; so that the Egyptian part of the desert[3] is also includ-

---

[1] Descr. t. 11. p. 291, seq.

[2] Very correctly J. H. Michaelis says : nempe qua Aegyptum attingit.

[3] What Rüppell says (Reise, S. 209,) shows that the Eastern part of Egypt deserves this name, as well as Arabia Petraea. The west coast of the Gulf of Suez and its continuation to Cosseir, may be said to be without inhabitant, and the almost entire want of drinkable water along the coast of the sea is a cause sufficient to prevent settlements there. But it is specially important to compare the treatise " de la geographie comparée et de l'ancien état côtes de la mer rouge," by Rozière, in t. 6 of the Descr. p. 267 : The contrast with the adjoining region first arrests the attention when the traveller enters upon the Isthmus of Suez. As long as he is in Egypt, notwithstanding the heat of a scorching sun, he beholds a fresh plain, permeated by flowing water, shaded by palm trees, clothed with grass, flowers, or the golden harvest; a smiling and animated region, where everything reminds him of only abundance and fruitfulness. When he comes upon the Isthmus under the same sky, how great the change ! There is no trace of cultivation or of inhabitant, no shade, no verdure, no flowing water, in a word, nothing which can sustain life. So as he proceeds farther, he seeks with anxiety some more fertile spot of ground in the distance, but the eye glances over the whole unending expanse of the horizon in vain ; even to both seas, on every side is a dry, leafless land,

ed, yet this is to be considered only as an exception to the general rule. "The desert" is generally the Arabian desert. 2. The phrase, "which lies at the edge of the desert," was evidently designed to show that the Israelites had already arrived at the border of Egypt, when they reached Etham. The expression, "they encamped in Etham at the edge of the desert," is followed in both places by the declaration, that the Israelites turned back, i.e. instead of crossing the boundary, they went again further into Egypt, as in Num. xxxiii. 7 : "And they removed from Etham, and turned back to Pi-hahiroth," &c. But the words do not correspond to their evident design, unless by the desert the Arabian is specifically understood. 3. The passage, Num. xxxiii. 8, is entirely decisive. Yet, in order to perceive its full force, it must be considered in connection with what goes before : verse 5, "And the children of Israel removed from Rameses, and pitched in Succoth." Verse 6, "And they departed from Succoth, and pitched in Etham, which is in the edge of the desert." Verse 7, "And they removed from Etham and returned to Pi-hahiroth, which lies before Baal-zephon, and pitched before Migdol." Verse 8, "And they departed from before Pi-hahiroth, and passed through the midst of the sea to the desert, and went three days' journey in the desert of Etham, and pitched in Marah." According to verse 8, the part of the Arabian desert which lies on the eastern shore of the Arabian Gulf bore the name of the desert of Etham. How can this well be otherwise explained than by supposing that the place from which the desert takes its name lies at the north end of the Arabian Gulf, and consequently on the borders of the desert named from it ? The sense is evidently this : At the end of the second day they had already arrived at the borders of the Arabian desert, at Etham, from which the tract of country lying next to Egypt receives the name, desert of Etham. But instead of advancing directly into the desert, they turned down again farther into Egypt to the Arabian Gulf. Afterwards, instead of going

---

barren rocks, glimmering sand, a plain bare everywhere. We find just the same contrast between Egypt and the desert in Ex. xiv. 12 : "Because there were no graves in Egypt, hast thou taken us away to die in the desert? Wherefore hast thou dealt thus with us, to carry us forth out of Egypt? Is not this what we did tell thee in Egypt, Let us alone that we may serve the Egyptians ; for it is better for us to serve the Egyptians, than to die in the wilderness."

round the sea, they proceeded through it unto the desert of Etham.

Supposing it now certain, that the Israelites at the end of the second day's march had reached the northern point of the Arabian Gulf, we are then, according to the common hypothesis, that the Raamses from which the Israelites began their march lay in the region of Heliopolis, brought into no small difficulty. The distance is then far too great.[1] It amounts from the Nile to the Red Sea to twenty-six hours, if we suppose, with *Sicard* and *von Raumer*,[2] that they passed through the valley of Wandering, and to as much, at least, if, with *Niebuhr*, they are allowed to have taken the common caravan route at the present day which leads from Cairo by Suez to Sinai. *Niebuhr*[3] says: "We spent twenty-eight hours and forty minutes, deducting the time of resting, on our way from Birket el Haj (four hours from Cairo)." Evidently much too great a distance for so heavily laden a train as was that of the Israelites.

But if we place Raamses[4] on the site of the present Abu Keisheid, this difficulty entirely vanishes. The distance from this

[1] "We were quite satisfied from our own observation, that they (the Israelites) could not have passed to the Red Sea from any point near Heliopolis or Cairo in three days, the longest interval which the language of the narrative allows. Both the distance and the want of water on all the routes, are fatal to such an hypothesis. We read, that there were six hundred thousand men of the Israelites above twenty years of age, who left Egypt on foot. There must of course have been as many women above twenty years old; and at least an equal number both of males and females under the same age; besides the 'mixed multitude' spoken of, and very much cattle. The whole number, therefore, probably amounted to two and a half millions, and certainly to not less than two millions. Now the usual day's march of the best appointed armies, both in ancient and modern times, is not estimated higher than fourteen English or twelve geographical miles; and it cannot be supposed that the Israelites, encumbered with women and children and flocks, would be able to accomplish more. But the distance on all these routes being not less than sixty geographical miles, they could not well have travelled it in any case in less than five days."—*Bib. Res.*, Vol. I. pp. 74, 75.

[2] See von Raumer, S. 11, and Ritter, S. 859.

[3] Beschreibung von Arabien, S. 408.

[4] It may be proper to say here, that in this volume Remeses is spelt in three ways. When it is the name of a king, it is, on the authority of *Wilkinson*, Remeses. In the other two cases, the method of the verse in the Bible, to which allusion is made, is retained.

place to the Red Sea is about thirteen French leagues.[1] This distance appears not too great,[2] but just sufficient, if it is considered that the Israelites departed "in haste."

We remark further, that the opinion of the French scholars who look for Etham on the site of the present Bir Suweis, has much probability.[3] This place is described by *Le Père*[4] in the following manner: "The traveller comes finally out of the valley and reaches the plain of Suez. The city as well as the sea is in sight, and a gentle declivity leads down to Bir Suweis or the wells of Suez; these wells are only an hour from Suez." Etham must have been situated somewhere in this region, on account of the designation, " which is at the edge of the desert." What *Du Bois Aymé* says applies especially to Bir Suweis: " Sweet water is very scarce in this whole region, and the wells must determine the stations of the caravans."

"BETWEEN MIGDOL AND THE SEA."

Finally also, Ex. xiv. 2 deserves a discussion in our geographical section: " Speak to the children of Israel that they turn back and encamp before Pi-hahiroth between Migdol and the sea over against Baal-zephon, before it shall ye encamp by the sea." Compare with Num. xxxiii. 7: " And they removed from Etham and returned back to Pi-hahiroth which is before Baal-zephon, and they pitched before Migdol."

An insuperable difficulty appears to lie here in the phrases " between Migdol and the sea," and " they pitched before Migdol." Migdol is, doubtless, as even the Seventy perceived, identical with Magdolum. But this place lies, according to the declaration of the Itinerarium *Antonini*, only twelve Roman miles southward from Pelusium. The general correctness of this declaration is confirmed by Ex. xxix. 10, xxx. 6, where in the words from " Migdol to Syene" these places are opposed to each other; Syene as being the most

---

[1] See Le Père in the Description, t. 1. p. 84, who also on pages 74 seq. gives a description of the way from Abu Keisheid to Heroöpolis.

[2] "From thirty to thirty-five miles, which might easily have been passed over in three days."—*Bib. Res.*, Vol. I. p. 80.

[3] See, for example, Du Bois-Aymé in a treatise: On the residence of the Hebrews in Egypt, Descr. t. 8. p. 113.

[4] P. 61.

southern border of Egypt, and Migdol the most northern, also by the passage in *Herodotus* where Magdolum, as the acknowledged border town of Egypt towards Palestine, is interchanged with Megiddo.[1] If Migdol was so far distant from the place where the Israelites were encamped—nearly the whole breadth of the Isthmus of Suez lies between—how can it be said, that the Israelites "encamped between Migdol and the sea," and "pitched before Migdol?"

The difficulty here is removed by the remark, that "between Migdol and the sea," and "before Migdol," do not serve for the geographical designation of the place where the Israelites were encamped, but rather call attention to the peril to which they exposed themselves by their foolish march.

That Migdol was a fortress, the name itself shows, since it signifies tower or fortress. Probably the border garrison against Syria, which in later times was removed to the neighbouring Daphne, was stationed here. *Herodotus* says: "Under king Psamaticus guards were stationed at Elephantine against the Ethiopians, as in the Pelusiac Daphne against the Arabs and Syrians, and in Marea in like manner against Lybia. And even to this hour Persian guards are stationed at the very same places where they were under Psamaticus; for Persians are on guard at Elephantine, and also in Daphne."[2]

Upon the phrase "between Migdol and the sea" is founded the saying of Pharaoh, "The desert has shut them in." They ought to have sought to free themselves as soon as possible from this unfortunate dilemma—to go around the north end of the Arabian Gulf before the garrison marching out from Migdol could block up their way—and they had already nearly escaped. Then they thrust themselves, through an inexplicable misunderstanding, again into the midst of danger.

Thus also here, that which appears at first view to be opposed to the author's knowledge of Egypt, is a proof of it, when more particularly examined.

---

[1] 2. 159, Καὶ Σύροισι πεζῇ ὁ Νεκὼς συμβαλὼν ἐν Μαγδόλῳ ἐνίκησε.
[2] B. 2. chap. 30.

HISTORY OF JOSEPH—CONTINUED.

KINGS AND PRIESTS, THE POSSESSORS OF THE LAND IN EGYPT.

We proceed now, after finishing our inquiry concerning the references of the Pentateuch to the geographical features of Egypt, in the explanation of the Egyptian allusions in this portion of sacred history, in the order of the chapters. We first turn our attention to Gen. xlvii. 13—26.

Joseph, according to this account, purchased for Pharaoh of his subjects the right of possession to their land, so that the whole country henceforth belonged to Pharaoh. " Only the land of the priests bought he not; for the priests had a portion assigned them of Pharaoh, and did eat their portion which Pharaoh gave them; wherefore they sold not their lands," verse 22. The land was divided out to its former possessors by lease; they were compelled to pay a fifth of its yearly produce. " And Joseph made it a law over the land of Egypt to this day, that Pharaoh should have the fifth part, except the land of the priests only, which became not Pharaoh's," verse 26.

Among the accounts of profane writers which extend over this same ground, those of *Herodotus* and *Diodorus* are of particular importance. The first of these authors says: " The same king (Sesostris) had also divided the whole land among the Egyptians, they said, and had given to each one a square portion of equal extent, and in this way he obtained his income, for he collected from each individual a yearly rent. And when the flood took away something from the portion of one, he must come to the king and make a representation of the calamity. The king then sent some of his servants to examine it and measure how much less the land had become, that the tenant might pay from what remained in proportion to the whole amount of the imposed rent."[1] According to *Diodorus*[2] all the land in Egypt belonged either to the priests or the kings, or the military caste.

---

[1] B. 2. c. 109.   [2] l. 73.

An important point of agreement between the Biblical account and profane writers comes here directly into view. There is an entire accordance with regard to the prominent thing, namely, that the cultivators were not the possessors of the soil. *Strabo*[1] also says, that those who were employed in agriculture and trade held their land subject to rent. In the sculptures, as *Wilkinson*[2] shows, only kings, priests, and the military order, are represented as landowners. Contracts of sale lately discovered, according to which towns seem to have had their separate territories,[3] belong to a very late condition of things, (a certain, although a limited right of possession will always arise, in process of time, from the condition of tenants,) and at most warrant only the assertion that the rule was not without exceptions.[4] " We can affirm with certainty," says *Heeren*,[5] " that if not all, yet surely the greatest and best part of the land belonged to the king, the temples, the priests, and the military order. It is further certain that these lands were cultivated by tenants, whose precise condition, whether they were fee-farmers or temporary occupants of the land, we do not know. Their condition may have been similar to that of the present Fellahs, who by no means have full ownership of land.[6] But it can-

[1] 17, p. 787. [2] I. p. 263.
[3] Böckh Erklärung einer Aeg. Urkunde, S. 27.
[4] Anything further is not desired by Böckh. That Herodotus does not recognise any special caste of cultivators, he explains by the fact that the peasants were not land-owners, and consequently could not constitute a special caste. He supposes that the kings, priests, and soldiers, all possessed real estate in the country, and a part of that in the towns, but that the inhabitants of towns in their very limited provinces also had possessions in land.
[5] S. 142.
[6] We will here quote what Girard says in the Description, t. 17, p. 189, "upon the right of possession in Egypt," since it aids in the explanation of the meaning of our passage : Such is also the condition of that which they here call private possessions. They remain in the same family less by right of inheritance, than as a testimony of the favour of the ruler, in whose hand it always remains to dispose of them according to his will. These possessions are, as it seems, only a kind of revertible and therefore entirely unalienable fief. We cannot here then, with the expression 'sale of real estate,' connect the idea of an invariable and absolute abdication, but merely that of a temporary mortgaging for a sum of money which is borrowed. The real estate will belong to the lender until the repayment of the money. Then the owner receives the avails of the land which he had abandoned.

not be doubted that the culture of the soil, if it was not entirely, yet was certainly for the most part performed by tenants. These therefore constituted the Egyptian peasantry," &c.

The narration in Genesis, and the consequent accurate acquaintance of the author with the condition of Egypt contended for by us, receive further confirmation from profane writers, since they attribute to the priests possessions in land as their own, and consequently rent free. "So much is certain," remarks *Heeren*,[1] "that a greater, perhaps the greatest and best part of the land, was in the possession of the priests."

But, on the other hand, there are important apparent contradictions between our narrative and the accounts of profane writers:

1. *Herodotus*, it might be said, ascribes the partition of the land to king Sesostris; but he cannot possibly be the king in whose time the administration of Joseph falls. But, although *Heeren*[2] seeks to sustain this statement of *Herodotus*, it must be considered as a fixed result of modern investigation, that Sesostris is not a historical but a mythic personage,[3] to whom it was the custom to trace back all the important measures and the great successes of the ancient Pharaohs. And this *Heeren* himself has also more recently acknowledged.[4]

If, further, *Herodotus* appears to know nothing of an original possession of the land by the Egyptian cultivators, but rather considers the king as the original possessor, the advantage is so decidedly on the side of the Book of Genesis, that the contradiction of *Herodotus* confirms its credibility and places in a clearer light the author's knowledge of Egypt, which extends back far beyond the time approached by profane writers. The fact confirmed by *Herodotus*, that the king was possessor of the land occupied by the cultivators, implies a historical fact through which it was brought about. That the king should be the original possessor of the whole land is not conceivable, and is contrary to the analogy of history in a country like Egypt, not obtained by conquest.

2. According to the representation in Genesis, there were only two classes of land-owners, the kings and the priests. *Diodorus*, on the contrary, whose declaration is confirmed by the monuments, mentions three classes, kings, priests, and the military caste. But

---

[1] S. 131.
[2] S. 142.
[3] Bähr upon Her. IV. S. 563.
[4] Gött. Anz. 1834. S. 39.

Herodotus furnishes us with the data for reconciling this apparent contradiction. According to him the real estate of the military order differed from that of the peasants, since it was free of rent; but otherwise belonged to the kings, and was given by them in fee to the soldiery. According to book 2. chap. 141, the land of the military order was given to them by the kings, and taken away by one of the same, named Sothon. That this land was instead of pay, is said in chap. 168: "They alone, of all the Egyptians except the priests, had the following special privilege, namely: each one had twelve acres of good land, free of rent."

3. It appears from the account in Genesis, verse 22, that the priests received their support from the king. On the contrary, *Herodotus*[1] says, as, at least, it is affirmed by *Heeren*,[2] whom most in modern times, as for example *Drumann*,[3] *Rosenmueller*,[4] and *Bähr*[5] follow: The support of the priests is obtained from the revenues of the land belonging to the temples, from the temple-treasures.

This contradiction would disappear of itself, if we could, with *v. Bohlen*,[6] translate verse 22 differently from what we have done above: "Only the lands of the priests he did not purchase, for that is a legacy to the priests on the part of Pharaoh, and they enjoyed their privilege which Pharaoh gave to them, therefore they sold not their land." According to this interpretation there is indeed no account in this passage of the daily portion which the priests received from the king. The reason that Pharaoh did not purchase the grounds of the priests, is this: they were already themselves crown-lands. But we could not well avail ourselves of this advantage. In the place of the contradiction removed, a new one would immediately arise. In opposition to other declarations, and to the whole situation of the Egyptian priests, all possessions in land, properly so called, would be denied them in this passage.

Moreover, this explanation is wholly inadmissible.[7] According

---

[1] 2. c. 37.
[2] S. 132. [3] Ueber die Inschrift zu Rosette, S. 158.
[4] Alt. u. Neu. Morgen. 1. S. 222. [5] Zu Herod. B. 2. c. 37.
[6] S. 60.
[7] The Hebrew word חק is also used to designate an allowance of food in Prov. xxx. 8., and xxxi. 15. The word *that* is arbitrarily inserted by v. Bohlen. The phrase, "the land of the priests," when compared with verse 20, can mean only the land which belongs to the priests as their own

to sound interpretation, the passage can mean only as follows; only the land of the priests he did not purchase; for the cause, which compelled the remaining Egyptians to sell their land, did not affect them, since they received an allowance from Pharaoh, so that, so long as he had bread, they also had it.

But the contradiction may be removed in another way, and become perfect agreement. In the passage of *Herodotus*[1] especially relied on, the meaning is not what it has been affirmed to be. It is there said: "And yet many thousand other usages, I might say, must they observe. But for this there is also much favour shown them. For neither their means of support, nor their other expenses, are derived from their own wealth. But they have their holy bread baked, and each one receives a great quantity of goose and neat's flesh every day; wine is also given them." The distinction is not here between the "common treasures" and "private wealth" of the priests, but between their own property and that which they receive in common with others out of the public treasures, from the king. It is precisely the distinction between the wealth of the priests existing in lands, and their salary made up of natural productions, which appears in Genesis; so that this passage of *Herodotus*, very far from contradicting our representation, serves rather as a strong confirmation of it. The phrase, "For neither their means of support nor other expenses are derived from their own wealth,"[2] then leads decidedly to this conclusion. For, since in what precedes the passage quoted, individual priests are not spoken of, but priests in general, so it is entirely arbitrary to understand by "their own wealth" the private property of individuals. The wealth of the priesthood, in distinction from the allowance which was given them as a reward for their service, can alone then be designated here. This declaration: "There is much favour shown them," (lit. they suffer

property, and also the expression "except the land of the priests alone, became not Pharaoh's," in verse 26, shows that the land of the priests was in the fullest sense their own. After comparing the words אֶת־חֻקָּם אֲכָלוּ with verse 18 seq., according to which the Egyptians sold their land in order to procure food, no one will interpret them by "they enjoyed their privilege." Finally, it cannot, from the nature of the case, be supposed, that the same author who makes the Egyptian peasants landowners, will deny to the priests all such possessions.

[1] 2. 37.
[2] Οὔτε τι γὰρ τῶν οἰκηΐω τρίβουσι οὔτε δαπανέωνται.

SUPPORT OF THE PRIESTS.

much good),[1] contributes further to this argument. For, since the party receiving, the suffering subjects are the priests in general, the activity must come from some other source than from themselves. Just so this: "There is to them," "there is given them." But did there any doubt remain with regard to the correctness of the foregoing explanation, it would be cleared away by the explanation of *Herodotus* himself in another place. He says,[2] The soldiers alone, *besides the priests*, receive a salary from the king. Now, since the land of the priests was their own property, their salary could consist only of the portion which was given them.

But other accounts also show that the priests received their support from the king. "The thirty judges," says *Drumann*,[3] "priests of Heliopolis, Thebes and Memphis, were maintained by the king,[4] and, without doubt, the sons of the priests also, all of whom over twenty years of age, were given to the king as servants, or more correctly, to take the oversight of his affairs.[5] As a general rule, every one in the immediate service of the court is maintained by the king; for example, the two thousand soldiers, who alternating yearly, formed the body guard of the king."[6] The ministers of court were in Egypt the priests, just as the state was a theocracy, and the king was considered as the representative and incarnation of the Godhead.

Diodorus says indeed, that the whole maintenance of the priests, as also the expenses for the offerings, &c., were derived from the revenues of the lands. But this is true, at any rate, only of later times, when the priesthood had lost much of their income, and of the respect previously shown them.[7]

We have hitherto shown that the author exhibits in the narrative which we are considering the most accurate knowledge of the condition of Egypt—such a knowledge as Moses may more easily be supposed to possess than any other one. But we cannot stop here. We must also show that the Egyptian usages here referred to, were the groundwork of those of the Israelites under discussion

---

[1] Πάσχουσι δὲ καὶ ἀγαθὰ οὐκ ὀλίγα.
[2] 2. chap. 168. [3] S. 159.
[4] Diodorus 1. 75. Συντάξεις δὲ τῶν ἀναγκαίων παρὰ τοῦ βασιλέως τοῖς μὲν δικασταῖς ἱκαναὶ πρὸς διατροφὴν ἐχορηγοῦντο· τῷ δὲ ἀρχιδικαστῇ πολλαπλάσιοι.
[5] Diod. 1. 70. [6] Herod. 2. 168. [7] Drumann, S. 159 ff.

in the Pentateuch, and that a copy of them can only be accounted for when the legislation attributed to Moses truly proceeded from him, since it was natural that he and no law-giver of more modern times should have regard to the Egyptian institutions in forming his laws. We will here quote what has been already said in another place[1] upon this point. "*Michaelis*[2] indeed finds a reference in the two-tenths in Gen. xlvii. to an Egyptian law. 'In Egypt,' he says, 'the lands all belonged to the king, and the husbandmen were not the proprietors of the fields which they cultivated, but farmers or tenants who were obliged to give to the king one-fifth of their produce. Gen. xlvii. 20—25. Just so Moses represents God, who honoured the Israelites by calling himself their king, the sole possessor of the soil of the promised land, in which he was about to place them by his special providence; but the Israelites were mere tenants, who could not alienate their land for ever.[3] In fact, they were obliged to give God, as also the Egyptians Pharaoh, two-tenths,' &c. Indeed the copiousness of the account must awaken the supposition of some design; and if we compare Lev. xxv., it can scarcely be doubted, that the representation of the relation in which Egypt stands to its visible king is applied to the relation of Israel to its invisible king, the king who is also God." As Pharaoh, we also add, furnished support for the priests out of the fifth which he received, so also did Jehovah.

EMBALMING,[4] LAMENTATION FOR THE DEAD, &C.

In Gen. l. 2, 3. it is said: "And Joseph commanded his servants the physicians to embalm his father, and the physicians embalmed Israel. And forty days were fulfilled for him; for so are fulfilled the days of those who are embalmed, and the Egyptians mourned for him seventy days."

This passage gives occasion for the following remarks: 1. The

[1] Th. III. der Beiträge zur Einl. ins Alt. T. S. 411, 412.
[2] Mos. Laws, Vol. I. § 73.
[3] Lev. xxv. 23. Compare verses 42 and 55.
[4] Additional information upon the topics discussed in this section may be found in *Wilkinson*, Vol. II. Sec. Ser. p. 451 seq. and 402 seq., with which compare *Lane's* Mod. Eg. pp. 285—311.

phrase, "Joseph commanded his servants, the physicians," is not to be understood to mean that all the physicians of Joseph took part in this operation. The command was rather obeyed by those among the physicians of Joseph to whom this business belonged. It is remarkable that we find among the domestics of Joseph a large number of physicians. Even *Warburton* has compared with this account what *Herodotus*[1] says of the healing art among the Egyptians: "The medical practice is divided among them as follows: each physician is for *one* kind of sickness, and no more, and all places are crowded with physicians; for there are physicians for the eyes, physicians for the head, physicians for the teeth, physicians for the stomach, and for internal disease." Therefore, remarks *Warburton*, it ought not to appear strange that Joseph had a considerable number of family physicians. "Every great family, as well as every city, must needs, as *Herodotus* expresses it, swarm with the faculty. A multitude of these domestics would now appear an extravagant piece of state, even in a first minister. But then we see it could not be otherwise, where each distemper had its proper physician."[2] The medical men of Egypt were renowned in ancient times. Cyrus had a physician sent him from Egypt,[3] and Darius always had Egyptian physicians with him.[4]

2. That the custom of embalming was very ancient in Egypt, is shown from the practice of cutting the bodies with an Ethiopian stone.[5] Some mummies also bear the date of the oldest kings.[6]

3. The embalming is here performed by the servants of Joseph, the physicians. According to the accounts of classical authors, on the contrary, the embalmers were a hereditary and organized class of men in Egypt, in which different duties were assigned to different persons. According to *Diodorus*, the Taricheuta were the most distinguished among them.[7] If a proper distinction of time is observed, there is no contradiction here. It is entirely natural to suppose, that in the most ancient times this operation was per-

---

[1] 2. 84. [2] Warburton's Divine Legation, Book IV. 3. 83.
[3] Herod. 3. 1. [4] Ibid. 3. 129.
[5] Herod. 2. 86. Biod. 1. 91. [6] Rosellini, II. 3. p. 306.
[7] Rosenm. Altertbumsk. II. 3. S. 352 ff. Upon this difference Zoega remarks, De Obeliscis, p. 263: At that time the college of Taricheuta seems not to have been formed, but embalming was performed by slaves.

formed by those to whom each one committed it. But afterwards, when the embalming was executed more according to the rules of art, a distinct class of operators gradually arose.

4. The embalming continued, according to the declaration of the author, forty days, the whole mourning seventy days, in which the forty days of the embalming are evidently included. The account of *Diodorus* agrees in a remarkable manner with this. With reference to embalming, he says: "They prepare the body first with cedar oil, and various other substances, more than thirty (according to another reading, forty) days; then, after they have added myrrh and cinnamon and other drugs, which have not only the power of preserving the body for a long time, but of imparting to it a pleasant odour, they commit it to the relatives of the deceased."[1] Of the mourning, the same author says: "When a king died, all the Egyptians raised a general lamentation, tore their garments, closed the temples, offered no sacrifices, celebrated no festivals for seventy-two days."[2] *Herodotus*,[3] in opposition to both these accounts, seems to limit the time of retaining the body in natron alone to seventy days. But if the passage referred to is more closely examined, it shows that he limited the whole time in which the body was under the embalmers to seventy days. Since this time began with the death and ended with the burial, while the mourning began and ended at the same time, there is the most perfect agreement between this passage of *Herodotus* and ours, which limits the time of lamentation to seventy days.[4]

---

[1] 1. 91.   [2] 1. 72.   [3] 2. 86.

[4] Herodotus says: ταῦτα δὲ ποιήσαντες, ταριχεύουσι λίτρῳ, κρύψαντες ἡμέρας ἑβδομήκοντα· πλεῦνας δὲ τουτέων οὐκ ἔξεστι ταριχεύειν. That these seventy days of Herodotus have reference, not merely to the time of retaining the body in natron, but to the whole time of the embalming and mourning, has been asserted by some who are by no means guided by a respect for the Mosaic account, as for example, by Zoega, De Obeliscis, p. 253, and by Heyne, Spicilegium antiquitatis mumiarum, in Commentt. Götting. III. p. 85. The time is not only too long for retaining the body in natron, but it is also improbable that Herodotus would give the time of salting, which was so far from being the prominent thing that Diodorus does not mention it at all, and not that of embalming and of the whole operation. Besides, seventy, as a round and sacred number, is much more suitable for the whole than a single, proportionally unimportant part, which under the embalming in its restricted sense, of which alone the Pentateuch makes mention, (the חנט means, according to the Arabic, bonis odoribus condivit mortuum, and consequently designates the opera-

5. The Egyptians mourned for Jacob, according to the above passage, seventy days. In verse 4 it is said: "And when the days of his mourning were past," &c. In verses 10 and 11: "And they came to the threshing floor of Atad, which is beyond Jordan, and mourned there with a great and very sore lamentation; and he made a mourning for his father seven days, and the inhabitants of the land, the Canaanites, saw the mourning in the floor of Atad, and said, This is a grievous mourning to the Egyptians; wherefore the name of it was called Abel Mizraim (mourning of Egypt)." The classical writers also show that the Egyptians appointed for themselves a very solemn mourning for the dead, especially for those of high rank. *Herodotus*[1] says: "Lamentations and funerals were celebrated. When a man died in a house, that is, *one of rank*, all the females of his family co-

tion of which Diodorus speaks,) held so inferior a place. But Creuzer, to whom Bähr accedes, has attempted to prove that the explanation which is most in accordance with the facts in the case, is inconsistent with the words. "Ego si quaeris," he says in Comment. upon Herodotus, p. 45, "vereor ut hae explicationes conciliari queunt cum verbis Herodoti, qui quidem h. 1. diserte dicit ταριχεύουσι λίτρῳ, quod posterius vocabulum cogitando videtur repeti debere cum ad sequens κρύψαντες, tum ad ταρικεύειν, ita ut ταρικεύειν h. 1. proprie salitionem videatur significare." According to Creuzer, therefore, we must translate: "When this is done, they lay it in natron and leave it therein 70 days, but they are not allowed to salt it longer." But this interpretation is not admissible, much less then necessary. With κρύψαντες, λίτρῳ cannot be implied, for the dead body was not put into the natron, but that was applied to it. Ταρικεύειν without λίτρῳ can the more appropriately be taken in a general sense, since it is always so used in what precedes and follows. Compare c. 85: οὕτω ἐς τὴν ταρίχευσιν κομίζουσι, c. 86: ὧδε τὰ σπουδαιότατα ταριχεύουσι, e. 89: τὰς δὲ γυναῖκας τῶν ἐπιφανέων ἀνδρῶν, ἐπεὰν τελευτήσωσι, οὐ παραυτίκα διδοῦσι ταριχεύειν,—οὕτω παραδιδοῦσι τοῖς ταριχεύουσι. Compare upon the meaning of ταριχεύειν, primarily to salt and then to embalm in general, Creuzer, p. 10 seq.; Heyne p. 81. We must translate: "When this is done, they embalm it in natron, having concealed it (in all) 70 days; but it is not permitted to embalm it longer." The expression "having concealed it 70 days," refers to the whole time in which the dead body was removed from the view of the relatives, and was under the operation of the embalmers. The phrase "they are not allowed to embalm it longer," is explained by the remark, that to the ταρίχευσις the treatment with natron also belonged, which began after the embalming in its more limited sense was at an end, and continued until the burial, or to the end of the mourning.

[1] B. 2. c. 85.

vering their faces with mud, and leaving the body in the house, ran through the streets, girded up, and striking their bare breasts and uttering loud lamentations. All their female relations joined them. The men beat their breasts in like manner, and also girded up their dress." *Diodorus*[1] says: "If any one dies among them, all his relatives and friends cover their heads with mud, and go about the streets with loud lamentations, until the body is buried. In the meantime, they neither use baths, nor even take wine, or any other than common food; they also do not put on beautiful garments." The same author gives an account of the lamentation of the Egyptians on the death of a king. Men and women, to the number of 200 or 300, went around in companies, sung twice every day the funeral dirge, honoured him with eulogies, and repeated the virtues of the dead. In the meantime, they neither taste meat nor wheaten bread, and abstained from wine, and every species of sumptuousness. No one used the bath or ointments or a soft bed, but every one was full of the deepest sorrow, as if a beloved child had died, and spent the prescribed time in sorrow. Meanwhile everything which pertained to the burial was made ready, and on the last day they placed the coffin which contained the body before the entrance of the tomb," &c.[2] The monuments[3] also show how violent and solemn the lamentation was among the Egyptians. Many of the ceremonies of mourning have been transmitted even to the modern Egyptians.[4]

In chap. l. 4, we read: "And when the days of his mourning (the mourning for Israel) were past, Joseph spake unto the house of Pharaoh, saying, If now I have found grace in your eyes, speak, I pray you, in the ears of Pharaoh," &c. It is worthy of remark here, that Joseph makes not his request directly to the king, but has recourse to the house of Pharaoh, while at other times he goes directly to Pharaoh; and even his brothers and his father were brought before Pharaoh, so that the fact cannot be explained on the ground of the hatred of the Egyptians to strangers. The correct explanation is as follows: It belongs to the Egyptian sense

---

[1] B. 1. c. 91.
[2] Diod. B. 1. c. 72.
[3] See the Representation of a mourning scene, from Thebes, in Wilkinson, Vol. I. p. 286.
[4] Heyne, p. 81, and De Chabrol, Essai s. les moeurs des habitants modernes de l'Egypt. Descr. t. 18. p. 180.

of propriety to go with shorn head and beard, and only so is it allowed to appear before the king. Compare chap. xli. 14, where Joseph shaved himself and changed his garments before he went to Pharaoh, and the remarks upon that passage above.[1] But while mourning, they were not permitted to shave. *Herodotus*[2] says: "Among other nations it is the custom in mourning for the relatives to shear the head, but the Egyptians, when an individual dies, leave the hair which was before cut off, to grow both upon the head and chin." Such peculiar customs are especially suited to fix the opinion with regard to the relation of the Pentateuch to Egypt.

In chap. l. 7 and 8, it is said: "And Joseph went up to bury his father; and with him went up all the servants of Pharaoh, the elders of the house, and all the elders of the land of Egypt. And all the house of Joseph and his brethren," &c. "The custom of funeral trains," says *Rosellini*,[3] "was peculiar to all periods, and to all the provinces of Egypt. We see the representations of funeral processions in the oldest tombs at Eilethyas, and similar ones are delineated in those of Saqqarah and Gizeh; we also find others of a like nature in the Theban tombs, which belong to the eighteenth, nineteenth, and twentieth dynasties." When we behold the representations of the processions for the dead upon the monuments, we seem to see the funeral train of Jacob.[4] The distinction between the elders of the house of Pharaoh, his court-officers, and the elders of the land of Egypt, the state-officers, is also worthy of notice. According to other accounts, the court of the Egyptian king was made up of the sons of the most distinguished priests; those called Nomarchs and Toparchs by the Greeks belonged to the state-officers.[5]

In chap. l. 26, it is said, "And Joseph died,—and they embalmed him, and he was put in a coffin in Egypt." Compare with this what *Herodotus*[6] says: "Now the relatives take away the body, and make a wooden image in the shape of a man, and place the body in it. When it is thus inclosed, they place it in the apartment for the dead, setting it upright against the wall." A doubt with regard to the Egyptian knowledge of the author might be awakened by the fact, that he permits Joseph to be placed in a

---

[1] P. 30. [2] B. 2. c. 36. [3] II. 3. p. 395.
[4] See in Taylor, p. 182. [5] Heeren, Ideen S. 337 ff. [6] B. 2. 86.

wooden sarcophagus,[1] while one of stone would be expected. But a closer examination shows that this expression is directly in favour of the credibility of the Pentateuch; coffins made of wood in Egypt, as indeed the passage already quoted from *Herodotus* shows, were the common ones, and those of basalt a rare exception;[2] and in the case of Joseph, his order that the children of Israel should at a future time carry his bones with them to Canaan, furnishes a separate reason for giving the preference to wood rather than stone. Besides, the custom of putting the dead in sarcophagi was by no means a general one, only rich and distinguished persons received this honour. Compare *Heyne*,[3] and notice that the Egyptian knowledge of the author appears here, since he permits Joseph to be a sharer in this honour that belongs to those who are highly esteemed.

[1] The Hebrew word אָרוֹן designates such a one. Plutarch employs the entirely synonymous word λάρναξ the same thing to designate. See Zoega de Obeliscis, p. 330.

[2] "Sarcophagi," says Heyne, p. 86, " e basalte rarissimi et ditissimorum fere : plerique e sycamoro, (compare upon the Sycamore wood as the common material of coffins for the dead, Creuzer Comm., Herod. p. 61,) ad formam corporis facti, ex uno caudice dimidiato, ut altera pars pro capuli fundo, altera pro tegumine sit ; alii e pluribus asseribus coassati." Compare upon the quality of coffins for the dead, Rosellini II. 3. p. 344. But the most copious collections upon wood, as the very common material of the Egyptian sarcophagi, are found in Zoega, p. 317 ; latissime autem patere videmus consuetudinem mortuos includere in arcas oblongas cadaveris staturae accommodatas, et sic sub terram condere, aut in sepulcro reponere super solo exstructo, aut vero hasi suffultas collocare sub divo. *Ligni ad hoc usus frequentissimus;* eoque Aegyptii ut plurimum contenti fuisse videntur, dum et sycomorus arbor, ejus regionis incola, materiem praeberet diuturnae durationis, et loca ubi condere solebant cadavera ab aëre atque humore ita essent praeclusa, ut quodvis lignum in iis perdurare potuisse videatur. Ideoque non alias quam ligneas arcas commemorat Herodotus, The same author says, p. 333 : Intelligimus et hinc in magno honore apud Aegyptios fuisse arcas ligneas cum arte factas et pulcre exornatas dum ipsum Osiridem hujusmodi conditorio delusum et captum inque eo sepultum traderent ; quare et regum cadavera ligneo loculo intra lapideum inclusa fuisse conjicio. The coffin of king Mycerinus, discovered in the year 1837 in the third pyramid of Memphis, is of sycamore wood. Compare Lenormant, Eclaircissemens s. le Cercuil du Roi Mycerinus, p. 4, Paris 1839.

[3] De sarcophago olim ita tradi solebat acsi omne mumiae sarcophago conditae essent ; atqui paucissimae ei inclusae sunt nec nisi in quas major impensa facta. Compare Maillet in Rosenm., A. u. N. M. Th. I. S. 257.

At the close of this chapter, we would also call attention to the wonderful change in the spirit of the Egyptian people, which appears in the narrative of the Pentateuch. Abraham found an easy entrance into Egypt and a friendly reception, and no distinction between him and the Egyptians is manifested. In the time of Joseph the spirit of the Egyptian people had acquired a more decided character; already are the shepherds an abomination, and Joseph must be freed from the ignominy of his origin by an alliance with the daughter of a priest of the highest rank. But still that such an alliance is possible, shows that the repulsive severity of the Egyptians against strangers had not yet reached its greatest height. The manner in which Pharaoh answers the request of Joseph for the admission of his family into Egypt, proves the same thing. But just at the beginning of the Exodus, we see the hatred and contempt of the Egyptians against all foreigners, and their strong national egotism, which is so conspicuous in the circumstance, that the term *man* is used exclusively for their people, designating them as of the highest rank.[1] Every one must confess that this gradual development is perfectly in accordance with nature, and that the representation of the Pentateuch carries with it the proof of its authenticity and credibility.

APPENDIX TO CHAPTER I.

BY THE EDITOR.

As the theory of a gradual spirit of exclusiveness, having grown spontaneously up among the Egyptian people, is contrary to all historical experience, it is to be regretted that the author should not have more closely examined the nature of the proofs which he has adduced in its support. Had he done so, it is probable that he would have altered or modified his views, for, when closely investigated, his authorities will be found to indicate an inference directly contrary to that which he has adduced. But in truth, the learned author adopted this hypothesis in order to support another equally unfounded. It is therefore advisable to examine both together; and having already done so in a popular periodical, the Editor

[1] Salvolini Campagne de Rhamsés, Paris, 1835, p. 261.

deems it his duty to republish what he has there said, simply adding, that a subsequent examination of the subject has only confirmed him in the opinions which he had formed.

Although the professed object of Dr Hengstenberg is to refute the cavils of Von Bohlen and other neologists, he is himself so far a rationalist, as to attempt to solve the problem of miracles by natural phenomena, and to deny the originality, and consequently the divine authority, of the Levitical law. In order to establish this point, he is driven to deny the existence of any national hatred between the Hebrews and the Egyptians, and to reject totally the received account of the Hycsos, or shepherd kings. On this he stakes the issue between the schools of biblical criticism in England and Germany, and he thus invests the question with sufficient importance to justify its minute investigation.

Hengstenberg's theory is essentially the same as that which was long ago started by Perizonius, that the account of the Hycsos was a fable invented after the translation of the Pentateuch into Greek, by some enemy of the Jews, in order to remove the infamy of the circumstances attending the Exodus from the Egyptians, and fix it on the Israelites. There is no doubt that many such forgeries were devised for this purpose; we have a specimen of them in the strange account given of the Jews by Justin, and in the tales of Apion refuted by Josephus. We may also safely concede, that very little reliance can be placed on the authority of Manetho as an historian, wherever anti-Jewish prejudices were likely to interfere, and that we must reject his story of the Israelites having been lepers expelled from Egypt; we may even go further, and grant that the whole history of the Hycsos must be given up, if we do not find it in some degree confirmed by the monuments. Still, we assert, in opposition to Dr Hengstenberg, that traces of Egypt having suffered from a foreign foe, are to be found in the Pentateuch. We have stated the question fairly, and are not aware of having omitted any material point in issue.

The monuments indisputably establish that there was some Asiatic race which the Egyptians viewed with detestation; they are constantly brought before us in the most humiliating and degrading situations; we find them crushed under the chariot-wheels of the kings, trampled beneath the feet of the warriors, and massacred without mercy. Captives of the hated race are represented as the worst of slaves; they are figured as Caryatides, supporting vases and other articles of domestic furniture, particularly the foot-baths; they are even painted on the soles of shoes or sandals, as if to intimate that they should be for ever trodden down under the feet of their enemies. We see them on the monuments represented as the supporters of a throne or chair of state, and the artist has indulged the national enmity, by adding to this degradation chains, fetters, and a most painful posture. Peculiarity of colour and physiognomy, connects these hated captives with the Semitic tribes of Syria and northern Arabia, while their costume clearly distinguishes them from the Jewish prisoners depicted on the monuments. The cause of this hatred is sufficiently obvious; Egypt, on its north-eastern frontier, was exposed to the ravages of the nomade tribes of south-western Asia, whose plundering propensities have varied very little during the course of thirty centuries. It was from this quarter alone that the valley of the Nile was exposed to danger from invasion and conquest. Through it came successively the Persians, the Macedonians, the Arabs, and the Turks; and we shall now show, that in the age of Joseph, it was regarded as the most vulnerable point of the empire of the Pharaohs.

When the ten sons of Jacob appeared before their brother, Joseph, assuming the character of an Egyptian, treated them with what appeared both to them and the bystanders, not unreasonable suspicion—" Joseph remembered the dreams which he had dreamed of them, and said unto them, Ye are spies; to see the nakedness of the land ye are come. And they said unto him, Nay, my lord, but to buy food are thy servants come. We are all one man's sons; we are true men, thy servants are no spies. And he said unto them, Nay, but to see the nakedness of the land ye are come." (Gen. xlii. 9—12.)

The phrase, "nakedness of the land," (את־ערות הארץ *Eth Gneruth Haäretz,*) signifies, "the defenceless part of the country," that is, the part through which the brethren had come on their way to the court. Again, when Pharaoh granted the land of Goshen to the Israelites, he particularly inquired whether there were "any men of activity," (that is, "warriors," as the phrase is elsewhere translated,) because such only were fit to be intrusted with the care of the cattle on an exposed frontier.

Dr Hengstenberg asserts that the Egyptians refused to eat with the brethren of Joseph, simply because they were shepherds, but he forgets that the objection, as originally stated, is to their race, and not to their profession. "And they set on for him by himself, and for them by themselves, and for the Egyptians, which did eat with him, by themselves; because the Egyptians might not eat bread with the Hebrews; for that is an abomination unto the Egyptians." (Gen. xliii. 32.)

Here "Hebrews," not "shepherds," are declared to be "an abomination to the Egyptians;" for the name "Hebrews," עברים (from עבר *Habar,* to pass,) signifies "passengers" or "wanderers," and was applied to the family of Abraham, because they were nomades from beyond the Euphrates. It was therefore because they were connected by their mode of life with the natural enemies of the Egyptians, and not because they followed the same profession as a despised caste, that contact with them was shunned as an abomination. Now it would be contrary to the whole course of history to ascribe such intense and pertinacious hatred to anything but a long continuance of national injuries and hostilities; there is therefore a strong probability for the truth of the invasion of the Hycsos, but there is reason to believe that their dominion did not extend beyond Lower Egypt.

Heeren has remarked, that Egypt might have been attacked on the side of the Red Sea, and he refers to a picture of a naval engagement, to show that its frontiers were not quite so secure as they are generally represented. But it is not quite clear from the representation, whether the Egyptians were the assailants or the assailed in this battle; indeed many circumstances,—particularly the superior trim of their ships, arguing previous preparation, while the enemies are only provided with rude rafts—

would seem to prove that in this instance the Egyptians are invaders. But in neither case is Dr Hengstenberg's case served, for the hostile race here depicted has no resemblance whatever to the Hycsos; they wear head-dresses of feathers, such as are described in ancient Hindû records, and such as the Indian caciques wore when America was discovered by Columbus.

Having fully proved that there was a hostile Asiatic race peculiarly odious to the Egyptians, we shall for the future speak of them as the Hycsos, without at all pledging ourselves to the propriety of the term, for our concern is not with the name but with the fact. Joseph's reference to the nakedness of the land, that is, to its want of fortresses and other means of defence, will appear peculiarly appropriate when we learn that the chief strength of the Hycsos consisted in their castles and towers erected on the hills of Idumea and Southern Syria. Jerusalem itself was originally a mountain castle, erected by the plundering tribe of Jebusites as a fastness to secure their booty on the top of Mount Zion; and so great was the strength of the place, that when David besieged it, the Jebusites tauntingly declared that they would intrust the defence of the place to the lame and the blind. (2 Sam. v. 6—8.) It has been plausibly conjectured, that the various places in Canaan to which the epithet Kirjath, "an edifice," is attached, were the places of strength belonging to the smaller tribes of Palestine; and hence the conquest of them was proposed as a prize deed of arms to the young warriors of Israel. An example of this occurs immediately after the death of Joshua. " Caleb said, He that smiteth Kirjath-sepher, and taketh it, to him will I give Achsah my daughter to wife. And Othniel the son of Kenaz, the brother of Caleb, took it; and he gave him Achsah his daughter to wife." (Josh. xv. 16, 17.)

The affiliation of nations and their various migrations in the earlier ages of the world, must be expected to present many problems of difficult solution, particularly when recorded in the exaggerated style of the Oriental nations. The titles of the ancient kings of Asia and Africa are far from affording a fair indication of the extent of their dominions: many proclaimed themselves sovereigns over countries of which they possessed as little as the monarchs of England did of France, or the kings of Spain did of Jerusalem. When Dr Hengstenberg speaks of mighty armies, systematic plans of conquest, and extensive organization of military power, as necessary to the existence of the Hycsos, he merely conjures up shadows of his own imagination, to dismiss them again as unceremoniously as Gulliver did the ghosts of Glubbdubdub. Who ever dreamed of looking for vast armaments and political combinations among the northern sea-kings? yet their conquests of England, Ireland, and Normandy are matters of history. What these pirates were by sea, the Hycsos were by land—desultory marauders, to whom a fortuitous combination of circumstances may have given a temporary supremacy.

The Hebrews were not only a distinct race from the Egyptians, but they were so separated by prejudices, social institutions, and all that constitutes the individual existence of races, that a fusion of the two was morally impossible : indeed, so far was Moses from adopting a code of laws which would have Egyptianized the Israelites, that it would be easy to point out many institutions which had no other object than to induce habits directly contrary to those which the Israelites had learned in Egypt.

It is quite clear from the narrative, that Joseph had taken extraordinary pains to naturalize himself in Egypt. As a stranger is said to have been recognised in Athens from the superior purity of his Attic dialect, so the chief means by which Joseph could be recognised as a foreigner, was his greater strictness in adhering to purely Egyptian usages. This strictness had nearly led to his detection, when he caused his brethren to be marshalled at the banquet in the order of their age. "And they sat before him, the first-born according to his birthright, and the youngest according to his youth : and the men marvelled one at another." (Gen. xlii. 33.) The mention of the posture used at table, proves that the writer of the history was well acquainted with Egyptian customs, for the patriarchal usage was to recline at meals. (Gen. xviii. 4.) There are indeed frequent instances of couches on the Egyptian monuments, but these were only used for sleeping ; in all the representations of entertainments, the ladies and gentlemen are depicted sitting on stools or chairs. It is also mentioned that Joseph sat apart from the rest, and we find from the monuments that a separate table was usually placed before each of the distinguished guests present. The number and variety of dishes set on each table were proportioned to the rank of each guest, or to the estimation in which he was held by the person who gave the entertainment. To this custom allusion is distinctly made by the sacred writer. (Gen. xliii. 34.)

Dr Hengstenberg renews the subject in his Appendix, and we shall then have occasion to show, that the invasion of the Hycsos is as well established as any fact in ancient Egyptian history.

CHAPTER II.

EXODUS, Chapters I—VII.

THE FEARS OF PHARAOH AND HIS SEVERITY TO THE ISRAELITES.

IN chap. i. 10, Pharaoh says to his people: "Come on, let us deal wisely with them, (the people of the children of Israel,) lest they multiply, and it come to pass that when there falleth out any war, they join also unto our enemies, and fight against us, and so get them up out of the land." These words are spoken perfectly in accordance with the state of things in Egypt. Fruitful and cultivated Egypt has for its natural enemies the inhabitants of the neighbouring deserts, and it is never in greater peril than when these enemies find allies among its own inhabitants. The history of the Arabian Bedawin in Egypt shows how very confident the Egyptian king might be that he had ground for his fears, and that he must make regulations in accordance with them. Of these Bedawin *Prokesch*[1] says: "They made common cause with the Arabs against the communities who possessed the land, and who were the enemies of the Arabs as soon as the latter became themselves land-tillers. They fought against the Saracen dynasty in Egypt, against the Turkomans as soon as they had acquired the ascendancy, against the Memlook Sultans who were the successors of the Turkomans, and they have been at war with the Osmanlies without intermission, since they first set foot upon Egypt more than three hundred years ago."

The measures which Pharaoh adopted for the oppression of the Israelites are entirely in accordance with the spirit of the Pharaohs, whose proud severity against hated and despised foreigners knew no bounds. According to *Diodorus*,[2] Sesostris placed upon all his buildings erected by captives an inscription, showing that no native citizens had been engaged in this servile employment. According to *Pliny*,[3] Sesostris harnessed captive kings to his

---

[1] Erinnerungen aus Aeg. und Kleinas. Th. 2. S. 231.
[2] 1. 56.
[3] 33. 15.

chariot.[1] Upon the sculptures, in the temple at Medeenet Haboo, representing the triumphal return of Remeses III., after his conquests in the Eastern war, three captives appear tied under the axle of his chariot, while others, bound by ropes, walk by the side of his horses, as an offering to the deity of the place.[2]

According to chap. i. 14, Pharaoh embittered the life of the Israelites with hard bondage in mortar and brick. We see from chap. v. 7,[3] that straw was used in the preparation of these bricks. 1. We have already shown that the use of brick was very general in Egypt, as is here implied.[4] 2. Bricks were made in Egypt under the direction of the king or some privileged person, as appears from the impressions found upon many of them.[5] A great multitude of strangers were constantly employed in the brick fields of Thebes, and other parts of Egypt. 3. But the most remarkable agreement with the Pentateuch is in the fact, that a small portion of chopped straw is found in the composition of the Egyptian bricks. This is evident from an examination of those brought by *Rosellini* from Thebes, on which is the stamp of Thothmes IV., the fifth king of the eighteenth dynasty.[6] "The bricks," remarks *Rosellini*,[7] " which are now found in Egypt, belonging to the same period, always have straw mingled with them, although in some of those that are most carefully made it is found in very small quantities." According to *Rosellini*, straw was used in order that the bricks (they were not for the most part burned, but dried in the sun) might be more firm, especially those of coarse clay and more roughly formed. *Prokesch*[8] says, "The bricks (of the first pyramid at Dashoor) are of fine clay from the Nile, mingled with chopped straw. This intermixture gives the

---

[1] Sesostris Aegypti rege tam superbo, ud prodatur annis quibusque sorte reges singulos e subjectis jungere ad currum solitus, atque ita triumphare. Diodorus also relates the same thing, 1. 58.

[2] Wilkinson, 1. p. 106, and plate.

[3] Luther has incorrectly translated in chap. v. 7 : That they might *burn* brick, from which the false opinion might easily arise that the straw served as fuel. It should be : Ye shall no more give the people straw to *make* brick with, &c.

[4] See p. 1.—Also concerning the use of brick in Egypt, Quatremère de Quincy, état de l'Architest, Egypt, p. 64. seq.

[5] Wilkinson, II. 97. [6] Ros. II. 2. p. 252.

[7] II. 2. p. 259. [8] In der Erinn. Th. 2. S. 31.

bricks an astonishing durability." The *inquirer* will not leave unnoticed such little and entirely undesigned circumstances as these.

We are carried much farther by the comparison of our history with a picture discovered in a tomb at Thebes, of which *Rosellini*[1] first furnished a drawing and an explanation: " Explanation of a picture representing the Hebrews as they were engaged in making brick." We will first give an abstract of the account of *Rosellini*. " Of the labourers," says he, " some are employed in transporting the clay in vessels, some in intermingling it with the straw, others are taking the bricks out of the form and placing them in rows, still others with a piece of wood upon their backs and ropes on each side carry away the bricks already burned or dried. Their dissimilarity to the Egyptians appears at the first view: their complexion, physiognomy, and beard, permit us not to be mistaken in supposing them to be Hebrews. They wear at the hips the apron which is common among the Egyptians, and there is also represented as in use among them a kind of short trowsers, after the fashion of the מכנסים *Miknesim*. Among the Hebrews, four Egyptians, very distinguishable by their mien, figure, and colour, are seen; two of them, one sitting and the other standing, carry a stick in their hand ready to fall upon two other Egyptians, who are here represented like the Hebrews, one of them carrying on his shoulder a vessel of clay, and the other returning from the transportation of brick, carrying his empty vessel to get a new load. The tomb belonged to a high court-officer of the king, Rochsceré, and was made in the time of Thothmes IV., the fifth king of the eighteenth dynasty. The question, " How came this picture in the tomb of Rochsceré ?" *Rosellini* answers as follows: " He was the overseer of the public buildings, and had, consequently, the charge of all the works undertaken by the king. There are found represented therein still other objects of a like nature; two collossal statues of kings, a sphinx and the labourers who hewed the stone,—works which he, by virtue of his office, had caused to be performed in his lifetime."

To the question, " How came the representation of the labours of the Israelites at Thebes ?" it is answered: " We need not sup-

---

[1] II. 2. p. 254 seq.

pose that the labours were performed in the very place where they are represented, for Rochscerê was overseer of the royal buildings throughout the land, and what was done in the circuit of his operations, could, wherever performed, be represented in his tomb at Thebes. It is also not impossible that the Hebrews went even to Thebes. In Ex. v. 12, it is said, that they scattered themselves through the whole land of Egypt in order to procure straw."

So far *Rosellini.* The agreement of this painting with our account, in many very striking points, appears at first view. We, consequently, select from them only two.

1. It is said in the narrative, the Israelites were subjected to severe labour in mortar and brick. Just so this servile labour appears throughout the painting as twofold, some are employed upon the clay from which the bricks were made, and some upon the finished brick. 2. We have in this painting an explanation with regard to the Egyptians who accompanied the Israelites in their Exodus. Of these Egyptians we read, first, in Ex. xii. 38, " And also a great rabble (עֵרֶב רַב *ereb rab)* went up with them." In Numbers xi. 4, " The mixed Egyptian populace (הָאסַפְסֻף *hasphuph)* led astray the Israelites in the desert to discontentment." In Deut. xxix. 10, 11—let it be observed how accurately these remote and disconnected passages agree with each other—the Egyptian aliens appear as very poor, as the lowest servants, as hewers of wood and drawers of water. The designations *rabble* and *populace* in the first passages, also show, that these attendants of the Israelites belonged to the lowest grades of society. Just such people we should naturally expect to find in Egypt. Their existence is the necessary consequence of strongly marked *castes* in society. The monuments indeed place vividly before us most manifest distinctions in station. A part of the people appear to be in the deep degradation which now presses upon the Fellahs.[1] According to *Herodotus,*[2] the caste of swineherds, a native tribe, was unclean and despised in Egypt. All intercourse with the rest of the inhabitants, even entrance into a temple, was forbidden, and they were as much despised as the Parias in India.[3] The contempt in which they were held was not certainly the consequence of their occupation, but their occupation of the disdain which was felt for them. Already unclean, they

---

[1] Wilk. Vol. I. p. 285. [2] B. 2. c. 47. [3] Heeren, S. 150.

had no reason for avoiding the care of unclean animals. But full light first falls upon these notices of the Pentateuch through our painting. We see upon it Egyptians who are placed entirely on an equality with the hated and despised foreigners. What is more natural than that a considerable part of these Egyptians, bound close to their companions in sorrow by their common misery, should leave with them their native land, such now to them only in name.[1]

He who has carefully examined the engraving in *Rosellini*, the great importance of which has been acknowledged by such historians as *Heeren*,[2] perceiving its striking accordance with the Pen-

---

[1] Compare upon the bondmen of Egypt, who, like the Helots in Sparta, were in ignominious servitude, Böckh, Erklärung Einer Aeg. Urkunde S. 27, 28. Many reasons render it very probable that the Pharaoh who tyrannized over the Israelites in the age of Moses, was not a native Egyptian, but a foreign conqueror, probably belonging to the intrusive dynasty of the Hyksos. He is described as "another, or an alien king, who knew not Joseph;" and it would be hard to believe that any native prince could be ignorant of the advantages which the Egyptian monarch and people derived from the administration of that patriarch. He is represented as saying, "The people of the children of Israel are more and mightier than we;" it is very possible that a warlike race of conquerors, such as the Hyksos of old, or the Turks of modern times, might be inferior in number even to the least division of the races subject to their sway, but it is utterly improbable that the Israelites should have multiplied so fast in the land of Goshen, as to exceed in number all the inhabitants of Egypt. One of the labours which he imposed upon the Israelites, was, to erect "treasure cities," that is, fortresses to secure his plunder; Joseph took no such precaution when he received all the money of Egypt in exchange for corn, but of course it became necessary under the iron rule of a foreign conqueror. Finally, we find this Pharaoh actually proposing to Moses to violate the laws and customs of Egypt, by sacrificing the sacred animals within their land. The remonstrance of the Jewish legislator is, as we shall see, very appropriate when addressed to a foreigner, but scarcely within the bounds of credibility if we suppose that any such speech could be made to a native prince. "And Pharaoh called for Moses and for Aaron, and said, Go ye, sacrifice to your God in the land. And Moses said, It is not meet so to do; for we shall sacrifice the abomination of the Egyptians to the Lord our God: lo, shall we sacrifice the abomination of the Egyptians before their eyes, and will they not stone us? We will go three days' journey into the wilderness, and sacrifice to the Lord our God, as he shall command us." (Exod. viii. 25—27.) T.

[2] He says, Gött. Anz. 1835, S. 1328: If this painting represents the servitude of the children of Israel in these labours, it is equally impor-

tateuch, will ask first of all, whether then this picture is really genuine, whether it is not probably a supposititious work, prepared after the Pentateuch was written. This question, almost sufficiently answered by the condition of the painting itself, is, by the judicious *Wilkinson*, who made a new examination on the spot, decided entirely in favour of the picture. This decision is the more to be relied on, since *Wilkinson*,[1] while he questions whether the painting has direct reference to the labours of the Israelites, does not deny the significance of it for the Pentateuch. But the arguments with which he contends against its referring to Israelites, are of so little importance, that we can scarcely avoid thinking that he is influenced by something foreign from the thing itself; and they are decidedly outweighed by the evident Jewish bearing and cast of physiognomy, which can be traced even in the common wood-cuts such as are found in Taylor.[2] *Wilkinson*, first, makes the place where the painting is found, a matter of importance. That it cannot represent work done in another part of Egypt, the hieroglyphic inscription shows. According to this, the bricks are made for a building in Thebes. But at least as given by *Rosellini*,[3] the inscription does not so definitely affirm this; and even if it did, what valid objection is there to the assumption that the Israelites were carried even as far as Thebes for the sake of their work? That Egypt in all times, even the most ancient, formed *one* kingdom, is now, since the witness of the Holy Scriptures in this respect has received so strong a con-

tant for exegesis and chronology. For exegesis, because it would be a strong proof of the great antiquity of the Mosaic writings, and especially of the book of Exodus, which in chapters one and five gives a description that applies most accurately to this painting, even in unimportant particulars. For chronology, since it belongs to the eighteenth dynasty, under the dominion of Thothmes-Moeris, about 1740 before Christ, and therefore would give a fixed point both for profane and sacred History.

[1] Vol. II. p. 98 seq: "It is curious," he remarks, "to discover other foreign captives occupied in the same manner, overlooked by similar 'taskmasters,' and performing the very same labours as the Israelites described in the Bible; and no one can look at the paintings of Thebes, representing brick-makers, without a feeling of the highest interest."

[2] P. 79.

[3] II. p. 262. Commendamento, che rechino—i mattoni? verso le construzioni della divina casa [del tempio] del—Dio.

firmation from the monuments, generally acknowledged.[1] It was for the interest of the oppressor to scatter the Israelites as much as possible through his whole land. Even now, the Fellahs are often collected in troops from the most remote provinces in Egypt, when any great work is to be executed. Secondly, the beard is wanting, which is so marked in the people of Syria on the Egyptian monuments and in the case of the prisoners of Sheshonk. But in *one* individual the beard is certainly represented, and if it is wanting in the case of the others, it is easy to account for it by supposing that they were compelled to accommodate themselves to Egyptian customs.[2] There is a plain difference between the Israelites and those just made captives, who naturally appear upon the monuments in the costume of their own nation. Thirdly, the argument from Jewish physiognomy is not decisive; for the Egyptians, who generally did not give the same attention to the

[1] Compare Plath, Quaestiones Aegypt. Gött. 1829, Rosellini, Wilkinson, and others.

[2] Even Wilkinson, Vol. III. p. 358, says: "Although foreigners, who were brought to Egypt as slaves, had beards on their arrival in the country, we find that as soon as they were employed in the service of this civilized people, they were obliged to conform to the cleanly habits of their masters; their beards and heads were shaved," &c. The Fellahs exhibit the sadness of men accustomed to suffer, the timidity and fear of wretches who have no refuge or protection. In vain does the Nile lavishly distribute its treasures, none of them fall to the share of the peasant. In the midst of all the wonders of fertility, the Fellah keeps his eyes fixed upon the ground, as if he lived in an accursed country. There are in Egypt myriads of labourers who reap abundant harvests, and who never eat anything but herbs, linseed cakes, and boiled beans. The celebrated Amrú compared the Egyptians to bees working diligently for the advantage of others, but enjoying no fruit of their toil; and since the days of Amrú, the condition of the cultivators of Egypt has undergone but little change. An idea can scarcely be formed of the number of wretched creatures in the villages; everywhere are seen men almost naked, or covered with rags worse than nudity,—countenances furrowed with grief—youth in premature sadness—women in whom misery has effaced the traits of their sex. The traveller in Egypt requires a very varied vocabulary of expressions to describe the intense misery which is presented to him at every fresh step, in a new shape. Nevertheless the population continues to increase, for the happy climate of Egypt seems of itself sufficient to support life, and supply man's prime necessities; the most miserable villages are filled with multitudes of children,—a circumstance seeming to prove, that there will be always men born to suffer, and that despotism will never want slaves.—*Correspondance d'Orient*, V. 73. T.

countenance as to costume, weapons, &c., but rather, for the most part, employed a certain general style of features, for the inhabitants of a particular region,[1] have adopted the same characteristics for all the inhabitants of Syria, as appears from the sculptures. Assuming the correctness of this position, which seems to us very doubtful, would the Egyptians, since the Jewish cast of physiognomy throughout can by no means be denied, have borrowed the type for the Syrians generally, from the Jews? This at least is certain, that a people from the region in which the Israelites dwelt were found in Egypt in the circumstances represented in the painting, and, by a comparison of the picture with the account of Moses, we should be perfectly justified in the assumption that these persons were real Israelites.

It is also characteristic of Egypt, when, in this same 14th verse, it is said, that the life of the Israelites was also embittered " through all manner of service in the field." There is scarcely a country in which the cultivation of the land requires so much peculiarly *servile* labour as in Egypt. Irrigation especially, is here very laborious.[2]

USE OF THE PAPYRUS AND BITUMEN IN EGYPT.

According to chap. ii. 3, the mother of Moses, taking a chest of *papyrus*, smears it with *bitumen* and pitch, lays the child in it, and put it down among the reeds on the shore of the Nile. That the author names the papyrus as the material of the chest, is a strong argument in his favour. In Egypt, and there only, was the papyrus employed in the manufacture of many articles of use. Mats, baskets, sandals, and various other things, were made of it.[3] Even boats were constructed of it.[4] The use of the papyrus be-

[1] Wilkinson, I. p. 386.
[2] See the more recent Commentators on Deut. xi. 10.
[3] Wilkinson, Vol. III. pp. 62, 146.
[4] Herod. 2. 96. Plut. de Is. et Osir. p. 395; according to which Isis is borne upon a boat of papyrus. Wilk. Vol. III. p. 61. Ros. II. 3. p. 124. The papyrus boat in which Moses was exposed, was " daubed with slime and pitch," that is, with both mineral and vegetable substances, to serve as caulking. A mineral tar frequently used for this purpose, is produced on the coasts of the Red Sea; it is remarkable for its antiseptic properties, and has been successfully used in the preparation of mummies. A human hand preserved by this substance, may be seen in the Museum of

longs to the earliest times. Even in the most ancient sculptures it is found with writing upon it.[1] Bitumen was one of the principal ingredients in embalming in Egypt.[2] In a passage in the Travels of *Minutoli*,[3] giving a description of the "analysis of the resinous composition of a black shining figure from the body of a mummy" by John, it is said: "The resinous mass is composed of the pitch-wood mentioned in a preceding note, and of a kind of bitumen which the Egyptians might have obtained from the Dead Sea, Babylon, Susa, or even from Phœnicia, or at least of an entirely analogous substance." John also found bitumous substances in the embalming materials in connection with a child-mummy.[4] According to *Rosellini*,[5] there have been found in the tomb of Usirei, or Menephthah,[6] many small statues of wood in the form of a mummy, covered with a stratum of bitumen.[7] That pitch was known at this time in Egypt, we cannot doubt, since it is found in objects which belong to the oldest times.

THE DAUGHTER OF PHARAOH FINDS THE CHILD, MOSES.

According to chap. ii. 5, the daughter of Pharaoh finds the child, Moses, as, accompanied by her maidens, she goes to bathe in the Nile. That the women in Egypt were far less restrained than in the rest of the East, as this fact implies, we have already shown.[8] That the king's daughter went to the Nile to bathe, is explained by the Egyptian notion of the sacredness of the Nile. Of this we shall speak in a subsequent part of this volume. A representation of an Egyptian bathing scene—a lady with four female servants who attend upon her and perform various offices, is found in *Wilkinson*.[9]

THE ISRAELITES DIRECTED TO BORROW OF THE EGYPTIANS ORNAMENTS, &c.

In chap. iii. 22, and the parallel passage where the Israelitish

---

the Royal Asiatic Society; it is so very perfect, that the shape of the nails, and even the mark of the place where a ring was worn, may be clearly distinguished.   T.

[1] Wilk. III. 150. [2] Diod. 19. chap. 99. [3] S. 373.
[4] S. 344. [5] Vol. I. 1. p. 249. [6] Ros. II. 3. p. 350, seq.
[7] Wilk. Vol. III. p. 186. [8] P. 26. [9] Vol. III. p. 389.

women are directed to borrow of their Egyptian neighbours gold and silver ornaments, it is implied that such ornaments were even then in very general use among the Egyptians. This has been fully confirmed by late discoveries. On the monuments, remarks *Rosellini*,[1] vases of costly metal are found, not merely in the representations of religious ceremonies and the offerings of kings to the gods, but also among the objects of household use. Very many such things are found in the tombs of mere private individuals. Therefore it is clear, that not the great only, but all who possessed any wealth, had such articles among their household furniture.[2]

MOSES' ROD.

According to chap. iv. 2, Moses carries a rod, and this we find to be afterwards his inseparable companion. That he follows an Egyptian custom in this, is evident from chap. vii. 12, where

---

[1] II. 2. p. 345. Jewels were anciently used as money, and are sometimes so employed at the present day; hence the weight of the jewels given by Abraham's steward to Rebekah is specifically recorded, apparently intimating that they were designed, not only as ornament, but as part of the purchase-money paid for a wife: "It came to pass, as the camels had done drinking, that the man took a golden ear-ring of half a shekel weight, and two bracelets for her hands of ten shekels weight of gold." Gen. xxiv. 22. That the jewels were thus given as money, is still more evident from a subsequent verse, describing the payment of Rebekah's dowry: "The servant brought forth jewels of silver, and jewels of gold, and raiment, and gave them to Rebekah: he gave also to her brother, and to her mother, precious things." Gen. xxiv. 55. These circumstances enable us to explain the true meaning of a passage, which, from a slight inaccuracy of translation, has been frequently the object of sceptical cavils. When God, immediately before the tenth plague, gave Moses directions respecting the leading out of the Israelites, part of his injunctions was: "Speak now in the ears of the people, and let every man borrow of his neighbour, and every woman of her neighbour, jewels of silver and jewels of gold." Exod. xi. 2. The word שאל *(Shaal)* translated "borrow," literally signifies "ask" or "demand;" and the "jewels," as we have seen, were current coin: the meaning then is, that the Israelites should demand payment of the hire justly due to them for their labour—a demand with which the Egyptians, terrified by the slaughter of the first-born, readily complied. Thus this transaction, so frequently represented as a loan fraudulently obtained, was in fact a simple demand of strict justice.   T.

[2] Wilkinson, Vol. III. p. 223.

each of the magicians carries his rod. According to the monuments, the Egyptian nobles generally carried a stick from three to six feet long when they went out. One of them, preserved to our time, is of cherry-wood; but they generally preferred, as it appears, the acacia wood.¹ Egyptian priests, and others persons of rank, are represented as walking with sticks.²

WRITING MUCH PRACTISED IN EGYPT.

The name of the Israelitish officers, which the task-masters of Pharaoh placed over them, שֹׁטְרִים *(Shaterim,) the writers*, is derived from the verb שָׁטַר *(Shater,) to write*.³ This is highly characteristic of the state of things in Egypt. In no land of the old world, was facility in writing so great, and the materials for writing by any means so perfect, as in Egypt. " Stone-workers were accustomed," says *Rosellini*,⁴ " to engrave upon each square block an inscription in hieroglyphics; an impression was made upon the bricks, (which besides very frequently bore inscriptions),⁵ —even oxen were represented,—the steward of the house kept a written register. They probably wrote more in ancient Egypt, and on more ordinary occasions, than among us." " The Egyptians," says the same author,⁶ " differ specially from all other people, in that they constantly cover the interior and exterior of their houses, and the walls of all the innumerable apartments, of their wonderful subterraneous burial places, with images and writing." " Upon the implements, and even garments of the Egyptians, the name of the owner is frequently wholly or in part inscribed." The proper name of the profession of the men is written on these implements as they appear on the monuments, the name of animals upon their representatives, and that of implements of every sort upon the figures which represent them." " We must shut our eyes against the clearest light, if we would deny that the art of reading and writing was generally studied and practised in ancient Egypt, to as great a degree at least as it now is among us." Proof from the monuments is also furnished by *Rosellini*,⁷ that

---

¹ Wilk. III. 396-8.
² Wilk. III. 386.
³ See the arguments for this in Th. II. der Beiträge zur Einl. S. 449 ff.
⁴ II. 3. p. 241.
⁵ P. 252, 3.
⁶ P. 239.
⁷ Vol. II. 3. p. 272 seq.

in judicial transactions every thing was transacted in writing. The scribes, who meet our eyes wherever we look, act an important part.[1] The judges of the under-world all carry upon their heads the symbolic pen of truth and justice.[2] The passion for writing was so incorporated with the business of Egypt, that even now the last remains of the Egyptians, the Copts, are in exclusive possession of all secretaries' posts, and, as it were, form a nation of scribes.[3] These Coptic scribes compose a numerous community, with a kind of hierarchy. These references show, that these and the remaining passages of the Pentateuch, which imply a great extension of the art of writing among the Israelites in the time of Moses,[4] only make known what cannot have been otherwise, and thus are a strong confirmation of the narrative. These passages, so far from witnessing *against* the Mosaic period, have now become just so many proofs for the same. The little foundation there is at the present time for the argument against the authenticity of the Pentateuch, from the non-existence, or at least the limited diffusion of the art of writing, is shown by such facts as this, that *Salvolini*[5] allows that the manuscript of *Sallier*, containing a description of the expedition of Rameses the Great against the Scheta and their allies, was written about the year 1565 before Christ! Whether in this particular case he is in error or not, is, for our argument, a matter of indifference. For, it is sufficient that an inquirer so generally esteemed for discrimination, can suppose such a date possible,—that he did not even consider it necessary to question whether writing existed at that time in Egypt.

We will here make some additions to our Essay concerning writing materials in the Mosaic period.[6] The Egyptians wrote with reddish ink.[7] The common material on which they wrote was paper made of the papyrus plant, which is found in great quantities in the common tombs. The great abundance of coarse

---

[1] Ros. p. 272 seq.
[2] Ros. II. 500.
[3] See e. g. Girard in the Descr. t. 17. p. 192.
[4] They are found collected in Th. 2. der Beiträge, S. 457 ff.
[5] Campagne de Rhamsés, Paris 1835, p. 123.
[6] Th. 2. der Beiträge, S. 481 ff.
[7] Ros. II. 2. p. 207, with which, in order to call to mind that the use of ink is implied in Num. v. 23, compare what was said on this passage, Beiträg, Th. 2. S. 489.

and fine paper which, from the dates, belonged to the different dynasties of the Pharaohs, as least as far back as the 18th, make it certain, that the use of paper in Egypt at the time of Alexander was very old, and therefore refutes the declarations of *Pliny*. The Egyptians also wrote with ink and red chalk upon cloth. We have in our possession, wrappers of mummies of byssos, written over with the ritual for the dead.¹ They also wrote catalogues, accounts, and other such like things, with ink upon wood, vessels of Terra Cotta, pieces of limestone, &c.² Finally, they also wrote on parchment.³

PREPARATION OF STONE FOR INSCRIPTIONS.

The passage, Deut. xxvii., according to which the stones to be written upon were to be first covered with lime, has already been explained and verified from the antiquities of Egypt.⁴ We here add also, a reference to *Wilkinson*, Vol. III. p. 300, where the sandstone of the Egyptians is said to have had a kind of stucco spread over it before the paintings were made, and even granite was covered with a similar composition. *Prokesch*⁵ says, "I saw one, (among the tombs in the pyramids of Dashoor,) where a red mortar is first laid upon the stone, and then the hieroglyphics and a figure of the apis are impressed upon this coating."

THE BASTINADO.

The scene in chap. v. 14, where the officers of the children of Israel, whom the Egyptian overseers of Pharaoh placed over them, were beaten because those under their charge had not performed their task in brick-making, is placed vividly before our eyes in the representation of an Egyptian bastinado in *Wilkinson*.⁶ With this compare another representation,⁷ where "the labourers are stimulated to work by the persuasive powers of the stick." The first painting shows conclusively, that the mode of inflicting stripes, described in Deut. xxv. 2, (the guilty person is laid down flat upon the ground before the judge and beaten,) was precisely

---

¹ Ros. p. 227. ² Ros. 228.
³ Wilk. Vol. III. p. 152. ⁴ Beiträge, Th. 2. S. 464.
⁵ Erinnerungen aus Aeg. und Kleinas, Th. 2. S. 31.
⁶ Vol. II. p. 41. ⁷ Wilk. II. p. 42.

the Egyptian mode. *Wilkinson* describes it in the following words: " Men and boys were laid prostrate on the ground, and frequently held by the hands and feet, while the chastisement was administered."[1]

THE SHOTERIM OF THE ISRAELITES, THE SAME AS THE MODERN SHEIKH EL-BELED.

Analogy, for the taking of officers from the oppressed people themselves, who are made responsible for the performance of prescribed labour, may be found in modern Egypt. This same thing is done among the Arab fellahs, whose condition, under the government of the Turks, as the description of *Michaud*,[2] for example, shows, agrees in many respects remarkably with that of the Israelites. In each village, one of the Arabs, under the title of Sheikh el-Beled, occupies the place of mediator between the government and the people. He must see that the men perform

[1] Compare Rosellini, II. 3. p. 274, and concerning the presence of a magistrate at the execution of the punishment, the same author, p. 278. From the monuments, we find that this descent of the bastinado in due subordination was the established rule of ancient Egypt, which, like modern China, was governed by the stick. The Moslems, who are well acquainted with its efficacy, have a favourite proverb, which says, "The stick came down from heaven, a blessing from God." The rulers of Egypt in every age have taken care that their subjects should have full enjoyment of that blessing. Ammianus Marcellinus informs us, that in his days endurance of the bastinado was a point of honour. "An Egyptian," says he, " blushes if he cannot show numerous marks on his body, which evince his endeavours to evade the taxes." Matters have not changed much since his time. "Nothing," says M. Michaud, "can equal the severity with which the imposts are levied. I have often seen the fellahs pursued by the merciless tax-gatherers, who exclaimed, 'Pay, pay!' '*Ma Fich*,' (I have nothing,) was the answer. 'You must pay,' retorted the officer, and forthwith a shower of heavy blows fell on the peasant's shoulders. The instrument of punishment on these occasions is a whip, made of the hide of rhinoceros. The fellahs make no doubt that this whip may claim the most remote antiquity, and that it was used in the time of the Pharaohs to enforce the payment of these imposts. Crowds of inspectors, and multitudes of agents, are met everywhere: one-half of the population seems employed to watch and torment the other. What will surprise you is, that the tax-gatherers, when convicted of malversation, receive the bastinado like the fellahs, and are shut up with them in the same prison." T.

[2] Correspondance, t. 5. p. 254.

the prescribed labour, and collect from them the taxes which the government imposes upon them. The *Sheikh el-Beled* is often seen under the stick of the Kaim-makam, the Kashif or the Mamoor, in the place of some individual of the common people, of whom he in turn afterwards takes vengeance.[1]

THE DUTIES OF THE SHOTERIM.

Since we are now occupied with the *Shoterim*, we will also add, that the position, hitherto not properly understood, which they, according to the precepts in Deut. xx. 1 seq. must have held with reference to warlike affairs, (they had the care of levying soldiers, and excusing those unable to perform military service, and they delivered the troops over to the military chiefs, the " captains of the armies," in verse 9th,) is explained by the post which the scribes occupy in the same sphere in modern Egypt, and in all probability the whole institution of the *Shoterim*, as it is entirely alien to patriarchal customs, is of Egyptian origin. The scribes in the representation of Egyptian warlike scenes, act an important part. In levying soldiers, for instance, they write down the names of those who are brought before them by their commanders.[2] They count, in the presence of the king, the hands of the slain which have been cut off, and sometimes also their tongues and other members of the body; they make a statement of the weapons, the horses, and the rest of the booty, and present it to the king,[3] and they perform whatever such like things there are to be done.

THE ARROGANCE OF THE PHARAOHS.

The insolent pride with which Pharaoh received the message communicated by Moses, as: " Who is Jehovah, that I should hear his voice, to let Israel go ? I know not Jehovah, and will not let Israel go," in chap. v. 2 ; the obstinacy which he afterwards exhibits, when the divine punishments fall upon him, one after another, in deciding to go to destruction with his land and people, rather than yield, are proved on the monuments in vari-

---

[1] Ros. II. 2. p. 257. [2] Ros. II. 3. p. 218. [3] Wilk. I. p. 339.

ous ways, to be in accordance with the genuine spirit of a Pharaoh. A comparison of the representation of the victory of Remeses Meiamun, in Thebes, explained by *Champollion*,[1] is of special interest in this connection. The Pharaoh, it is there said, at whose feet they lay down these trophies of victory, (the severed right hand and other members of the body,) sits quietly in his chariot, while his horses are held by his officers, and directs a haughty speech to his warriors : " Give yourselves to mirth ; let it rise to heaven. Strangers are dashed to the ground by my power. Terror of my name has gone forth ; their hearts are full of it ; I appear before them as a lion ; I have pursued them as a hawk ; I have annihilated their wicked souls. I have passed over their rivers ; I have set on fire their castles ; I am to Egypt what the god Mandoo[2] has been ; I have vanquished the barbarians ; Amun Re, my father, subdued the whole world under my feet, and I am king on the throne for ever." It is said that we mistake the whole character of *Champollion's* work, if we assert the literal truth of this translation ; but the spirit which the speech breathes may always be recognised from it.

The ancient Egyptian kings named themselves in their pride, Kings of the whole world,[3] and what is yet more, they in this arrogance claim divine honours for themselves. This can be proved by a multitude of arguments, of which we will here give only a few. The Menephtheum at Thebes has a double character,[4] that of a temple and palace. It is in all its plan destined for the dwelling of a man, and yet it reminds one, by its decorations, of the consecrated residence of a god. Even the name Pharaoh is a monument of this idea. It cannot be doubted that it designates the king, as the incarnation of the sun, which the Egyptians named Phre. The proof of this *Rosellini*[5] furnishes, relying specially upon the fact, that among the royal emblems, a disk, representing the sun, takes the first place. This is, accordingly,

---

[1] In den Briefen aus Aeg. p. 227.
[2] "The Pharaohs frequently styled themselves ' Mandoo towards the Gentiles ; ' from which it appears that he was the avenger or protector against enemies, the Mars of Egyptian mythology, with the additional title of *Uker*, ' avenger,' like the Roman god of war."—*Wilkinson*, Vol. II. Sec. Ser. p. 34.
[3] Champollion, p. 231.   [4] Champollion, p. 267.   [5] I. 1. p. 115.

the first title which all the kings of Egypt bore. Phre also occurs, Gen. xli. 45, in the name of the priest at On or Heliopolis, city of the sun, Potiphera, that is, consecrated to Phre. This name is also very common on the Egyptian monuments.[1]

[1] See also Wilkinson, Egypt and Thebes, p. 5, note, and Manners and Customs, Vol. I. p. 43.

CHAPTER III.

THE SIGNS AND WONDERS IN EGYPT.

THE CONNECTION OF THE SUPERNATURAL WITH THE NATURAL IN THE PLAGUES OF EGYPT.

THE part of Exodus which we now proceed to examine, is of great importance for our object, first and principally in that the supernatural events described, all find a foundation in the natural phenomena of Egypt, and stand in close connection with ordinary occurrences, and also on account of the many separate references in the narrative, which show how very accurate the author's knowledge of Egypt was.

As respects the first point, many have wished to make the connection of the wonders with the natural phenomena of Egypt, an argument against the Pentateuch. So indeed the English deists have done, as, for example, *Morgan*.[1] Among those more recent, *v. Bohlen*[2] is conspicuous. Moses, he remarks, in order to avoid the suspicion of self-deception, was at least obliged to express himself in the mildest manner possible among his contemporaries, who were so well acquainted with Egypt, if he wished to make the commonly observed natural phenomena avail as miracles. But it is perfectly clear, that these occurrences, as they are related, notwithstanding their foundation in nature, always maintained their character as miracles, and consequently are sufficient to prove what they are intended to prove, and to accomplish what they did accomplish. Attempts to merge the supernatural in the natural, such as have been made by *Du Bois Aymé*,[3] and then by *Eichhorn*,[4] will not accomplish their design. Indeed, the unusual force in which the common exhibitions of nature here manifest themselves, and especially their rapid succession, while at other times only a single one exhibits

---

[1] Comp. Lilienthal, die gute Sache der göttl. Offenb. Th. 9. S. 33.
[2] S. 56. der Einl.
[3] Notice sur le séjour des Hebreux en Egypte, Description, t. viii.
[4] In his Treatise, De Aegypti Anno mirabili.

itself with unusual intensity, as well as the fact that *Eichhorn*, notwithstanding all the unnatural misrepresentations in which he allowed himself, yet found material for a treatise on the wonderful year of Egypt,—if we at the same time consider these events in connection with the changing cause of them, and also take into account the exemption of the Land of Goshen,—bring us to the limits of the miraculous ; for the transition to the miraculous is reached by the extraordinary in its highest gradation.[1]

But we are brought into the sphere of the miraculous itself, by the circumstance that these things are introduced and performed by Moses, that they cease at his request, and a part of them at a time fixed upon by Pharaoh himself.[2] Hence the connection with natural phenomena can be made to avail against the Pentateuch, only when, going beyond the present narrative, we limit what in it can be explained by the natural occurrences of Egypt, and establish the presumption, that the remainder belongs to fiction. But this assumption wants all foundation. Not until the historical character of the Pentateuch is disproved, is it necessary, in conformity with the natural philosophy of Egypt, to separate truth and fiction from one another, although it is then better to transfer the whole narrative to the province of mythology, since the natural in it acquires its significance merely through its connection with the supernatural. And so soon as it shall be separated, we can no longer comprehend how Moses could make use of this to prove anything, and how it produced the consequences ascribed to it.

But, that the natural is in itself a presumption against the supernatural, and thus furnishes an argument against the historical veracity of the Pentateuch, cannot be affirmed. If we exert ourselves to bring forward any one tenable reason for this, we shall soon see that we have allowed an entirely arbitrary assumption. On the contrary, that the connection with the natural

---

[1] Even Du Bois Aymé in a manner acknowledges this. He says, Descr. t. 8. p. 110 : " Que l' on écarte donc de la description des plaies d' Egypte les exaggérations poétiques permises à celui, qui decrit avec transport les phénomènes qui ont servi à la délivrance de son peuple, et l' on verra tout prestige s' évanouir ; mais le concours de tant d' événemens extraordinaires quoique naturels, et leur résultat sur le cour, endurci du Pharaon, pourrout nèanmoins être considérés comme une preuve frappante de la protection divine."

[2] See Ex. viii. 5 seq.

serves for confirmation to the supernatural, is clear from the following reasons.

Since we have shown that the natural ground-work of these wonderful events cannot be made an argument *against* the Pentateuch, it belongs to us also to point out how far it is in favour of the same. Here comes into view, first, the fitness of this character of the miracle to the end designed. The *supernatural* presents generally in the Scriptures, no violent opposition to the *natural*, but rather unites in a friendly alliance with it. This follows from the most intimate relation in which natural events also stand to God. The endeavour to isolate the miraculous can aid only impiety. But there was here a particular reason also for uniting the supernatural as closely as possible with the natural. The object to which all of these occurrences were directed, according to chap. viii. 20., was to show that Jehovah is Lord in the midst of the land. Well-grounded proof of this could not have been produced by bringing suddenly upon Egypt a succession of strange terrors. From these it would only have followed that Jehovah had received a momentary and external power over Egypt. On the contrary, if the events which annually return were placed under the immediate control of Jehovah, it would be appropriately shown that He was God in the midst of the land, and the doom of the false gods which had been placed in his stead would go forth, and they would be entirely driven out of the jurisdiction which was considered as belonging to them.[1]

Further, later fiction would aim specially at the dissolution of all connection between the supernatural and the natural, on the supposition that the dignity of the former would be marred, and that the omnipotence of the Lord and his love for Israel would be obscured, through this connection. It would make it an object to

---

[1] Even the earlier commentators have occasionally hinted at this reason for a connection of the supernatural with the natural, yet without giving to the thought its full importance. Thus, Calvin, for example, in his remarks upon the account of the plague of frogs, says: Aegyptios ante quasi precario vitam duxisse ostendit deus, quia singulari beneficio protexerat ab incursu ranarum. Scimus Aegyptum ob multas paludes et lentum ac prope stagnantem Nilum multis ranis et venenatis bestiis fuisse refertam. Nunc quum subito erumpunt ingentes turmae, agrorum superficiem obtegunt, penetrant etiam in domos et cubicula, denique in regium palatium conscendunt: facile apparet fuisse ante cohibitas sola dei manu *atque ita deum Hebraeorum fuisse regni illius praesidem et custodem.*

concentrate upon Egypt the strangest terrors. The consideration of the significance of the connection of the supernatural with the natural, which has just been pointed out, would not be sufficient to counterbalance this advantage, even if it could be supposed that this delicate manner of considering the subject, so far removed from common observation, would have been understood. And even aside from this view, a fictitious account could never succeed in sustaining so accurately the Egyptian character in connection with the supernatural, in preventing the obtrusion of an element which was not Egyptian. Were it even probable that individual Israelites of later times had an accurate acquaintance with Egypt, it would be of little advantage, since the thing would necessarily not take its shape from them merely, but far more from the prevailing ignorance of Egypt. Thus, therefore, the connection of the supernatural with the natural, throughout the whole, is an argument for the credibility of the narrative, for its composition at the time it purports to have been made, and consequently for its Mosaic origin.

MOSES' ROD CHANGED TO A SERPENT.

After these general remarks, we turn to particular explanations. A sign which is of a harmless nature, precedes, in Ex. vii. 8—13, the signs which are comprehended in the number ten as a perfect number, and which are also plagues. Trial is first made, whether Pharaoh, in reference to whom *Calvin*[1] so strikingly says, "There is presented us in the person of *one* abandoned, an example of human arrogance and rebellion," will not become wise without severe measures. Moses' rod is changed into a serpent ; the Egyptian magicians accomplish, at least in appearance, the same thing : but Moses' rod swallows up their rods. This counter-wonder of the Egyptian magicians is founded on the peculiar condition of Egypt : much more is the Mosaic sign,—the same by which indeed Moses had already, by the divine command, proved his commission from God, among the elders of his people. Moses was furnished with power to perform that which the Egyptian magicians most especially gloried in, and by which they most of all supported their authority.

[1] Nobis in unius reprobi persona superbiae et rebellionis humanae imago subjicitur.

The incantation of serpents has been native to Egypt from the most ancient even to the present time.[1] The French scholars, in their Description, have given the most accordant accounts of it. Even those who entered upon an examination of the subject with most absolute unbelief, have been forced to the conviction that there is something in it,—that the Psylli are found in possession of a secret charm, which places them in a condition to bring about the most wonderful consequences. "We confess," it is said, "that we, far removed from all easy credulity, have ourselves been witnesses of some things so wonderful, that we cannot consider the art of the serpent-tamers as entirely chimerical. We believed at first that they removed the teeth of serpents, and the stings of scorpions, but we have had opportunity to convince ourselves of the contrary."[2] "I am persuaded," says *Quatremère*,[3] "that there were a certain number of men found among the Psylli of antiquity, who by certain secret preparations put themselves in a condition, not to fear the bite of serpents, and to handle the most poisonous of them uninjured." "In Egypt and the neighbouring countries," says the same author, "there are men and women, who truly deserve the name of Psylli, and who uninjured handle the cerastes and other serpents, whose poison produces immediate death."[4] That they do not probably break out the poisonous teeth, *Hasselquist* also testifies from personal observation. According to the account in the Description,[5] the art passes from father to son. The Psylli form an association claiming to be the only individuals who are able to charm serpents, and to free houses from them. Never does any other than the son of a Psylli attain to this ability. Serpents in Egypt often conceal themselves in the houses, and then become very dangerous. When any thing of this kind is suspected, they have recourse to the Psylli. "The French commander-in-chief wished at a certain time to examine the affair to the bottom. He called for the Psylli, and commanded them to produce from the palace a serpent, which,

---

[1] Compare Aelian, 17. 5, and the summary of the accounts of the ancients, concerning the Psylli, in Quatremère, Mémoires sur l' Egypte, t. I. p. 202 seq.

[2] In a Treatise, De l' art des ophiogènes ou enchanteurs des serpens, in t. 18. of the Descr. p. 333 seq.

[3] As above quoted, p. 204.   [4] Quatremère, p. 210.

[5] T. 24. p. 82 seq.

from traces discovered, was supposed to be there. The moist places were especially examined. There the Psylli called, by imitating the hissing, sometimes of the male and sometimes of the female serpent. After two hours and a quarter, a serpent truly presented itself. In the religious festivals, the Psylli appear entirely naked, with the neck, arms, and other parts of the body coiled around by serpents, which they permit to sting and tear their breast and stomach, and effectually defend themselves against them with a sort of frenzy, pretending to wish to eat them alive. Their sleight of hand is very various. They are able, according to their assertions, to change the Haje[1]—i. e. the species of serpent which they especially make use of for their tricks—into a rod, and compel them to feign themselves dead. When they wish to perform this operation, they spit in the throat of the animal, compel it to shut up its mouth, and lay it down upon the ground. Then, as if in order to give a last command, they lay their hand upon its head, and immediately the serpent, stiff and motionless, falls into a kind of torpor. They wake it up when they wish, seizing it by the tail, and rolling it roughly between the hands." *Du Bois Aymé*[2] gives his testimony to the same thing.

That which is related to us of the condition of modern serpent-charmers, in the practice of their sleight of hand, is entirely sufficient to give an insight into the condition of the Egyptian magicians who withstood Moses. The state of these last, no less than the first, was certainly that of the highest enthusiasm, and cannot be attributed to a merely deliberate attempt to deceive ; although deception, as is shown to be the case with the modern Egyptian Psylli, is by no means excluded by enthusiasm, but rather often goes hand in hand with it. That the condition of the

---

[1] It is worthy of notice, that this species of serpent, the asp of the ancient Egyptians, was considered sacred throughout the whole country. " It was worshipped," says *Plutarch*, De Isid., "on account of a certain resemblance between it, and the operations of the divine power. It was the emblem of the god Neph, and the goddess Ranno. The asp was easily tamed, and came from its place of concealment by the snapping of the fingers." *Aelian* (Lib. vi. c. 33) speaks of the power of the Egyptians to charm serpents, and call them forth from their lurking places, &c. " Mummies of them have been discovered in the Necropolis of Thebes." Compare *Wilk*. Vol. 1. Sec. Ser. p. 237—242, also upon the Cerastes or horned snake, mentioned on p. 101, see 245 seq.

[2] Page 108.

Psylli is one of ecstacy is indeed clear from the passages already quoted. According to *Minutoli*,[1] "the people consider them as holy. At certain festivals, e. g. on the day before the departure of the great caravan to the Holy Caaba, they go forth in procession with live snakes around their necks and arms, having their faces in contortions like an insane person, until foam falls from the mouth. They sometimes also tear the serpents with their teeth.[2] When they are in this condition, the people press around them, especially the women, in order, if it is possible, to touch their foaming mouths with their hands." The same author describes one of the Psylli, who had been sent for to free a house from serpents, in the following manner: "The appearance of this man was that of a true magician. In the beginning of his operation he stripped himself naked even to a little apron about his hips: upon his breast hung a chain of black coral: his head was shorn to a bunch of hair, which stood up like bristles upon the top of his head; his body was dark-brown and muscular. Rolling his eyes and with the rod of divination in his hand, he now walked forth with a grave demeanour, and, in the meantime, whilst casting forth louder and louder imprecations, and thrusting against the ceiling and walls with his divining rod, he searched thoroughly the chambers and corners, now of the upper and now of the lower story. His fumigations of meal, sulphur, and onion parings were at last so stupifying that a hard cough often interrupted the formula of incantation, and he was several times obliged to invigorate himself by smoking a pipe of tobacco."

It is entirely contrary to the spirit of antiquity in general, and

---

[1] S. 266, ff. der Reise.

[2] *Lane*, in his "Modern Egyptians," Vol. II. p. 207, says: "Serpents and scorpions were not unfrequently eaten by Sáadees, during my former visit to this country. The former were deprived of their poisonous teeth or rendered harmless, by having their upper and lower lips bored, and tied together on each side with a silk string, to prevent their biting; and sometimes, those which were merely carried in procession, had two silver rings put in place of the silk strings. Whenever a Sáadee ate the flesh of a live serpent, he was, or affected to be, excited to do so by a kind of frenzy. He pressed very hard, with the end of his thumb, upon the reptile's back, as he grasped it, at a point about two inches from the head; and all that he ate of it, was the head and the part between it and the point where his thumb pressed; of which he made three or four mouthfuls: the rest he threw away."

of Egyptian antiquity in particular, to explain the phrase, "This is the finger of God," chap. viii. as meaning, "This is accomplished by God," so that the magicians say, that until now they have contended with Moses and Aaron upon earthly ground, with human means, and there they have overcome, but now God appears.[1] It should rather be explained: By the power of God have they obtained the victory. They certainly also ascribe to Elohim (not Jehovah) their former success; the whole contest was a contest of God, Gen. xxx. 8, and therefore their present inability must be to them of just so much greater significance.

It deserves to be noticed also, that the present condition of the Psylli in Egypt is entirely one of decay. It is torn loose from its natural connection, the soil of natural religion, from which it originally sprung. It exists in a land in which even now modern illumination has variously exerted its influence and hindered its freedom. Accordingly nothing is more natural than that very much that is artificial should be added to the exstatic condition, and that very much charlatanry should creep in. But what now remains of ecstacy is entirely sufficient to convince us of the intensity of it, as it existed in the time of the glory of the Egyptian religion and priesthood.

The opinion expressed upon the proceedings of the modern Psylli, which we find among observers who are most free from prejudice, and also among those who, on the other hand, are decidly under the dominion of prejudice, guide us in explaining the fact, that the author of the Pentateuch does not speak definitely upon the nature and origin of the results produced by the Egyptian magicians. Were the thing so simple as it is generally considered to be, were it either common jugglery or something really miraculous, performed by the permission of God through Satanic influence, then the author of the Pentateuch would not, it may be presumed, fail to express an opinion upon it. But, since the ground on which these things rest—a very dark and difficult one —is not yet indeed but imperfectly explained by the most thorough investigations, it was preferable to remain standing at the outer edge without going deeper into the nature of these results.[2] As respects the thing itself, a further insight into the

---

[1] Calvin says; Digitum dei opponunt suae solertiae et peritiae. Pudebat enim fateri quenquam mortalium scientia praecellere.

[2] The word בְּלַטֵיהֶם *Belteyhem*, in chap. vii. 22, and viii. 3, 14, in

nature of these consequences avails nothing. Whatever opinion they had of it, this is certain, that even in the first three signs, the superior power of the God of Israel made itself sufficiently known to any one who did not studiously seek a support for his unbelief and rebellion. They change, it matters not whether really or in appearance, their rods into serpents, but the rod of Moses swallows up their rods; they also change, at least on a small scale, water into blood, but they are not able to restore the blood to its former state; in like manner, imitating on a small scale the miracle of Moses, they brought up frogs upon the land, but they were not able to free it from the plague of frogs. "For the punishment of the Egyptians," says *Theodoret*, "God gave also to magicians power, but not for removing punishment: since the king had not enough of his plagues, but even commanded the magicians to increase the chastisement, so God also punished him through these: Thou art not yet satisfied with the punishment inflicted by my servants, so punish I thee also by thine own." And the relative power of the Egyptian magicians in the beginning, must serve to show in so much clearer light their entire impotence as it was first exhibited in the little gnats and then continued invariable. The contest was first intentionally carried on in a sphere in which the Egyptian magicians, as we certainly know with reference to the first sign, had hitherto shown their principal power. After they had there been vanquished, the scene was changed to a sphere in which they could not at all further contend, and the doom which in this way came upon them, fell through them upon their gods.[1]

THE FIRST PLAGUE—THE WATER OF EGYPT CHANGED TO BLOOD.

We turn now to the *second* sign, which is also the first *plague*. It consists in changing the waters of the Nile, and the other waters of Egypt, into blood. It appears from Joel iii. 4, according to which the moon shall be changed into blood, that there is no reason to suppose that literal blood is here meant. On the con-

which it is often affirmed that a verdict of the author upon this matter is found, contains no such thing; and the whole contest is a vain one, since there is nothing existing which can give us any information concerning his opinion.

[1] Ex. xii. 12.

trary, the change into blood can properly only have reference to the blood red colour: so that the blood here is the same as the water red as blood in 2 Kings iii. 22. The designation is here evidently chosen for the sake of the symbolic character which this plague bears, as also the water red as blood in the passage referred to in the book of Kings has a symbolic significance, announcing destruction to the enemies of Israel. To the Egyptians shall the reddened water be blood, reminding them of the innocent blood which they have shed, and pointing to the flowing guilty blood to be shed. In this characteristic this plague is coupled with the darkness which afterwards covered the whole land, as both also appear connected in Joel iii. 4: "The sun shall be turned into darkness and the moon into blood." In the symbolic colours arranged by the Egyptians, black was the colour of death and mourning,—for that which was base and its author, the red colour was chosen, probably as the colour of blood.[1]

That there is found something analogous to this plague in the natural phenomena of Egypt, has already long ago been said. The water of the Nile, a short time before the inundation, takes a green, and at the beginning of the inundation a red colour. The cause of this change of colour has not yet been sufficiently investigated.[2] According to *Antes*,[3] the inhabitants name the water when the flood has reached its highest point of increase, ما أحمر *(ma ahmar)* red water. In the year 1673 the Nile reddened as early as the beginning of July, and continued of a red colour to the end of December, when it assumed again its usual hue.[4]

In common years the water, when it is green and red, is drink-

---

[1] Drummann, Ueber die Inschrift in Rosette, S. 108, 109.

[2] Le Père Ainé, in the Memoir sur la Vallée du Nil, in the Descr. t. 18, p. 571, says: "The water at Cairo is found by analysis to be five times purer than that of the Seine at Paris. It, however, has this degree of purity only at the time when the inundation begins to diminish. The noxious qualities which are attributed to it, at the time when the water is low and stagnant, and when it begins to increase, appear to proceed from an innumerable multitude of insects which the heat generates in it. The causes which destroy the purity of the water, at different seasons of the year, are not yet sufficiently investigated. The *red* colour originates, probably, from the earthy particles which the flood brings along with it from Sennaar."

[3] In De Sacy upon Abdollatiph, p. 346.

[4] Hartmann, Aegypten, S. 128.

able. *Sonnini*[1] says: "During the continuance of my journey, I with my companions had no other drink than the unmingled water of the Nile. We drank it without any one of us experiencing inconvenience, at all seasons of the year, even when the inundation so fills it with slime that it is thick and reddish, and appears truly loathsome."

But sometimes, in years of great heat, this peculiarity of water becomes a great calamity. Thus *Abdollatiph*[2] relates: "In the year 596 (1199) the increase of the Nile was smaller than had ever been known. About two months before the first indications of the inundation, the waters of the river assumed a green colour. This increased by degrees, and it became putrid, and offensive to the taste. Sick people avoided drinking from it, and drank well-water.[3] By boiling, its smell and taste became worse. There also appeared in it worms and other animals, which live in stagnant water."

That in our account the common plague existed in an entirely uncommon degree is evident, since the ordinary means of purification did not at all take effect, verse 19. The Egyptians could not drink at all from the river, verse 21, and the fish also died in it, verse 18. Of this last effect there is no other example on record. But what passes beyond the boundaries of the barely extraordinary, and carries the occurrence into the region of the miraculous, is, that the changing of the waters took place, not merely suddenly, while it commonly is gradual,[4] but it also was in accordance with the prediction of Moses, and just at the moment when he lifted his rod.

The circumstances which are also sometimes referred to, as proof of the difference between this change of the water, and the one which is common, namely, that it occurred at an entirely unusual time, and that it also ceased far more suddenly than common, are shown on closer examination to be without foundation. For with reference to the time of this first plague, there is nothing said in the account, and it is therefore most probable that in this respect it offered nothing extraordinary. The reason which *De Wette*[5] adduces, that the first plagues, in reference to time, must

---

[1] Th. 2. S. 13. [2] De Sacy, p. 332. [3] See Ex. vii. 24.
[4] Compare the interesting cases of the change of water to a red colour in other countries. Rosenm. A. u. N. Morgenl. Th. I. S. 281 ff.
[5] Krit. der Isr. Gesch. S. 193.

border nearly on the last which took place some time between the end of **February**, and the beginning of **April**: 'They must follow each other at short intervals, if they shall produce wonder and fear,' has little force. For the facts were of a kind, that could not fail to make a deep impression, if they were separated from one another by even longer intervals; and besides, it had a peculiar significance, if Jehovah went through, as it were, an entire course with the Egyptians—following now with his miracles, the customary, revolving circle of nature in their land. Let it be remarked, as the account says nothing of the time of the first plagues, the assumption of *v. Bohlen*: "Since the Exodus of the Israelites was in the month Abib, just at the time of the passover, the most of these plagues, which first appear in midsummer, can be devised only by one who has a merely casual acquaintance with the land," is baseless. But were such specifications of time found, it would be pertinent to call attention to the fact, that the author nowhere asserts that those extraordinary events are confined to the time in which the common events belong. The second asserted difference is founded on verse 25: "And seven days were fulfilled after that the Lord had smitten the river." But we have no right to infer[1] from this, that that condition of the Nile lasted only seven days. The words are rather to be closely connected with what follows, and the meaning is only, that seven days after the beginning of the first plague, concerning the end of which nothing is related, the announcement of the second follows.

Although it belongs not to our immediate purpose, yet we wish to remark here, briefly, upon the ridiculous contradiction which has been found in this narrative. How could the Egyptian magicians, it is said, after Moses has changed *all* the waters to a red colour, do the same. Setting aside all forced solutions, this objection is easily and simply annulled by the remark, that the pressing of the word *all*, upon which this contradiction entirely rests, stands in opposition to the usage in the Hebrew historical writings in general, and especially in narrating the great deeds of the Lord in Egypt, concerning which the heart, full of gratitude and astonishment, was allowed to have no little influence. That

---

[1] With Jonathan who supplies: Et postea sanavit verbum domini fluvium.

no rule is without exceptions, appears to the writer so self-evident, that he supposes there is no necessity to avoid the full expression, on account of exceptions, which with him are entirely in the background. So he proceeds throughout. According to chap. ix. 25, for example, all the trees of the field were broken by the hail. According to x. 5, the locust eat *all* the trees. If we here press the significance of the *all*, we shall have a contradiction for the explanation of which even the most boundless carelessness is not sufficient.

Besides this most prominent Egyptian reference, already noticed, several others are found. We will begin with the one most striking among them, which is contained in verse 19. It is there said, Blood shall be in all of Egypt, "both in wood and stone." (Luther: both in vessels of wood and stone.) These words have at first view something very remarkable, and they lose it only when they are explained by the Egyptian customs, to which they refer, as has already been remarked.[1] In common times they are accustomed to purify the turbid water of the Nile in vessels of wood or stone, generally in the latter. When it is desirable to purify it quickly, a ball of crushed almonds is thrown in ; when there is time for the purification, it is done without them. The purification with almonds is particularly described by *Prosper Alpinus*, *Pococke*,[2] and *Savary*. Of the simple process speaks *Helfrich*, as quoted by *Hartmann*:[3] "*Helfrich* remarks, that the water in large vessels of wood, earth, and also of unburned clay, even without the addition of almonds, settles in two or three days. According to others, this is done even quicker." And then *Mayr*[4] says: "The water which comes upon the table is passed through vessels of a kind of earth, which forthwith permits the liquid to filter through." *Le Bruyn*[5] says that it is considered as very fortunate to be in possession of such a vessel of white earth. It is also said, that the water becomes so putrid that it admits no purification. But it is of far more importance, than that the author knows the common method of purifying water among the Egyptians, to consider the precise manner in which he speaks of it. He does not obtrude this knowledge. He supposes

---

[1] In den Beob. a. d. Orient, Deutsch von Faber, Th. 2. S. 315.
[2] 1. 312.   [4] P. 130.   [5] Reise, Th. 2. S. 19.
[3] Tom. II. p. 103. Thevenot, t. 1. p. 245, 00.

that a mere hint is enough for his immediate readers, who were themselves acquainted with the peculiarities of Egypt, and it does not occur to him as necessary to add anything of explanation. Certainly these two words, *wood* and *stone*, are of no small importance with respect to the authorship of the Pentateuch.

The same verse furnishes us also another proof of the author's acquaintance with Egypt. The Lord commanded Moses to take his rod, and stretch out his hand "upon the waters of Egypt, upon its streams, upon its canals, upon its pools, and upon all its collections of water." The classification of the waters of Egypt, which is here given, appears to be entirely accurate and complete.

The streams, נְהָרֹת *Neharoth*, says *Faber*,[1] are the arms of the Nile; the ditches, יְאֹרִים, *Garim*, are the artificial canals;[2] the pools, אֲגַמִּים, *Agamim*, are the stagnant ponds, which the Nile makes, called in Egypt, Birke,—of these there are many; the collections of water, כָּל־מִקְוֵה מַיִם, *Kol-Mikvè-Maim*, are all the other standing water, or that which is left behind by the Nile, the lakes and puddles, from which the peasants, who live at a distance from the Nile, water their land; and indeed, even the inhabitants of Cairo are compelled to pay for and drink this water, since the carriers bring it to them on camels, instead of the Nile water, which is farther off.[3]

The threat of Moses, and the described inconveniences which its fulfilment brought upon the Egyptians, is founded on the importance which the Nile water has for the Egyptians, and upon the enthusiastic love of the inhabitants of Egypt for it. The Nile water is almost the only drinkable water in Egypt. For the water of the few wells is distasteful and unwholesome. The Turks, according to *Mascrier*, find the water so pleasant that they eat salt in order to be able to drink more of it. They are accustomed to say, if Mohammed had drank thereof, he would have asked immortality of God, so that he might always drink of this water. If the

[1] Zu Harmar, S. 326-7.
[2] Compare upon יְאֹרִים, with the signification of *canals*, Ges. Thes. s. v.
[3] Thevenot, t. 1. p. 173. In reference to the Egyptian lakes, Hartmann, S. 146, may be compared. He remarks: "Also upon them, the inundation of the Nile has a considerable influence, supplying them with water where they are dry, and increasing it where any yet remains." See also Le Père, Mém, s. les Lacs de la basse Egypte, in the Descr. t. 16. p. 199 seq.

Egyptians undertake a pilgrimage to Mecca, or travel elsewhere, they speak of nothing but the delight which they shall experience when, on their return, they again drink of the Nile water, &c.[1] It is very justly said, after these circumstances have been referred to, "He who has never understood any thing of the pleasantness of the Nile water, and does not know how much of it the Egyptians are accustomed to drink, will now find in the words of Moses, 'the Egyptians shall loathe,' &c. a meaning which he has not before perceived. The sense is, they loathe the water which they at other times prefer before all the water in the world, even that which they have previously longed for. They prefer to drink well-water, which in their country is so unpleasant."[2]

In verse 15, it is said: "Go to Pharaoh in the morning, behold he goeth out to the water, and meet him on the banks of the Nile." In like manner, in chap. viii. 16 (20): "Rise up early in the morning, and stand before Pharaoh; behold he goeth forth to the water." Both passages are founded on the divine honours which the Egyptians paid to the Nile. Moses is commanded to meet Pharaoh, with a commission from the true God, whom Pharaoh wickedly resists, just when he is preparing to bring his daily offering to his false gods. In the first passage, this moment appears to be the more fitly chosen, since the threatened demonstration of the omnipotence of Jehovah is exhibited directly upon the false god. The Egyptians, even in the most ancient times, paid divine honours to the Nile. Especially was he zealously

---

[1] See Maillet, t. 2. p. 103. The salubrity and excellence of the water of the Nile have been ever the theme of praise, both with natives and foreigners. So nutritious were its qualities supposed to be, that the priests withheld it from their sacred bull Apis, lest the use of it should make him too fat. The natives at the present day frequently stimulate themselves by adding salt to fresh draughts from the delicious stream, and the Egyptians in foreign land speak of nothing with so much enthusiasm as the delight which they will experience from the Nile water on their return. The Egyptians, during the continuance of the plague, were not wholly without a resource; we read that "all the Egyptians digged round about the river for water to drink; for they could not drink of the water of the river." (Exod. vii. 24.) But though the waters of the Nile are remarkably good, that of all the wells in Egypt is so brackish as to be scarcely fit for use. See *Lam.*, I. 293. T.

[2] In den. Beob. a. d. Orient, S. 311. Comparo also Oedmanns verm. Sammlungen, Th. 1. S. 130. Rosenm. A. u. N. Morgenl. Th. 1. S. 276 ff.

honoured, according to *Champollion*,[1] at Nilopolis, where he had a temple. *Herodotus*[2] mentions the priests of the Nile. "What the head is to the body," says *Horapollo*,[3] "the Nile is to the Egyptians." "He is," continues the same author, "according to representations whose antiquity cannot be determined, identical with Osiris,[4] and the highest god."[5] *Lucian*[6] says: "Its water is a common divinity to all of the Egyptians." The monuments bear witness to the same effect as the ancient authors, they indeed very particularly represent, that even the kings paid divine honours to the Nile. According to *Champollion*,[7] there is in a chapel at Ghebel Selseleh (Silsilis,) a painting of the time of the reign of Remeses II., which exhibits this king "offering wine to the god of the Nile, who, in the hieroglyphic inscription, is called, Hapi Môou, the life-giving father of all existences." According to the inscription, this chapel is specially dedicated to this god. Remeses is called in it, "beloved of Hapi Môou, the father of the gods." "The passage which contains the praise of the god of the Nile, represents him at the same time as the heavenly Nile, the primitive water, the great Nilus, whom *Cicero*[8] declares to be the father of the highest deities, even of Ammon; and of this I am myself also convinced[9] from other inscriptions on the monuments."

Yet far more convincing than the knowledge of Egyptian affairs which the author exhibits, is here also the unpremeditated manner in which he exhibits this knowledge, and the want of every explanatory remark, resting upon the supposition, that such a thing is not necessary for his immediate readers.

---

[1] Eg. sur les **Pharaons**, t. 1. p. 321.
[2] In B. 2. c. 90: Οἱ ἱρέες αὐτοὶ οἱ τοῦ Νείλου. See Bähr on this passage.
[3] Bei Drumann, Inschrift von **Rosetta**, S. 100.
[4] Plut. de Is. et. Osir. p. 363 D.
[5] Heliodorus, Aeth. 9. p. 435. Athen. 5. 203: "Αἰγύπτιε ζεῦ Νεῖλε."
[6] In the Jupiter Tragoed. opp. t. 2. p. 699. Edid. Reitz.
[7] In den Briefer aus Egypten, S. 121, D. Uebers.
[8] De nat. Deor.
[9] "Anaglyphum in vico **Karnak** repertum," remarks Creuzer, (in Comm. Herod. p. 212,) who also, pp. 186—188, treats expressly of the divine honours paid to the Nile, "terna Pharaonis initia exhibit. Etenim primo loco sacerdotes eum aspergunt lustrantque sacra unda Nili," &c. Compare also upon the deity of the Nile, Jabl. Panth. t. 2. p. 171.

THE SECOND PLAGUE—THE FROGS.

The account of the second plague, the frogs, furnishes us far less abundant spoil than that of the first. It is implied in the account itself, in chap. viii. 5, that the waters of Egypt, even in ordinary circumstances, contain many frogs; and from the nature of these waters, we could scarcely imagine it to be otherwise. The statements of travellers in regard to this are, however, very scanty. *Hasselquist*[1] mentions frogs among the Mosaic plagues, which even now visit both natives and foreigners. According to *Sonnini*,[2] the stagnant waters about Rosetta are filled with thousands of frogs, which make very much noise.[3]

That a sudden appearance of animals,—which though always present in a land, ordinarily are scarcely noticed at all,—in untold numbers so as to become a plague, has not been unknown in Egypt at other times, is shown by what *Macrizi*[4] says of the destructions by worms: "In 791-2, the worms which destroyed books and woollen cloth, multiplied in a wonderful manner. A credible man assured us, that these animals ate 1500 pieces of cloth,—more than fifteen camel loads. I was persuaded from what I myself saw, that this declaration was not exaggerated, and that the worms had destroyed in the region of the sea, a great quantity of wood and cloth. I saw at Materiah, garden-walls which were entirely pierced through by these little animals. About the year 821, this plague made its appearance in the quarter of Hosainiah, just out of Cairo. The worms, after they had consumed provisions, cloth, &c. which caused an incalculable loss to the inhabitants, seized upon the walls of the houses, and gnawed the rafters until they were pierced entirely through. The owners quickly tore down the buildings which the worms had spared, so that the quarter near was entirely laid waste. These animals carried their devastations even to the houses which stand hard by the Gate of Conquest and Victory."

---

[1] P. 254.
[2] Th. III. S. 365.
[3] An account of the different kinds of frogs in Egypt, is found in the Descr. t. 24. p. 134 seq.
[4] In Quatremère, t. 1. p. 121.

THE THIRD PLAGUE—THE כִּנָּם, GNATS.

As respects the third plague, it is now generally agreed, that by כִּנָּם, *kinnim*, gnats are meant. These are, even in ordinary years, very troublesome in Egypt. *Herodotus*,[1] as early as his time, speaks of the great trouble which the gnats cause, and of the precautions which are taken to guard against them. The passages in modern travellers are collected in *Oedmann*,[2]—according to the testimony of *Maillet* and *Pococke*, they often darken the air in Cairo,—in *Hartmann*,[3] and last in *Eichhorn*.[4] *Hartmann* comprises the results in the following words: "All travellers speak of these gnats as an ordinary plague of the country. In cool weather they are especially bold. They pursue the men, prevent them from eating, disturb their sleep, and cause swellings which are sensibly painful. What *Sonnini*[5] says of these gnats, in his account of his abode in Rosetta, is of peculiar interest: "It is asserted that the multitude of gnats, with which the streets and the inside of the houses were then filled, owe their origin to this employment (the drying of rice about the end of October.) Indeed, there are fewer of them at other times. After the rice harvest, they go forth in multitudes from the overflowed fields in which the preceding generation laid their eggs. They come to trouble men, they make wounds, in order to suck their blood, not less burning than those of the Maringonins of South America." These passages show that the time of the extraordinary public calamities corresponded merely to that of the extraordinary plague. The first plague, the changing of water to blood, transfers us to the period of the increase of the Nile, the gnats begin to multiply at the end of the inundation.

THE FOURTH PLAGUE—THE FLIES.

The animals which constitute the fourth plague, are designated by עָרֹב, *arob*. This word originally can scarcely have any other signification, than *the mingling*, but it was secondarily applied to a distinct species of animals, which in Egypt especially compose

---

[1] B. 2. c. 195.   [2] I. S. 74 ff.   [3] S 250.
[4] S. 17, 18.   [5] Th. 1. S. 246.

the vermin or insects. That they were flies is argued: 1. From the authority of the Septuagint, which translates ערב, *arob*, by dog-fly, Κυνόμυια. 2. From the appropriate connection of gnats and flies. 3. From the fact that flies belong to the common inconveniences of Egypt.

How troublesome flies are in Egypt even in ordinary circumstances, is most clearly shown by the description of *Sonnini*:[1] "The most numerous and troublesome insects in Egypt are the flies (musca domestica L.) Men and animals are grievously tormented by them. It is impossible to form an adequate conception of their fury when they wish to fix themselves upon any part of the body. If they are driven away they light again the same instant, and their pertinacity wearies the most patient. They especially love to light in the corners of the eyes, or on the edge of the eyelids, sensitive parts to which they are attracted by a slight moisture." The description of the dog-fly by *Philo*[2] is, for substance, entirely in accordance with this account. By this name insects incredibly monstrous are often designated. Aside from a little exaggeration, it is impossible to disbelieve in *Philo*. The name, dog-fly, is probably chosen to distinguish those insects from another very widely diffused species of flies, which is smaller and less troublesome.[3] *Abdollatiph*[4] says: "In consequence of the great dampness of the air, bugs, flies, and fleas continue here a great part of the year." In *Jomard*,[5] just as here, flies and gnats are associated together as plagues of Egypt: "The remark also that these cold seasons free the land from the plague of innumerable flies and gnats, whose bites are so troublesome and painful."

As the threatened plague made its appearance, Pharaoh caused Moses and Aaron to be called, and said to them: "Sacrifice to your God in the land." But Moses answered: "It is not meet to do so; for we shall sacrifice the abomination of the Egyptians to the Lord our God. If we sacrifice the abomination of the Egyptians before their eyes, will they not stone us?" Exod. viii. 22 (26). That there is here a reference to Egyptian customs, has always been acknowledged.

[1] Th. 3. S. 226.
[2] See in proof of this Michaelis Suppl. p. 1960.
[3] Sonnini, S. 227.
[4] P. 5. De Sacy.
[5] In the Descr. t. 18. p. 2, 512.

According to the common theory, the very bitter exasperation to be apprehended by the Israelites from the Egyptians, was because the latter sacrificed animals, which the former considered sacred. But there are two arguments against this supposition: 1. The designation—abomination, is not appropriate to the consecrated animals. This indicates that the animals which the Israelites slaughtered were not too good, but two bad for offerings. 2. The animals which were commonly taken among the Israelites for offerings, were also among the Egyptians not sacred. The only one of the larger domestic animals which was generally considered as sacred, the cow,[1] was also among the Israelites, except in the case in Num. xix., which is entirely by itself, not offered. The animals most commonly sacrificed—oxen, were also both sacrificed and eaten by the Egyptians.

The offence is rather, that the Israelites omit the inquiry concerning the cleanness of animals, which is practised with the greatest caution by the Egyptians. That only clean animals were sacrificed by the Egyptians, *Herodotus* says in 2. 45, where he acquits the Egyptians from the imputation of offering human sacrifices: "For since they are not allowed to sacrifice any animals except the swine, and the bullock, and calves, namely, those that are clean among them, and the goose, how can they offer men?" What stress is laid upon cleanness, and how truly it is considered as an abomination to offer an unclean animal, is seen from *Herodotus*.[2] Only a red ox could be offered, and a single black hair rendered it unclean. They also placed dependence upon a multitude of marks besides this; the tongue and tail were accurately examined, &c. Each victim must, after a prescribed examination in confirmation of its fitness, be sealed on the horns. To offer an unsealed ox was prohibited on penalty of death.[3]

---

[1] Compare Herod. B. 2, c. 41. Heeren, S. 363.
[2] B. 2. c. 38. See also Bähr on the passage.
[3] The intolerant fanaticism of the Egyptians, which the answer of Moses implies, is also proved from other sources. Herodotus says in B. 2, c. 65: "If any person kills one of these animals intentionally, he expiates his crime by death; if unintentionally, he must pay the fine which the priest imposes. But whoever kills an ibis or a hawk, whether intentionally or not, must die." Even in the days of the Ptolemies, a Roman ambassador narrowly escaped being torn to pieces for having injured one of the sacred animals.

FIFTH PLAGUE—THE DESTRUCTION OF THE ANIMALS IN EGYPT.

In reference to the fifth plague—the destruction of the cattle, there is not much to be said, since travellers have bestowed little attention upon the diseases of animals in Egypt. Only single scattered passages are found in the Description, and these indeed very general, so that it cannot be determined whether diseases make their appearance in Egypt, by which all kinds of the larger domestic animals are seized in like manner. It is said,[1] that murrain breaks out from time to time in Egypt with so much severity, that they are compelled to send to Syria or the Islands of the Archipelago for a new supply of oxen. It is also said,[2] since about the year 1786 a disease very much diminished the number of oxen, they began to make use of the buffalo in their place for watering the fields, and the practice is continued in later times.

That in the enumeration of the animals on which the plague shall seize, chap. ix. horses are assigned the first place, and that too without further remark, is again one of the little things, which, in such an inquiry as the one before us, is of so great importance, so soon as the scattered items are collected, and thereby rescued from the contingency to which each is subject.

THE SIXTH PLAGUE—THE BOILS.

That the sixth plague—the boils, was miraculous only in extent, is shown by a comparison of Deut. xxviii. 27, where the same disease, under the name of *boils* of Egypt, is represented as of common occurrence there. But a more exact defining of the nature of this sickness is difficult. *Rosenmüller*[3] considers it the elephantiasis, which, according to *Lucretius*[4] and *Pliny*,[5] was peculiar to Egypt. But the appellation boil[6] does not seem to be proper for this disease, still less the expression "breaking out in blains," in Ex. ix. 9. Besides, the elephantiasis does not attack cattle. *Eichhorn* appeals to a remark in *Granger*[7] *(Tourtechot)*: "In

---

[1] Descr. t. 17. p. 126.
[2] Upon Deut. xxviii. 27.
[3] He calls it in Book 26, c. 5: Aegypti peculiare malum.
[4] שחין *Shchin*, from שחן *Shahan* in the dialects, incaluit, inflammatus est.
[5] Descr. p. 62.
[6] B. 6. 112-13.
[7] Voyage de l'Egypte, p. 21.

autumn sores come upon the thighs and knees, which remove the patient in two or three days." These notices seem, however, to have reference to the plague, but it is uncertain whether this malady existed so anciently, and indeed it does not answer the circumstances, for the reference is evidently to a very painful, but not absolutely dangerous, sickness. Only a disease attended by feverish cutaneous eruptions can be meant, one which amid the variety of diseases does not easily admit of definition. But the destruction which small-pox and plague makes in Egypt, shows how very much the climate there disposes to such diseases. We are almost disposed to think of a disease which *Thevenot* describes: "There is besides," he says, "a sickness, or rather inconvenience, for it is more inconvenient than dangerous, which makes its appearance when the waters of the Nile begin to rise. Then hot postules, which are very troublesome, and sting terribly, appear upon the whole body, and when the patient thinks to comfort and refresh himself with drink, he feels, while drinking and afterwards, stings as painful as if he were pierced with two hundred needles all at once."[1] But this disease which *Thevenot*, perhaps, described with some exaggeration,[2] cannot be meant, since postules are not referred to, but a sore; and this disease is not the object of the curse, as our sickness appears to be in Deut. xxviii. Besides, the language in Deut. xxviii. 35, "with sore botch which cannot be healed," is not appropriate to the disease, as well as what is related in the passage before us, that the magicians are not able to stand, and the cattle no less than men were attacked with it. See upon diseases which are common to men and animals, *Mayner's* Anthropology.[3]

THE SEVENTH PLAGUE—THE TEMPEST.

The seventh plague was a severe tempest, attended with hail and rain. In the narrative itself, chap. ix. 18, 24, it is said that the phenomenon was unexampled only in degree, and it is implied that it is not uncommon in Egypt in a milder form. Other accounts agree with ours in showing that tempests in Egypt are not unfrequent, and that they, in general, differ from the one under

---

[1] Voyage du Levant, L. II. c. 80, p. 831.
[2] See other authors upon this same blotch in Hartmann, S. 59.
[3] Th. 2. S. 279.

consideration, only in severity. These notices are explanatory of our account, insomuch as they represent that tempests are most abundant just at the time in which, according to verse 31, the tempest here described occurred. The accounts of ancient travellers concerning tempests in Egypt, in January and March, are found carefully collected in *Nordmeyer*,[1] and especially in *Hartmann*:[2] "*Mansleben* and *Manconys* heard it thunder during their stay at Alexandria, the former on the 1st of January, and the latter on the 17th and 18th of the same month: on the same days it also hailed there. *Perry*[3] also remarks that it hails, though seldom, in January and February at Cairo. An account in the Notices[4] bears witness to the occurrence of the same thing in February. *Pococke* even saw hail mingled with rain, fall at Fium in February; compare Exodus ix. 34. *Korte* also saw hail fall. *Bruce*[5] heard at Cossir during the roaring of the winds through the whole of February, also afterwards on the Arabian Gulf, the crash of thunder. In March tempests are not uncommon at Cairo." During *Thevenot's* residence in Egypt, a tempest discharged itself, killing a man.[6] The residence of the scholars of the French Expedition in Egypt, was not continued long enough to make complete observations of this kind. *Du Bois Aymé*[7] affirms, that during the two years which he spent in Egypt, he did not hear a clap of thunder but once, and that was so faint that several persons with him did not notice it. *Coutelle*[8] says: "Natural phenomena succeed each other in this land with a constant uniformity. The same winds return regularly at the same time, and continue equally long. In the Delta it does not rain at all in summer, and scarcely at all in winter. We have very seldom seen it rain in Cairo. Rain in Upper Egypt is a wonder. A higher temperature than that designated below, a harder frost, and more copious rains, are extraordinary occurrences." *Jomard*[9] upon the climate of Cairo, says: "Rain falls by no means so seldom in Egypt as is commonly asserted. First of all, Lower Egypt must evidently be excepted, as it covers a

---

[1] Calendarium Aeg. Occon. p. 11, 12, 20, 27.
[2] S. 41.
[3] P. 255.
[4] I. 260.
[5] I. 267(?), II. 117.
[6] I. 344.
[7] l. c. p. 135.
[8] In Obss. Meteorologiques in the Descr. t. 19. p. 467.
[9] In Descr. 18. 2. p. 510 seq.

much more extended surface than the rest of the country, and lies where its greater or less proximity to the sea produces a more variable climate than than of Saïd. All phenomena, with the exception of hail and snow, follow there as in other countries, which are washed by the Mediterranean Sea. I have several times seen even hail at Alexandria. At Cairo the state of the atmosphere begins to be more settled, and in Upper Egypt it is almost invariable."

The account of this plague comprises also other separate but very striking references to Egypt. One is found, first, in chap. ix. 19, where Moses says to Pharaoh: "Send therefore now and gather thy cattle and all that thou hast in the field; for upon every man and beast which shall be found in the field and shall not be brought home, the hail shall come down, and they shall die." According to this verse, the cattle were not found in the stall but in the field, when the tempest commenced; verse 31 confirms this fact. With this agrees accurately our other accounts,—an agreement so much the more significant, since the time that the cattle were turned out was so short. *Niebuhr*[1] says: "In the months January, February, March, and April, the cattle graze, whereas, during the remaining months, they must be supplied with dry fodder." The author of the Egyptian calendar[2] shows the same thing. Also, according to the Description,[3]

---

[1] Reisebeschr. I. S. 142. The lotus was particularly useful as fodder for cattle. In the account of Pharaoh's dream, we read: "And, behold, there came up out of the river seven well favoured kine and fat-fleshed; and they fed in a meadow." (Gen. xli. 2.) Here the word *Achu*, rendered *meadow* by our translators, really signifies a succulent aquatic plant, such as the byblus or lotus. We learn from the monuments, and from history, that the fattening of cattle was extensively practised in the marshes, and that in other places stall-feeding was very common. This circumstance enables us to explain an apparent inconsistency in the history of the ten plagues. We are told, that "all the cattle of Egypt died" in the plague of murrain; but we read in the same chapter (Exod. ix.), that some cattle were destroyed by the plague of hail. The contradiction vanishes, when we look to the limitation with which the plague of murrain was announced: "Behold the hand of the Lord is upon thy cattle, *which is in the field;*" the plague, therefore, did not extend to the beasts which were in stalls and enclosures, and these consequently survived to become the victims of the plague of hail. T.

[2] In the Notices et Extraits, t. 1. p. 252. See also Nordmeyer, p. 17; Hartmann, S. 232; Le Bruyn, I. 570.

[3] Tom. 17. p. 126.

the cattle get green food only four months of the year, the rest of the time, dried fodder.

Not less important is the parenthetical remark of the author in chap. ix. 31, 32: "And the flax and the barley were smitten; for the barley was in the ear, and the flax was bolled. But the wheat and the spelt were not smitten, for these come to maturity later." In surveying what was destroyed, and what was to be destroyed, in case of persevering obstinacy, there is here named,— First, the products on which the weal and woe of ancient Egypt depended. Compare respecting spelt as one of the most important products of ancient Egypt, the corn from which they prepared their bread, *Herodotus*[1] with the remarks of *Bähr*. There are representations of the flax harvest in *Rosellini*.[2] The cultivation of the Durrah, from which the bread is made, upon which the common people for the most part live, is recent in Egypt.[3] Of the cultivation of rice there is scarcely a single certain trace found, and it cannot at least have been general.[4] Secondly, The author shows the most accurate knowledge of the time of the harvest in Egypt. Flax and barley are nearly ripe, when wheat and spelt are yet green. *Theophrastis*[5] and *Pliny*[6] say: In Egypt barley was harvested in the sixth month after sowing, wheat in the seventh month. *Sonnini*,[7] after remarking that with the cultivation of wheat, that of barley is very important, says: "It comes to maturity about a month earlier than wheat, and its harvest is especially abundant." Wheat and spelt come to maturity at about the same time.[8] Flax and barley were generally ripe in March, wheat and spelt in April. Such circumstances are not in keeping with the character of a mythic historian.

THE EIGHTH PLAGUE—THE LOCUSTS.

The narrative itself indicates, ch. x. 6, 14, that the animals, which constituted the eighth plague, the locusts, were at other times somewhat common in Egypt, and that only the abundance of them was unprecedented. Other accounts also confirm this fact.

---

[1] B. 2. c. 36, and also c. 77.
[2] De Sacy upon Abd. p. 120.
[3] 8. 3.
[7] Th. 2. p. 261.
[2] Vol. II. p. 333. seq.
[4] Sonnini, l. S. 251 ff.
[5] 18. 7.
[8] See Hartmann,

Hartmann[1] has collected the notices of ancient travellers, among whom *Norden*[2] has particularly described what he saw in the following words: "In common with Syria and other regions of Asia, Egypt suffers from the locusts, yet no account can be found of their producing such terrible desolation here as in Syria, Arabia," &c. But of especial interest is *Denon's*[3] account of a flight of locusts observed by him: "Two days after this calamity, (they had been suddenly overtaken by a heavy chamsin) we were informed that the plain was covered with birds, which flew in dense flocks from east to west. We in fact saw from a distance, that the fields seemed to move, or at least that a long current flowed through the plain. Supposing that they were strange birds which had flown hither, in such great numbers, we hastened our pace in order to observe them. But instead of birds, we found a cloud of locusts which made the land bald; for they stopped upon each stalk of grass in order to devour it, and then flew further for spoil. At a time of the year when the corn is tender, they would have been a real plague; as lean, as efficient, and as lively as the Arab Bedawin, they are also a production of the desert. After the wind had changed its course, so as to blow directly against them, it swept them back into the desert."

This account presents a striking agreement with ours, in three particulars: 1. In both passages, the locusts and chamsin appear in immediate connection with each other. 2. In both the flight is from east to west, which is even so much the more worthy remark, since some, as recently *v. Bohlen*,[4] have imputed it to the author, as a fault, that he represents the locusts as coming with the east wind. 3. In both, the locusts, by a change of the wind, are driven back whence they came.

THE NINTH PLAGUE—THE DARKNESS.

In the ninth plague—the darkness, it is scarcely possible to mistake the similarity to natural phenomena, since it has many other characteristic traits besides the one rendered most conspicuous here. The partial prominence given to the darkness in this plague is explained from the symbolic significance, which the occurrence

---

[1] S. 249. [2] S. 119.
[3] Vol. I. p. 287, London Edition.
 Compare page 8. seq. of this volume.

has in this particular. The darkness which overshadowed Egypt, and the light which shone upon the Israelites, were symbols of God's anger and favour. It cannot be doubted that the foundation in nature for this ninth plague is to be sought in the chamsin, whose effects, in a higher or lower degree, all-travellers who have visited Egypt have experienced.

Hartmann[1] has collected what is said by ancient authors. " The inhabitants of the cities and villages," it is there said, " shut themselves up in the lowest apartments of their houses and cellars;[2] but the inhabitants of the desert go into their tents, or into the holes which they have dug in the ground.[3] There they await, full of anxiety, the termination of this kind of tempest, which generally lasts three days. The roads during this time are entirely vacant, and deep stillness, as of the night, reigns everywhere."

Among modern writers we first refer to *Du Bois Amyé*,[4] who compares the Mosaic darkness to the chamsin. The phenomena of the latter he describes in the following manner: " When the chamsin blows, the sun is pale yellow, its light is obscured, and the darkness is sometimes so great, that one seems to be in the blackest night, as we experienced in the middle of the day at Cene, a city of Saïd." A second description we quote from *Sonnini*:[5] " The atmosphere," he says, " was heated, and at the same time obscured by clouds of dust: the thermometer of Reaumur stood at 27 degrees. Men and animals breathed only vapour, and that was heated and mingled with a fine and hot sand. Plants drooped, and all living nature languished. This wind also continued the twenty-seventh; it appeared to me to have even increased in force. The air was dark on account of a thick mist of fine dust, as red as flame." But of special importance for our object is the description of *Denon*:[6] On the eighteenth of May in the evening, I felt as if I should perish from the suffocating heat. All motion of the air seemed to have ceased. As I went to the Nile to bathe, for the relief of my painful sensations, I was astonished by a new sight. Such light and such colours I had never seen. The sun, without being veiled with clouds, had been shorn of its beams. It gave only a white and shadowless light, more

---

[1] S. 46 ff. [2] Volney. [3] Pococke.
[4] P. 110.   [5] Th. 3. p. 35 ff. [6] Vo̱ 7

feeble than the moon. The water reflected not its rays, and appeared disturbed.—Every thing assumed another appearance; the air was darker, a yellow horizon caused the trees to appear of a pale blue. Flocks of birds fluttered about before the clouds. The frightened animals ran about in the fields, and the inhabitants who followed them with their cries could not collect them. The wind, which had raised immense clouds of dust, and rolled them along before itself, had not yet reached us. We thought that if we went into the water, which at this moment was quiet, we should avoid this mass of dust which was driven towards us from the south-west; but we were scarcely in the river, when it began suddenly to swell as if it would overflow its banks. The waves broke over us, and the ground heaved under our feet. Our garments flew away when seized by the whirlwind, which had now reached us. We were compelled to go to land. Wet and beaten by the wind, we were soon surrounded by a ridge of sand. A reddish dusky appearance filled the region; with wounded eyes, and nose so filled that we could hardly breathe, we strayed from one another, lost our way, and found our dwellings with great difficulty, feeling along by the walls. Then, we sensibly felt how terrible the condition must be, when one is overtaken by such a wind in the desert. On the following morning the same cloud of dust was driven, in like circumstances, along the Lybian desert. It followed the mountain range, and when we believed ourselves free from it, the west wind turned it back. Lightnings shot feebly through these dark clouds; all the elements appeared to be in commotion; the rain mingled with the lightning gleams, with wind and dust; every thing seemed to be returning to chaos and old night."[1]

The severity of the chamsin is very different in different years.[2] *Dschemaleddin* describes, in the Chronicle quoted by *Rosenmueller* in his Commentary, cases which, seen merely in general, are considerably like those with which we are concerned. In reference to the one which took place in the eleventh century, it is said: "There occurred a great and violent storm, accompanied by darkness; edifices were destroyed, and houses demolished; moreover,

---

[1] See other descriptions in Mayer, Reise, S. 245, and in Michaud, Th. 7. S. 11.

[2] Hartmann, S. 51.

at the same time Egypt was covered with so thick a darkness that all believed that the resurrection had come." In the account of another wind of this kind in the twelfth century, he says: "There occurred such a darkness in Egypt, that the whole air was obscured with dimness, at the same time there arose so heavy a wind, that the men all expected the resurrection."

The time in which the three days' darkness falls, is just that in which the chamsin generally blows.[1]

THE TENTH PLAGUE—THE DEATH OF THE FIRST-BORN OF THE EGYPTIANS.

It may be proper to remark here, before we proceed with the tenth plague, that the phrase "all of the first-born" must not be pressed too far.[2] The whole tenor of the narrative is opposed to such a proceeding, and particularly the declaration, "There was no house where there was not one dead," in chap. xii. 30; since in every house there was not a first-born. It must not be inferred that none of the first-born remained alive in the land, or that none besides the first-born died.[3]

If we take into view the time in which the last plague, the destruction of the first-born, occurs, and farther also that it follows immediately the chamsin, we cannot deny that we find something analogous to it in a pestilence described by *Minutoli*.[4] It is not material whether it be allowed that the plague raged at so early a period, or that another similarly destructive disease existed in its place. The plague, he says, commonly makes its appearance at Cairo about the end of March, or at the beginning of April. The miasma is communicated merely by contact. Local causes, however, increase its malignancy, and even the prevailing winds have an important influence. With an uninterrupted chamsin the

---

[1] Hartmann, S. 47.   [2] See p. 109.
[3] The account of an especially destructive plague in Egypt, in the Description, t. 15, p. 180, may be compared: "Howls and shrieks were heard in every house; funeral processions met one at every step. Several dead bodies were oftentimes put together on the same bier, and I saw men who bore them, give over their burden to others, and lie down upon the ground with all the symptoms of the plague."
[4] S. 224.

plague increases frightfully, and speedily takes off those who are attacked by it.

Legh also gives a similar account: " A salutary influence (on the pestilence then raging) was also expected from the Nokla, or the rise of the Nile, which begun on the eighteenth of June. The unhealthiness of the season of the year preceding this month is ascribed to the chamsin, or the wind from the desert, which commonly begins to blow about Easter-Monday and continues fifty days, and to the stagnant condition of the Nile. This notion is so settled among the Arabs that they are accustomed when it ceases to congratulate each other on account of having survived this period.—The two or three months before the summer solstice are esteemed so unhealthy, that it is said, that the plague always rages during this time, even in Cairo. During the same period, the small-pox is also very dangerous."[1] Compare also the Description,[2] where, in accounting for this sickness, it is imputed mainly to the chamsin; and it is remarked, that great inundations which leave numerous morasses, always precede destructive epidemics.

That the Egyptians are swept off by an epidemic is indeed probable, and much more than probable, from chap. ix. 15. What the Lord there says he had long been able to do, that he now really does; since the reasons here given in verse 16, which, until now, have prevented him from proceeding to this last resource, have now ceased; since, in short, he has by a series of acts sufficiently unfolded his omnipotence and grace.

For the sparing of the Israelites, certain things in nature analogous may be referred to, but they by no means serve to obscure the divine favour in the preservation, since this divine favour insured nothing less than absolute safety. Here may be quoted, first, what *Minutoli* says in reference to the plague: " It is remarkable that fear increases the susceptibility to it, but fearlessness protects against it." Further, what *Prokesch*[3] says of the Egyptian Bedawy, is appropriate here: " His health is unalterably good. Some ascribe the disease of the eyes in Egypt, which rages among the Fellahs, and even in the cities, to the dew and dust of the desert. But the Bedawy sleeps in the open air, and

---

[1] Reise in Aeg. D. Weim. 1818, S. 142.   [2] T. 15. p. 179.
[3] Erinnerungen, Th. 2. p. 244.

ranges from desert to desert, and this pest has never spread among these tribes." With this agrees what *Michaud* says:[1] "The Bedawin are in general very temperate. They have no physicians and little sickness. The disease of the eyes, which is so prevalent an evil in Egypt, is almost unknown in the desert. The plague seldom extends its ravages among them."

Those who are disposed to take offence at the analogies in nature, which we have adduced for the plagues, are referred, first, to what we have said in the beginning of this chapter, concerning the miraculous character of these occurrences, notwithstanding the analogy of nature. They are also reminded, that it cannot be denied that similar analogies are generally allowed to exist in relation to the wonders of the desert, the manna and the quails. But we wish the advocates of the mythic interpretation of the Pentateuch to know, that precisely that part of it which appears to them the strongest bulwark for their view, is most decidedly opposed to it.[2]

---

[1] Th. 7. p. 29.

[2] It would require more space than the limits of a note allow, to examine the theory of the plagues, advocated by Dr Hengstenberg; it must however be remarked, that all the sacred writers who have referred to the Exodus, insist strongly on the direct interference of Jehovah to effect the deliverance of his chosen people, and speak of "the signs and wonders in the land of Ham," as marvels without a parallel in human experience. Dr Hengstenberg's effort to show that they were natural calamities in an exaggerated form, leaves still the greatest of all the wonders unexplained, the occurrence of ten such dreadful visitations in such rapid succession. T.

CHAPTER IV.

EXODUS, Chapters xiv. and xv.

THE MILITARY FORCE OF THE EGYPTIANS.

IN our section on the references of the Pentateuch to the geographical features of Egypt, we have spoken of some things which come within the range of our inquiry in connection with these chapters of Exodus. We have pointed out the agreement of the fact, that a considerable army stood ready, at the command of Pharaoh, to pursue the fugitive Israelites, with the declarations of *Herodotus*, which show that the principal stations of the military caste were in the vicinity of the scene of these transactions, in the Delta.[1] It remains for us to make *here* the following remarks.

1. "Wherever," says *Rosellini*,[2] "the armies are represented on the great monuments of Egypt, they are composed of troops of infantry, armed with the bow or lance, and of ranks of chariots drawn by two horses." Chariots appear also in *Homer*[3] as the principal strength of the Egyptian army. Upon the Egyptian monuments, says the same author,[4] neither a king nor any other person of consequence is represented in any other way, than on foot, upon a chariot or throne, or in a litter. The few figures upon horses almost all belong to foreigners. *Wilkinson*[5] agrees with *Rosellini* in the principal point, namely, that chariots composed the main military force of the Egyptians, and the cavalry took only a subordinate place. That the Egyptians had no horsemen at all he does not admit,—although he concedes that

---

[1] Page 48, 57 seq. Compare in reference to this last fact also Rosellini, II. 3. p. 200.

[2] II. 3. p. 232.

[3] Iliad, 9. 383, where it is said of Thebes: Αἳθ' ἑκατόμπυλοί εἰσι, διηκόσιοι δ' ἀν ἑκάστην Ἀνέρες ἐξοιχνεῦσι σὺν ἵπποισιν καὶ ὄχεσφιν.

[4] II. 3. p. 240.   [5] Vol. 1. p. 288, 335.

no representations of them are found on the monuments,—relying upon the authority of *Herodotus*, 2, 162, where Amasis appears on horseback, (the more important passage, chap. 108, he omits,) the declaration of *Diodorus*, according to which Sesostris had, besides 27,000 who fought upon chariots, also 24,000 horsemen, and the fact that in the hieroglyphics the "command of the cavalry" is represented as a very honourable post, generally occupied by the most distinguished among the sons of the king.[1] This last argument, however, *Rosellini*[2] attempts to set aside, by remarking that the designation is properly overseer of horses, and probably has reference to the care of the breed of horses. *Champollion*[3] says of the war chariots: "This was the cavalry of the age, cavalry properly speaking did not exist then in Egypt."

It is accordingly certain, that the cavalry, in the more ancient period of the Pharaohs, was but little relied on, and it is doubtful whether it generally existed. The question now is: What relation the declarations in our passage have to this result? Were the common view, according to which riding on horses is superadded with equal prominence to the chariot of war, in our passage, the right one, there would arise strong suspicion against the credibility of the narrative. But a more accurate examination shows, that the author does not mention Egyptian cavalry at all, that according to him the Egyptian army is composed only of chariots of war, and that he therefore agrees in a wonderful manner with the native Egyptian monuments. And this agreement is the more minute, since the second division of the army represented upon them, the infantry, could not, in the circumstances of our narrative, take part in the pursuit.

The first and principal passage concerning the constituent parts of the Egyptian army which pursued the Israelites, is that in chap. xiv. 6, 7: "And he made ready his chariot, and took his people with him; and took 600 chosen chariots, all the chariots of Egypt, and chariot-warriors upon all of them." Here Pharaoh's preparation for war is fully described. It consists, first, of chariots, and secondly, of chariot-warriors. Cavalry are no more mentioned than infantry. This passage, which is so plain, explains the second one, verse 9, where the arrival of this same army, in sight of

---

[1] Wilk. Vol. I. p. 292.   [2] II. 3. S. 259.
[3] Page 442 of the German Translation of his Letters. Brussels Ed.

the Israelites, is plainly and graphically described, in order to place distinctly before the reader the impression which the view made upon the Israelites: "And the Egyptians followed them and overtook them, where they were encamped by the sea, all the chariot-horses of Pharaoh and his riders and his host." If riders here be understood in the common sense, (chariot-warriors rather than riders upon horses might so much the sooner be mentioned, since the Egyptian war-chariot was very small and light,) where then are the chariot warriors? The author would not leave them out, since it is to his purpose to be minute, and since he evidently intended to accumulate circumstances as much as possible. Also in verse 17: "I will get me honour upon Pharaoh, and upon all his host, upon his chariots, and upon his riders," the riders again correspond with the chariot-warriors in verse 7. If there were then chariot-warriors *and* riders, how strange that they are never spoken of together.[1] In verse 23: "And the Egyptians pursued them and went in after them, all the horses of Pharaoh, his chariots and his riders," the three constituent parts of the Egyptian warlike preparation are fully designated. If riders were here understood in the common way, it would be surprising that horses and chariots were named, and that chariot-warriors, who are most important, were left out. Finally, the meaning of the passage, chap. xv. 1, "Horse and his rider hath he thrown into the sea," is clear from verse 4 of the same chapter, where only the overwhelming of the chariots and chariot-warriors is spoken of.

2. The number of chosen chariots of Egypt is limited in chap. xiv. 6 (7) to 600. If we compare with this other declarations with regard to the strength of the Egyptian hosts of war, we shall be the better prepared to appreciate these moderate statements, so inappropriate in a mythic representation. *Josephus* adds, from his own resources, to the 600 chariots which Pharaoh brought into the field, 50,000 horsemen and 200,000 footmen. The Jewish tragic poet, *Ezekiel*, says that the Egyptian hosts of war amounted to a million. According to *Diodorus*,[2] Sesostris had 600,000 footmen, and 24,000 horsemen, and 27,000 chariots of war. He gives an equally extravagant number in chap. xlv. 47.[3] It is cer-

---

[1] In the Illustrations of the Bible from the monuments of Egypt, I took a different view of this passage, but on further examination, I am convinced that I was wrong, and that Dr Hengstenberg is right.   T.

[2] 1. 54.   [3] Compare Rosellini, Vol. II. 3. p. 231.

tain that the 600 chariots are not the whole force with which Pharaoh pursued the Israelites. Besides, the 600 chosen chariots were also the chariots of Egypt. But the number of the last must also be fixed according to the analogy of the first.

3. The author in verse 7 makes a difference between the chosen chariots and the chariots of Egypt. The first evidently compose the guard of the king. We have already proved the existence of a royal guard in Egypt from *Herodotus* and the monuments.[1] From *Herodotus*:[2] " But they (the warriors) enjoyed these privileges in turn, never all at once—a thousand of the Calasaries and as many of the Hermotybies were the yearly guard of the king, and to these was given, in addition to their land, each day," &c., it is certain that at least in early times, these guards changed each year. It is however true, that this must not be understood as implying that the soldiers all succeeded to this employment, without selection, in successive divisions; but the rotation took place rather, only among chosen troops.

4. It may perhaps appear remarkable, that the Israelites, notwithstanding their very great numbers, at the appearance of the not very numerous Egyptian hosts of war, considered themselves as absolutely lost, and that the thought of withstanding them did not even occur to them. A remark in *Wilkinson*[3] assists in explaining this fact: " The civilized state of Egyptian society required the absence of all arms except when they were on service." If the Israelites were entirely unarmed when they departed, they could not think of making resistance.

MUSICAL INSTRUMENTS AMONG THE EGYPTIANS.

According to chap. xv. 20, 21, after they had passed through the sea, Miriam, the prophetess, the sister of Aaron, took the timbrel in her hand, and all the women followed after her with timbrels and dances, and Miriam answered them (Moses and the children of Israel:) " Sing to the Lord, for he hath triumphed gloriously ; the horse and the rider hath he thrown into the sea." Analogies for this scene, in more than one respect, are found upon the Egyptian monuments. First, we find upon them, as here,

---

[1] Pages 24, 67.   [2] 2. 168.
[3] Vol. I. p. 347. Compare a minute discussion of this circumstance, p. 402.

separate choirs of men and women. *Champollion*[1] discovered in the grottoes of Beni Hassan, "a picture which represented a concert of vocal and instrumental music; a singer is accompanied by a player upon the harp, and assisted by two choirs, one of which is composed of men and the other of women; the latter beat time with their hands."

Further; the timbrel or the tambourine was, according to the representations of the monuments, commonly the instrument of the women, as the flute of the men.[2] A description and drawing of the tambourine is given by *Wilkinson*.[3] We also find upon the Egyptian monuments, as here, the playing of the tambourine even unaccompanied by other instruments, in connection with the dance and singing. "Women," says *Wilkinson*,[4] in describing a scene in Thebes, "beat the tambourine and darabooka drum, without the addition of any other instrument, dancing or singing to the sound." Finally; the monuments and description show, that among the Egyptians generally, music had a decidedly religious destination.[5] Moreover, the tambourine was used among them in sacred music.[6] Religious dances were performed in Egypt in the worship of Osiris.[7]

[1] S. 53. der Briefe.
[2] Wilk. Vol. II. pp. 253, 314. Res. II. 3. p. 37 seq.
[3] Vol. II. p. 254.
[4] Vol. II. p. 240, where a representation of this scene is found.
[5] Rosellini, II. 3. p. 78.   [6] Wilkinson, II. p. 316.
[7] Ros. II. 3. p. 96. The players on the timbrels and cymbals always danced to the sound of their own music, and these dances formed part of the ceremonials used in religious worship, as well as in triumphal processions. Thus, David exhorting to the worship of Jehovah, says, "Praise him with the timbrel and dance." (Psalm cl. 4.) Though men did not often join in these religious dances, boys were indulged in this pastime. It was probably because dancing in public was regarded as unmanly, that David's doing so exposed him to the contempt of his wife; we are told, "David danced before the Lord with all his might; and David was girded with a linen ephod. So David and all the house of Israel brought up the ark of the Lord with shouting, and with the sound of the trumpet. And as the ark of the Lord came into the city of David, Michal Saul's daughter looked through a window, and saw king David leaping and dancing before the Lord; and she despised him in her heart." (2 Sam. vi. 14—16.) The Jews appear to have brought this custom of religious dances from Egypt, for we find that dancing was a part of the idolatrous worship offered to the golden calf. (Exod. xxxii. 19.) But festive dances were not confined to religious occasions; they were celebrated at stated

We will here add those things which the examination of Egyptian antiquity furnishes in explanation of the remaining passages of the Pentateuch, where music is mentioned.

According to Num. x. 2 seq. two silver trumpets, חֲצוֹצְרֹת, *chatzotzeroth*, were ordered to be made for calling together the congregation, to give the signal for breaking up the camp, for use in war, (see Num. xxxi. 6, where in the war against Midian the trumpets are taken,) and for festal occasions. By the blast of another kind of trumpets, called שׁוֹפָר, *shophar*, according to Lev. xxv. 8 seq., the year of jubilee was announced. From Joshua, chap. vi. verse 4, where the same instrument is interchangeably called trumpet and horn, we see that this last instrument had the form of a horn, and accordingly the *chatsotserah* must be the *straight* trumpet.

Among the Egyptians, remarks *Wilkinson*,[1] trumpets were already in use in the earliest times of the Pharaohs. The sculptures at Thebes show this. Trumpeters are often represented there in the battle scenes, sometimes standing still and summoning the troops to form, and at other times leading them to a rapid charge. *Rosellini* says: "The Egyptians were acquainted with the real straight trumpet, and made use of it for warlike purposes, as far as the monuments show, as the Tyrrhenians make use of it only in war." See the description of this trumpet in *Wilkinson*,[2] who also remarks that it was especially used in war. The *crooked* trumpet is not found on the Egyptian monuments, but *Eustathius* makes mention of an instrument in the fashion of a crooked trumpet, whose invention he ascribes to Osiris, and whose Egyptian name he gives, remarking that it was used for assembling the people to sacrifice.[3] It is remarkable that,

times by the villagers, especially at the season of the vintage, and it was at such a time that the Benjamites seized the virgins of Shiloh. (Judges, xxi. 21.) There were also dances and hymns to commemorate a victory, or to honour a conqueror; for when David fled from Saul, and sought shelter among the Philistines, "The servants of Achish said unto him, Is not this David the king of the land? did they not sing one to another of him in dances, saying, Saul hath slain his thousands, and David his ten thousands?" (1 Sam. xxi. 11.) T.

[1] Vol. I. p. 297.   [2] II. 260, 262.

[3] Upon the Iliad, Σ. 219, ed. Lips. t. iv. p. 63: δευτέρα ἡ στρογγύλη (σάλπιγξ) παρ' Αἰγυπτίοις, ἥν "Οσιρις εὗρε; καλουμένη, φασί, χνούη, χρῶνται δ' αὐτῇ πρὸς θυσίαν, καλοῦντες τοὺς ὄχλους δι' αὐτῆς.

as among the Egyptians, so also among the Israelites in the Mosaic times, only the straight trumpet was in general use, and especially among both, this only was made use of in war."

In Gen. iv. 2, Jubal is represented as the father of all who play the lute and the pipe; accordingly the invention of these instruments is referred to a primitive age. It serves indeed as a commendation of this passage, that it represents music as beginning with its natural beginning, the invention of stringed instruments.[1] But the great antiquity of stringed instruments in general, and especially of those named, receives special confirmation from the monuments. Among the Egyptians, we find, even in the most ancient times, very curiously constructed stringed instruments, especially a three-stringed guitar, which implies a long succession of imperfect attempts. Such instruments indeed are represented in the pyramids.[2] "The oldest perhaps," says the same author,[3] "found in the sculptures, are in a tomb near the pyramids of Gizeh, between three and four thousand years old." According to *Rosellini*,[4] there is represented in the tomb of Imai, at Gizeh, an eight-stringed harp, which must belong to the times preceding the last fifteen dynasties. In another very ancient tomb at Gizeh, there are represented players on a similar harp. Indeed, upon the oldest monuments instruments are found with the most diverse number of strings, and any advancement in the art of constructing them cannot be traced.[5]

[1] Burney in Wilk. II. p. 226.
[2] Wilk. p. 271.
[3] Wilk. II. p. 230.
[4] II. 3. p. 13.
[5] Pp. 12, 13.

CHAPTER V.

MATERIALS AND ARTS EMPLOYED IN THE CONSTRUCTION OF THE TABERNACLE AND PRIEST'S GARMENTS.

CULTIVATION OF THE ARTS AMONG THE EGYPTIANS AND ISRAELITES.

It has been adduced as an argument against the historical character of the Pentateuch, that the construction of the tabernacle and the priests' garments, implies a cultivation of the arts and an abundance of costly materials, such as we could not expect to find among the Israelites when they left Egypt. These materials consisted not merely of gold, silver, and brass, but also of costly stuffs, furs and spices, things which a nomade people are not accustomed to carry with them in their wanderings. It is accordingly argued, that the whole description of the tabernacle belongs not to history but to fiction.[1] The assertion was made with so much confidence that it has by degrees become established and traditional.

The foundation for its confutation we have indeed previously laid,[2] by showing that the prevalent view concerning the condition of the Israelites in Egypt, according to which they merely continued their nomade life, is a false one, since they there availed themselves of the advantages of Egyptian culture and civilization, and in some respects attained to considerable prosperity. To complete the structure, there is now nothing further requisite than to show, that the materials which were used in making the tabernacle and priestly robes were at that time already in use in Egypt, but most especially that the arts and contrivances which come into consideration were there already in existence and known. For the material and intellectual resources of the Egyptians, we justly consider as common to the Israelites with them.

[1] See Vater, Abhand. S. 648, De Wette, Beitr. I. S. 259. II. S. 260. Von Bohlen, S. CXII.
[2] Beiträge Th. 2. S. 430 ff.

But to furnish this information is not our only design in this chapter. We also aim at a more positive object beyond this. While we show that the Israelitish arts are connected with the Egyptian by many characteristic peculiarities, we prove that the situation of things is just such as it must be, if we suppose that Moses is the author of the Pentateuch, or at least, that it is historically accurate, while later fiction or fictitious narrative could not have originated or sustained this Egyptian relationship.

We begin with a general declaration of one of the most distinguished investigators of Egyptian antiquity. "It is a wonderful fact, that the first information which we have with regard to the history and manners of the Egyptians, shows us a nation which is far advanced in civilized life. The same customs and inventions which prevailed in the Augustine era of this people, at the commencement of the eighteenth dynasty, are also found even in the far distant age of Osirtasen, the contemporary of Joseph."

THE ART OF CUTTING AND SETTING PRECIOUS STONES.

The materials which were used in the construction of the tabernacle and priests' garments, were a part of them hard and a part soft. Among the former, precious stones take the first place. *Bezaleel* is spoken of in Exod. xxxiii. 36, as distinguished among other things for his skill "in the preparation of stones for setting." Precious stones, on which the names of the Israelites were engraven in the character engraven on the signet ring, were placed, according to Ex. xxviii. 9—11, 17, seq., in golden encasements upon the ephod and breastplate of the high priest.

The art of cutting precious stones, generally very early discovered, was practised in Egypt even in very ancient times.[1] "There are several necklaces of gold and cornelian in the new gallery of the Egyptian antiquities opened at the British Museum, whose exquisite workmanship could scarcely be surpassed by modern artists, though, as we see from the engraving, the apparatus of the jeweller was as simple as could well be imagined. This is still the case in Hindoostan, where the native jeweller, travelling from house to house with his little furnace and blow-pipe, produces or-

---

[1] See quotations from Winkelmann, Müller, and others, in Bähr Symbol. Th. II. S. 103.

naments of considerable beauty."[1] How very much genuine precious stones were valued, is indeed evident from the circumstance, that imitations of them were made in considerable numbers. The Theban artists were particularly distinguished in this employment of counterfeiting. As then, we find it common for the Egyptians to imitate the ornaments of the rich in cheaper materials for the use of the lower classes, it is very evident that the spirit of luxury, which belongs to an advanced state of civilization, was already at an early period widely diffused in Egypt.[2] That the art of the engraver was native to Egypt, is manifest from the data which *Wilkinson* has furnished with regard to the Egyptian signets. Of many of them he has also engravings.[3] There, for example, is described the signet, yet preserved, of one of the earliest of the Pharaohs. Upon one side of the plate the name of the king is engraved; upon the opposite, a lion with the motto, "The lord of strength," which is applied to the king; on one side is a scorpion, and on the opposite a crocodile.[4] Moreover, various other inscriptions are found engraved on Egyptian rings."[5]

THE ART OF PURIFYING AND WORKING METALS.

Among the hard materials, the metals hold the second place. Of Bezaleel it is said in Exod. xxxv. 32, "he had power to devise curious works, to work in gold, and silver, and brass." With this compare what *Rosellini*[6] says,: "From all such articles, as they are represented in the Egyptian tombs, it is manifest how anciently the art of casting and working metals was practised in Egypt."—And: "The greater part of Egyptian metallic articles are of bronze, not a few of gold, a smaller number of silver, very few of lead, and those made of iron are seldom found."[7]

The gold which was ordered to be used about the sanctuary, is commonly designated as *pure* gold.[8] A painting in the tomb at Thebes, which bears the date of Thothmes IV., appears to repre-

---

[1] Taylor, p. 88.   [2] Taylor, p. 88.   [3] Vol. III. pp. 373—4.
[4] The assertion of Pliny, 33 6: "Non signat Oriens aut Aegyptus etiam nunc, literis contenta solis," is by these discoveries shown to be false.
[5] Compare Wilk. III. p. 376.   [6] II. 2. p. 297.
[7] Ros. II. 2. p. 298.
[8] See Ex. xxv. 11, 17, 24, 29, and other passages.

sent the fusion and purifying of gold.[1] Many ornaments are found in the Egyptian collections, which are made of the purest gold. The monuments furnish clear evidence that gold was purified, and thus of course distinguished from that which was unwrought, and not purified. Incorrectly, therefore, have some, referring to some one old ornament, made of impure gold, denied to the Egyptians the art of preparing pure gold.[2] According to Exod. xxv. 11, the ark of testimony, and according to xxvi. 29, all the boards of the tabernacle, were to be overlaid with gold. "We find," says *Wilkinson*,[3] "that in Egypt substances of various kinds were overlaid with gold leaf, at the earliest periods of which the monuments remain even in the time of the first Osirtasen." Even the mummies were gilded.[4]

According to Ex. xxxix. 3, the high priest's ephod was interwoven with threads of gold. We find even gold wire attached to rings bearing the date of Osirtasen the first; and silver wire existed in the days of the third Thothmes.[5] Some of the coloured Egyptian dresses represented in the paintings are probably woven with gold threads.[6]

In the two upper golden rings of the breastplate, wreathed golden chains were inserted, for fastening the breastplate to the ephod.[7] Golden chains were very common among the Egyptians, and are often, for example, represented as necklaces.[8]

The golden candlestick was ornamented with flowers of gold, Ex. xxv. 31, seq. Representations of flowers were also probably made on the variegated cloths of the tabernacle.[9] The Egyptians had an extraordinary love for flowers, both natural and artificial. The lotus and other favourite flowers are found everywhere worn as ornaments. According to *Pliny*[10] they made artificial flowers, which received the name of "Ægyptiæ."[11]

In Exodus xxxv. 22, among the free-will offerings which both the men and women of Israel brought for the sanctuary, "nose

---

[1] Rosellini II. 2. p. 278.   [2] Ibid. p. 280.   [3] Vol. III. 224.
[4] See Pettigrew, History of Egyptian Mummies, London, 1834, p. 63.
[5] Wilk. III. p. 129.   [6] Wilk. III. p. 131.
[7] Ex. xxviii. 22. seq. Bähr Symbol. Vol. II. S. 105.
[8] Wilkinson, Vol. III. p. 376, with the engraving, 400, M.
[9] Bähr Th. I. S. 314.   [10] 21. 2.
[11] Wilk. Vol. II. p. 183.

rings and ear rings, and signet rings and pendants," all jewels of gold, first mentioned. Astonishment at this abundance of ornaments is at an end, when we read what *Rosellini*[1] says upon this point: "Costly and elegant ornaments abounded, in proportion as clothing in general was simple and scarce among the Egyptians. Girdles, necklaces, armlets, rings, ear rings, and amulets of various kinds suspended from the neck, are found represented in the paintings, and in fact still exist on the mummies. Figures of noble youth are found entirely devoid of clothing, but richly ornamented with necklaces," &c.[2]

[1] Vol. II. 2. pp. 419—20.
[2] Gilding was certainly understood by the Egyptians, for we find several examples of it on the mummies and the mummy cases. In the new Egyptian gallery just opened at the British Museum, there are masks on a mummy and a mummy case exquisitely gilt and burnished, which are among the richest specimens of the gilding art in any age. It would be too long a digression to examine whether the " overlaying the boards of the tabernacle with gold," (Exod. xxxvi. 34,) refers to gilding or a covering of thin plates; but, in support of the former view, we may notice that the weight of the plates would have rendered the tabernacle very difficult of transport, and a positive incumbrance to the Israelites in their journeying through the desert; the amount of gold, too, collected by Moses, would not have supplied sufficient material for plates, however thin, to cover the entire edifice; and, finally, the word here rendered "overlaying" is the same used to describe the decorating of the carved work in Solomon's temple, which must have been gilding, as plates, however thin, would have concealed the tracery and foliage described to have been wrought with so much artistic skill. The quantity of gold, indeed, which would have been required to cover all the parts of the temple which Solomon is said to have " overlaid," would be utterly incredible if we supposed that he covered them with plates, however thin; this is sufficiently clear from the description: "So Solomon overlaid the house within with pure gold; and he made a partition by the chains of gold before the oracle; and he overlaid it with gold. And the whole house he overlaid with gold, until he had finished all the house: also the whole altar that was by the oracle he overlaid with gold. And within the oracle he made two cherubims of olive tree, each ten cubits high. And five cubits was the one wing of the cherub, and five cubits the other wing of the cherub: from the uttermost part of the one wing unto the uttermost part of the other were ten cubits. And the other cherub was ten cubits: both the cherubims were of one measure and one size. The height of the one cherub was ten cubits, and so was it of the other cherub. And he set the cherubims within the inner house; and they stretched forth the wings of the cherubims, so that the wing of the one touched the one wall, and the wing of the other cherub touched the other wall; and their wings touched one another in the

The brazen laver, according to chap. xxxviii. 8, was made of the brazen mirrors which the holy women offered.[1] "One of the principal objects of the toilet," says *Wilkinson*,[2] "was the mirror. It was of mixed metal, chiefly copper, most carefully wrought and highly polished; and so admirably did the skill of the Egyptians succeed in the composition of metals, that this substitute for our modern looking-glass was susceptible of a lustre, which has even been partially revived at the present day, in some of those discovered at Thebes, though buried in the earth for many centuries." The mirror was nearly round, inserted into a handle of wood, stone, or metal, of various forms.[3] See also the same author,[4] upon looking-glasses discovered at Thebes, and upon the whole subject, *Rosellini*,[5] according to whom the Egyptian name of mirror, like the Hebrew, signifies the view of the face.

SKILL IN CARVING WOOD.

The third hard material is *wood*. The circumstance that the same kind of wood which was employed about the sanctuary, the acacia, (tamarisk, sant,)[6] was also commonly used in Egypt, is of but little importance, since this is the only wood which the desert furnishes. The Egyptians were greatly skilled in joiner and cabinet work.[7] *Rosellini* says on p. 38: According to the monuments, the *saw* was known and in use 2000 years before our era.

USE OF LEATHER.

Leather holds the first place among the soft materials. The covering of the tabernacle, which lay directly over that of goat's hair, according to Exodus xxvi. 14, was to consist of rams' skins

midst of the house. And he overlaid the cherubims with gold." (1 Kings, vi. 21—28.) Isaiah distinctly mentions that the goldsmith "spreadeth over" the molten image with gold, (Is. xl. 19.); and he also intimates that wood was also gilt over, for he speaks of the "carpenter encouraging the goldsmith." (Isaiah xli. 7.) T.

[1] Th. 3. der Beiträge, S. 133.   [2] Vol. III. p. 384.
[3] Engravings of them are found in Wilk. III. 365—6.
[4] Vol. III. p. 253.   [5] Vol. II. 2. 528 seq.
[6] Compare Herod. B. 2. c. 122. Jablonsky, Vocc. Aeg. ap. Script. Vett., s. v. Sant and Sittim, Rosellini, II. 2. S. 33. Wilk. Vol. III. p. 168.
[7] Compare Ros. II. 2. p. 32, and Taylor, p. 106 seq.

coloured red. Above that, was a covering of another kind of handsome leather, which cannot be accurately defined. The preparation of leather, says *Wilkinson*,[1] was an important branch of Egyptian industry. The fineness of the leather of the straps of a mummy discovered at Thebes, and the beauty of the figures which are stamped upon it, show conclusively the skill of the artist who prepared it. Some of these pieces of leather bear the name of the kings of the oldest times. *Rosellini*[2] also gives an account of the art of making leather. In the tombs at Thebes, a shop filled with leather-workers is found represented. They made bottles, quivers and pouches of different colours, and ornaments, shoes, and sandals, shields, &c. of leather. " The wood of the Egyptian harps was sometimes covered with coloured leather. In the museum of the Louvre, at Paris, an Egyptian harp is preserved, whose wood is covered with a kind of green morocco, cut in the form of a lotus blossom."[3]

SPINNING, WEAVING, AND EMBROIDERY.

We now turn our attention to their cloths of the tabernacle and priests' garments. Many passages mention the twisted byssus.[4] In the tombs of Beni Hassan, the process of preparing the thread and twining it, in preparation for weaving, is exhibited.[5] They were accustomed to beat the yarn with clubs so as to make it softer and more suitable for twining; they also boiled the thread in water to increase its softness, and at the same time give it greater consistence, and thus make it better for twisting and weaving. The byssus in particular was treated in this way. The inscription on a part of an Egyptian wall-picture is interpreted by *Rosellini*:[6] The preparation of the yarn of byssus. Then follows the representation of the twisting itself, which is performed partly by men and partly by women, and indeed in different ways, which *Rosellini* describes.[7]

The skill of the Egyptians in weaving, and the great renown of their cloths in all antiquity, is recognised and confirmed by

---

[1] Vol. III. p. 155.　　[2] Ros. II. 2. p. 355.　　[3] Ros. II. 3. p. 16.
[4] Ex. xxvi. 1, 31, and other passages.　　[5] Ros. II. 2. pp. 13, 14.
[6] P. 16.　　[7] Pp. 16 and 17.

the fact, that the ancient writers attribute to the Egyptians the invention of this art.[1]

Herodotus[2] mentions as one of the points in which the Egyptians differ from other nations, that among them the women perform the out-of-door's work, and the men weave.[3] Other ancient writers bear testimony to the same thing. " In ancient times the weavers of Panopolis, in Upper Egypt, were especially distinguished ; in later times, those in Arsinoë, Pelusium, and Alexandria."[4] Also very many men are seen on the monuments employed in weaving,[5] and when we not unfrequently also see women weaving,[6] this can, in view of the testimony of ancient writers, yet be considered only as the exception which destroys not the rule.—Now, in most perfect agreement with these notices of ancient writers, the preparation of the cloth for the sanctuary and the sacerdotal robes is represented throughout as under the care of men.[7]

The women, on the contrary, performed the spinning,[8] and this work generally belonged to them in Egypt.[9] *Wilkinson* gives engravings of women who are employed with the spindle. Yet this was not exclusively their work.[10]

It is evident from Ex. xxxv. 25, according to which the Israelitish women brought of the purple which they had spun, that the

---

[1] Aegyptii textilia (invenerunt.) Plin. B. 7. c. 56. Moses is the first who mentions the preparation of gold in threads to be interwoven with the more precious cloths. "And they did beat the gold into thin plates and cut it into wires, to work it in the blue, and in the purple, and in the scarlet, and in the fine linen with cunning work." (Exod. xxxix. 3.) Cloth of golden tissue is not uncommon on the monuments, and specimens of it have been found rolled about the mummies, but it is not easy to determine whether the gold thread was originally interwoven or subsequently inserted by the embroiderer. T.

[2] Chap. 2. 35. Compare c. 105 : Οἱ δὲ ἄνδρες κατ' οἴκους ἰόντες ὑφαίνουσι.

[3] Heeren, S. 388.

[4] Strabo, 17, 813. Drumann Inschrift von Rosette, S. 170.

[5] See, e. g. Minutoli, t. 25.

[6] Ros. II. 2. p. 30, and Wilk. Vol. III. p. 134, and the engravings, Vol. II. p. 60.

[7] See the phrase, "work of the weaver," in Ex. xxviii. 32 ; xxxix. 22, 27 : "work of the artificer," in xxviii. 6, 15 ; xxvi. 31, but especially ch. xxxv. 36.

[8] Ex. xxxv. 25.   [9] Herod. 2. 35, and Wilk. 2. 60.

[10] Wilk. Vol. III. p. 133. The same author also gives an engraving of Egyptian spindles, p. 136.

coloured fabrics which were employed about the tabernacle, were dyed before weaving. The same thing was also done among the Egyptians. In *Minutoli*[1] it is said: "From many experiments upon the ancient Egyptian cloth, it appears that the byssus was coloured in the wool before weaving, which also is shown by Ex. xxv. 4, xxvi. 1. The process which *Pliny*[2] describes for impressing different colours all at once upon the web after it is finished by the use of various preparations, appears therefore to be a later advancement in Egyptian art." *Wilkinson*[3] also shows that cloth was coloured in the thread among the ancient Egyptians.

The coloured figures in the cloth of the Israelites were partly the product of the weaver in colours, חשֵׁב, whose art appears the superior, and partly that of the embroiderer in colours, רֹקֵם.[4] Both methods are reproduced on the monuments, so that the objection which has been brought forward against rendering the word *rokem* by embroiderers, that the art of embroidering was generally unknown in earlier ages, and particularly among the Hebrews, is to be regarded as entirely groundless. "Many of the Egyptian stuffs," says *Wilkinson*,[5] "presented various patterns worked in colours by the loom, independent of those produced by the dyeing or printing process, and so richly composed, that they vied with cloths embroidered with the needle." The Egyptian sails, says the same author,[6] were some of them embroidered with fanciful devices, representing the phoenix, flowers, and other emblems. This, however, was confined to the pleasure boats of the nobles and king. That this was done even in the early ages, is evident from the paintings at Thebes, which show sails ornamented with various colours of the time of Remeses III. The devices are various, the most common one is the phoenix.[7]

In Ex. xxviii. 32, it is said of the outer garment of the high priest: "And its opening for the head shall be in the middle of it, a border shall there be to the opening round about, of woven work, like the opening of a habergeon shall it be, so that it be not

---

[1] S. 402.   [2] Hist. nat. pp. 35, 42.   [3] Vol. III. p. 125.
[4] Compare the passage in the LXX, and the proof that רֹקֵם signifies embroiderers, in opposition to Hartmann, Gesen. and others, in Bähr Symb. I. S. 267.
[5] Vol. III. p. 128.   [6] Ibid. 210.
[7] See engravings in Wilk. III. 210.

rent." No other than a linen habergeon can be meant; for no other would need a binding. The linen armour of the Egyptians was renowned in all antiquity. *Herodotus*[1] mentions a linen habergeon (or corselet,) ornamented with many animals, and worked with cotton thread and with gold, which Amasis sent to the Lacedemonians as a present, and also another which the same king dedicated to Minerva at Lindus. He designates this last as a "linen corselet worthy of admiration."[2] It is acknowledged, that the linen corselet was not peculiar to Egypt alone.[3] But yet an importance such as is here implied, the linen corselet had nowhere except in Egypt.

PREPARATION AND USE OF UNGUENTS.

We also remark, that what is said in Ex. xxx. 22 seq., concerning the holy ointment and its preparation, has received abundant explanation and confirmation from investigations in Egypt. Unguents were very much used among the Egyptians. This is evident in part from representations in the paintings, and in part from the vases for containing them which yet exist. Some of them still retain their odour. As far as can be determined from these last, unguents appear sometimes to have been made of nut oil, but it is probable that animal as well as vegetable oil was used for this purpose, while the other ingredients depended on the taste of the maker or purchaser.[4]

It is worthy of notice, that in the description of the holy ointment, the hin is first used as a measure, which afterwards often appears in the Pentateuch. It has no discoverable Hebrew etymology, and furthermore it appears probable that the name is not of Hebrew origin, since it is found, out of the Pentateuch, only in Ezekiel, in the description of the temple, where, like so many other words, it is not taken from the current language of the day but from the Pentateuch. According to *Leeman*,[5] the word is

---

[1] 3. 47.

[2] 2. 182. See also Wilk. III. 127 seq.

[3] Ajax is designated in the Iliad, 2. 529, as, $\lambda\iota\nu o\vartheta\omega\rho\eta\xi$. Compare the passages collected and referred to in Perizonius upon Sueton. Galba, c. 19.

[4] Wilk. II. p. 214, and III. 378.

[5] Lettre a M. Salvolini sur les Monumens Egyptiens, Leyden, 1838.

borrowed from the Egyptian language. The *hin*, he asserts, was originally the general name for a vessel which then was transferred by the Hebrews and Egyptians, to a certain measure of variable compass.

Hitherto we have occupied ourselves only with the materials of the tabernacle and priest's garments, and the arts which are known to have been employed upon them. Now, we will also show, that even in the religious institutions of the Books of Moses Egyptian references cannot be denied, notwithstanding the opposition of those who, in modern times, combating the practice, so hostile to sound criticism, of finding such references wherever there is the least semblance of a reason for it, have wholly denied their existence.

CHAPTER VI.

EGYPTIAN REFERENCES IN THE RELIGIOUS INSTITUTIONS OF THE BOOKS OF MOSES.

LAW AMONG THE EGYPTIANS AND ISRAELITES.

THE complicated character of the legislation of the Pentateuch directs us, in a general way, to Egypt.[1] So complex a code of laws could not have been given to a people who had not indeed, from former circumstances, been accustomed to a law regulating the whole life. If we fancy the Israelites as still occupying the position of the patriarchs, they are a complete enigma to us. Egypt was pre-eminently a land of law, and especially of written law. "There can be no doubt," says *Heeren*,[2] " after all that we know of Egyptian antiquity, that legislation in its main branches was there carried, as far at least as in any other land of the east."[3] But especially was the religious polity of the Egyptians carried out into the most minute details. *Herodotus*[4] says of the Egyptian priests: "The priests shave the whole body every third day ;—the priests also wear a linen garment and shoes of papyrus, and they are not permitted to put on any other clothing, and no other shoes. They bathe themselves in cold water twice a day, and twice every night. And yet many thousand other usages, I might say, they must observe."[5]

If we take into view the people from among whom the Israelites were removed, the complicated character of the Mosaic polity, very far from being an argument against its genuineness, must rather appear to us a necessary condition of it. For a people which had been in such a school, a simple polity was by no means suitable.

---

[1] In den Beiträgen, Th. 3. S. 623–4.   [2] S. 167.
[3] Concerning the Books of Legislation among the Egyptians, see Diod. I. 94, and Zoega, De Obeliscis, p. 520.
[4] B. 2, c. 37.
[5] "Άλλας τε θρησκείας ἐπιτελέουσι μυρίας, ὡς εἰπεῖν λόγῳ.

In the following institutions of the Books of Moses, special Egyptian references can be shown, or at least made probable.[1]

We begin with those things which are closely connected with the preceding chapter, without properly belonging to it.

THE STUFF AND COLOUR OF THE PRIESTS' GARMENTS.

The similarity which is found to exist between the Israelitish and Egyptian priests' garments, in respect to colour and material, is of no small importance. It is clear from many passages, that the Israelitish priests were clothed in white linen and byssus:[2] and that the Egyptians were also so clothed, is evident from *Herodotus*:[3] "But the priests wear merely linen clothing, and are not allowed to put on any other." In this passage linen includes also byssus.[4]

Two arguments have been made use of to show that this agreement between Egyptian and Israelitish antiquity is merely accidental. First, it is asserted, that these priests' garments did not probably belong to the Israelites and Egyptians *alone*, but they are rather the same which were diffused throughout the old world; a sure proof, that one people cannot be supposed to have adopted them from another, that they were rather, from the nature of the case, everywhere used. *Bähr*[5] says: "Everywhere, from India to Gaul, the priests' wear garments of vegetable material, consequently of linen or cotton, and of white, if possible, of brilliant white colour. It is the less necessary to refer to individual documents concerning these well known facts, as they have been already collected by several authors."

---

[1] We satisfy ourselves with the statement of the really tenable Egyptian references, for those which have been claimed as untenable by those who have preceded us, we refer to the "Symbolik des Mosaischen Cultus," by Bähr, where their inadmissibility has been shown oftentimes in a striking manner.

[2] As Ex. xxviii. 39—42. xxxix. 27, 28. Lev. vi. 10. Compare Braun de Vestitu Sacerdotis magni, I. p. 93: Vestes totius coetus lineae erant praeter balteum, qui ex lana et lino mixtus.   [3] 2. 37.

[4] Compare Heeren Ideen, I. 1. S. 107. II. 2. S. 133. Drumann, Ueber die Inschrift von Rosette, S. 169. Pliny, Hist. nat. 19. 1, vestis ex gossypio sacerdotibus Aeg. gratissimae.

[5] In der Symbolik, Th. II. p. 87.

But among those quoted, *Spencer* and *Braun,* in the passage cited,[1] speak only of the *white colour.* The former directly shows that linen clothing is, with the exception of the Israelites, peculiar only to the Egyptian priests. *Saubert*[2] only undertakes to prove that the priests everywhere have been accustomed to clothe themselves with white *linen* garments. But the passages which the inaccurate collector quotes, all have reference either to Egyptian or Israelitish antiquity.

The colour taken by itself, is indeed not without some importance. It is allowed that white priestly apparel is common among other nations of antiquity. But in this exclusiveness it is peculiar only to the Egyptians and Israelites. *Rosenmueller*[3] remarks: "Among the Greeks and Romans the colour of the pontifical robes was different according to the different gods to whom they sacrificed, and white garments were put on only when they offered to Ceres."[4] (?)

But if we look at the material of the priests' robes in connection with the colour, an accidental agreement of Israelitish with Egyptian antiquity can no longer be thought of. That their priests were clothed in linen, was considered in all antiquity as a remarkable and exclusive peculiarity of the Egyptians. The documents have already been so fully quoted by *Spencer,*[5] that we only need to refer to him. A priesthood clothed only in linen, cannot be shown to have existed elsewhere in all heathen antiquity; and if the new Pythagoreans, appealing to the alleged example of Pythagoras himself, gave the preference to linen clothing, instead of woollen,[6] this can certainly be accounted for only by supposing an imitation of Egyptian customs.

[1] 1. 179. [2] De Sacrificiis, 1. c. 9. p. 188.
[3] In dem. A. & N. Morgenl. Th. 2. S. 190.
[4] Ovid's Festb. 6. 619.
[5] P. 683 seq. He says: Addere liceat auctores illos antiquos, qui de veste linea sic loqui solent, quasi sacrificulis Aegypti propria esset et peculiaris. Nam *linigeri* tanquam proprius et peculiaris character sacerdotum Aegyptiacorum apud antiquos, poetas imprimis, frequenter usurpatur. Ideo enim Juvenali *grex liniger,* Ovidio linigera turba, Martiali *linigeri calvi,* qui et Senecae *linteati* senes appellantur. Herodotus aliique sacrum lineae vestis usum inter nativos et antiquos Aegypti mores referunt. Compare the copious collections upon linen as the peculiar dress of the Egyptian priests, in Perizonius upon Suetonis, Otho, c. 12.
[6] According to Philistratus, p. 1. ed. Olearii, Pythagorus would wear no clothing which was prepared from animal stuffs. Sic infra, remarks Olearius

Bähr[1] adduces a second argument against the dependence of the priestly robes of the Israelites upon those of the Egyptian. "In Egypt," he says, "the byssus was chosen in preference, and mainly on account of its origin, 'out of the indestructible earth,' while they despised animal clothing, since it is obtained from a creature subject to death, or since it implies the death of the animals which they suppose unallowed. The byssus garments of the Egyptian priests are therefore most intimately connected with the fundamental principles of the Egyptian natural religion, of which there is not the least trace to be found in the Mosaic law. Supposing therefore that the Egyptian priests only, besides those instituted by Moses, had worn the byssus garment, in consequence of the entirely different significance it had among them, it could yet furnish no proof of a borrowing or copying."

But allow that it is shown that the import of the garment of byssus was entirely different among the Egyptians and the Israelites, yet the latter might very properly have borrowed the custom. What good objection is there to the supposition that they applied to a form borrowed from the Egyptians a new significance?

But the assertion that the reasons for the preference of this kind of garment, both among the Israelites and Egyptians, are entirely different, is in the highest degree uncertain. That among the Israelites cleanliness is the ground of the use of garments of linen only, and the prohibition of woollen, is evident from Ex. xliv. 17, 18. The same thing is shown by *Bähr* himself. To the same cause *Herodotus*, the oldest witness, traces back the use of linen garments among the Egyptian priests. Both that which goes before the clause already quoted: "The priests wear only linen garments," and also that which follows, has reference to the

upon this passage, Pythagoricae disciplinae initiatus Apollonius λίνου ἐσθῆτα ἀμπίσχεται, παραιτησάμενος τὴν ἀπὸ ζώων. Et l. 1. 32, a Pythagora se habere ait γηίνῳ ἐρίῳ τούτῳ ἱστᾶλθαι, quod lana ex terra nata vestintur. In B. 6. c. 11 of the Pythagorean philosophy, Apollonius says: Sectatorem suam nec laena esse fovendum, nec lana quae animatis depocti solet. Olearius refers also to other passages. The passages which Braun refers to in one of various places before cited (l. p. 103,) in proof of the incorrect position: "Ejusdem quoque materiae plerumque fuerunt ethnicorum vestimenta sacra," can relate only to the Pythagoreans.

[1] Symbol. 2. S. 90, 91.

cleanliness, which, in the estimation of the Egyptian priests, was a matter of so much importance. It is said before : The Egyptians are excessively religious above all other people, and consequently practise the following usages : They drink from brazen cups, which they wash out thoroughly every day. They wear linen garments always newly washed, with regard to which they take peculiar care. They also practise circumcision for the sake of cleanliness, and prefer neatness to decorum. Moreover, the priests shave the whole body each third day, lest either a louse or any other vermin may be found on them, while they are engaged in the service of the gods." After follows : " They bathe twice a day in cold water, and twice every night."

Plutarch,[1] who lived so much later, upon whom *Bähr* relies for support in his claim for the most intimate connection of the linen garments of the Egyptian priests with their peculiar theology, reasons evidently on his own way, without reference to the priests, and as the comparison with *Philostratus* shows, more in the sense of the new Pythagoreans, than of the Egyptian priests. Besides, he also represents the linen as a pure garment which least of all generates vermin.[2]

But the reason assigned by *Bähr* is not even reconcilable with the Egyptian law. The contempt for animal material in itself, accords not with the divine honour which in Egypt was shown to animals. That the killing of animals in general in Egypt was considered as unallowed, is entirely incorrect. Animals were sacrificed and eaten in Egypt without scruple.

How one can suppose, in his zeal for the vindication of the Bible, that it is necessary to contend against the dependence of the Israelitish upon the Egyptian priests' garments, can scarcely be conceived. The more original, independent, and peculiar the Israelitish religion was in spirit, the less necessity had it to avoid with timid care, every external contact with the religions of other nations, the more freely could it appropriate to itself the suitable existing forms, and the more untrammelled might it avail itself of the advantages which familiarity with the religion of Egypt offered.

But we consider it certain that the Israelitish priests' garments, in respect to material and colour, were made in imitation of those

---

[1] De Iside et Osir. p. 352.   [2] Καθαρὰν ἐσθῆτα ἥκιστα φθειροποιόν.

of the Egyptian priests. Their independence of each other is excluded, since, in reference to these particular circumstances, these two nations stand alone in all antiquity.

The thought of an inverted order of things is, in addition to the general reasons already given, impossible, since the priesthood in Egypt, according to expressions in the Pentateuch itself, had already long existed when that of the Israelites was instituted, the material of the clothing is peculiarly Egyptian, and the garment of byssus, even in the time of Joseph, appears as the most common Egyptian clothing [1] Thus, we have an important result in favour of the Pentateuch. Such a reference to Egyptian customs can only be supposed, if the priesthood was instituted in the circumstances given in the Pentateuch; and modern views of the origin of the Israelitish priesthood must appear as entirely untenable, since in the time to which this is referred, so close a connection did not exist between the Israelites and Egyptians, as to render it possible for the former to borrow from the latter.

URIM AND THUMMIM.

The Egyptian reference in the Urim and Thummim, is especially distinct and incontrovertible. Of them it is said: "And you shall put in the breast-plate of judgment the Urim and the Thummim, (the light and the truth); and they shall be on Aaron's heart when he goeth in before the Lord: and Aaron shall bear the judgment of the children of Israel upon his heart before the Lord continually," Exod. xxviii. 30. According to *Aelian*,[2] the high priest among the Egyptians, as superior judge, wore around his neck an image of Sapphire, which was called *truth*. *Diodorus*[3] also confirms this fact. According to him, the chief judge (also according to *Diodorus* the office of judge belonging to the priests,[4]) wore around his neck an image of costly stones, suspended upon a gold chain, which was named truth.

[1] Gen. xli. 42.
[2] Var. Hist. L. 14. c. 34: Αἰγύπτιοί φασι παρ' Ἑρμοῦ τὰ νόμιμα ἐκμουσωθῆναι· δικασταὶ δὲ τὸ ἀρχαῖον παρ' Αἰγυπτίοις οἱ ἱερεῖς ἦσαν· ὧν δὲ τούτων ἄρχων ὁ πρεσβύτατος καὶ ἐδίκαζεν ἅπαντας. Ἔδει δὲ αὐτὸν εἶναι δικαιότατον ἀνθρώπων καὶ ἀφειδέστατον· εἶχε δὲ καὶ ἄγαλμα περὶ τὸν αὐχένα ἐκ σαπφείρου λίθου καὶ ἐκαλεῖτο τὸ ἄγαλμα ἀλήθεια.
[3] B.... [4] See Wesseling on this passage.

After both of two contending parties have laid open their case, the high priest must touch one of them with the image of truth. The same author,[1] in describing an Egyptian wall-picture, shows us in the midst of the judges, the chief judge, "who wears suspended from his neck the *truth* with closed eyes." By this it is shown that the chief judge must see only the truth. These declarations of the ancients have received confirmation from the new discoveries in Egypt. In proof of the statement of *Diodorus*, *Rosellini*[2] says: "Among the monuments of the tombs, representations of persons are found who filled the office of chief judge, and who wore the common little image of the goddess Thmei suspended from the neck. *Wilkinson*[3] gives, from the Theban monuments, an engraving of the goddess who was honoured under the double character of truth and justice, and was represented with closed eyes.

That a connection here exists between Egyptian and Israelitish antiquity,[4] even the Seventy probably perceived, since in Exodus

---

[1] B. 1. c. 48. [2] II. 3. p. 500. [3] II. p. 27.

[4] The general similarity of the sacerdotal institutions among the ancient Egyptians and the Israelites, is very noticeable. The ceremony of investiture to office of the priests, among the Israelites, is described in Ex. xxvii. 5—7, "Thou shalt take the garments, and put upon Aaron the coat, and the robe of the ephod, and the ephod, and the breast-plate, and gird him with the curious girdle of the ephod: and thou shalt put the mitre upon his head and put the holy crown upon the mitre. *Then* shalt thou take the anointing oil and pour it upon his head." The priest is anointed with oil after he has put on his entire dress. "The Egyptians" also, "represent the anointing of their priests and kings *after* they were attired in their full robes, with the cap and crown upon their head. Some of the sculptures introduce a priest pouring oil over the monarch, in the presence of Thoth, Hor-Hat, Ombte, or Nilus; which may be considered a representation of the ceremony, before the statues of those gods. The functionary who officiated was the high-priest of the king. He was clad in a leopard-skin, and was the same who attended on all occasions which required him to assist, or assume the duties of the monarch in the temple. This leopard-skin dress was worn by the high-priests on all the most important solemnities, and the king himself adopted it when engaged in the same duties."—*Wilkinson, Man. and Cus.*, 2d Ser., Vol. II. p. 280. Both the Egyptians and Israelites were purified with water before they assumed the sacerdotal robes. (Ex. xl. 12—15.) They were divided into different orders, among both nations, and the offering of incense was limited to priests of the highest rank. Priests were the judges, also, among the Israelites and Egyptians. *Wilkinson* says, Vol. I. p. 282:

xxviii. 30, they translated Urim and Thummim, by revelation and truth, δήλωσις καὶ ἀλήθεια. This relation also forced itself oven upon the ancient theologians. *Braun*,[1] for example, supposes that the Egyptians probably borrowed this symbol from the Israelites.

But recently *Bähr*[2] has denied that there is any connection between the two. The agreement, he asserts, depends on no other ground than the acknowledged false translation of Thummim by the Seventy, as meaning truth. But this "acknowledged false translation," since the word means perfectness or blamelessness in the moral sense, is proved on closer examination to be as completely correct, as the explanation given by *Bähr* is on the other hand false.[3]

"Besides their religious duties, the priests fulfilled the important offices of judges and legislators, as well as councillors of the monarch ; and the laws, as among many other nations of the East, forming part of the sacred books, could only be administered by them." So in Deut. xvii. 8,—"If there arise a matter too hard for thee in judgment, between blood and blood, between plea and plea, and between stroke and stroke, being matters of controversy within thy gates ; then shalt thou arise, and get thee up into the place which the Lord thy God shall choose ; and thou shalt come unto the priests the Levites, and unto the judge that shall be in those days, and inquire ; and they shall show thee the sentence of judgment."—Of the similarity of Urim and Thummim to the Egyptian symbol, *Wilkinson*, (Vol. II. 2d Ser. p. 28,) after speaking of the badge of the judge among the Egyptians, says : "A similar emblem was used by the high-priests of the Jews ; and it is a remarkable fact, that the word Thummim is not only translated 'truth,' but, being a plural or dual word, corresponds to the Egyptian notion of the 'two Truths,' or the double capacity of this goddess. According to some, the Urim and Thummim signify, 'lights and perfections,' or 'light and truth,'—which last present a striking analogy to the two figures of Rē and Thmei, in the breast-plate worn by the Egyptians. And though the resemblance of the Urim and the Uræus (or basilisk,) the symbol of majesty, suggested by Lord Prudhoe, is very remarkable, I am disposed to think the 'lights,' Aorim or Urim, more nearly related to the sun, which is seated in the breast-plate with the figure of Truth."

[1] De Vestitu, p. 508.   [2] Symb. II. S. 164.

[3] According to him, (see S. 165,) the word תֹם, *Thom*, must mean completeness, and תֻּמִּים, *Thummim*, in connection with אוּרִים, *Urim*, is a subordinate, accessory idea, both together meaning perfect illumination. The supposition of such a hendyadis, besides that it is in itself very harsh, and confirmed by no entirely analogous example, is excluded by Deut.

Besides, remarks *Bähr*, there is nothing more incongruous than the significance of the Urim and Thummim when compared with that badge of the judge, which evidently points to impartiality as his first duty. But the moral significance which later Greek writers, according to their custom, give the symbol, is not certainly the first and most important one. That symbol has first and principally a promissory significance. It refers to the special aid of the goddess of truth and justice, which the high priest and chief judge enjoyed. On the other hand, the promissory significance does not exclude the moral one in the Israelitish symbol. Upon the promise follows of itself rather the admonition. How intimately both are connected, is shown by Deut. xxxiii. 8, 9, in which the Urim and Thummim given to the tribe of Levi is considered as a pledge that God will guide him in the decisions given in his name, and then it is said: "who says unto his father and to his mother, I saw thee not, and his brother he recognises not, and his children he does not know," words which in a striking manner remind one of the Egyptian image of the goddess of justice with closed eyes, and of the statues of the judges at Thebes mentioned in *Plutarch*,[1] without hands with their president at their head, having his eyes directed to the ground.

How any one could even suppose that a denial of the affinity of these Egyptian and Israelitish symbols is of any importance in the vindication of the truth, can hardly be conceived. Through the outward similarity the internal difference is more clearly exhibited. As among the Egyptians the author of truth appears to be a mere personified abstraction, an image of their own fancy which can never have a true and perfect power over its own pro-

---

xxxiii. 8, where תֻּמִּים, *Thummim*, stands first: "Thy Thummim and thy Urim belong to thy holy one." The Urim (the plur. is the plur. majest., compare Beiträge Th. 2. S. 258,) therefore, refers to divine illumination, the Thummim to the perfect rectitude of the decision given by him, and integrity and truth are the designations of the same thing, considered from a different point of view. The circumstance that אוּרִים is used unaccompanied by Thummim, is very easily explained also by the moral element comprehended in the latter. Light has right and truth as its necessary concomitants, so that the Urim comprehends the Thummim in itself.

[1] De Isid. et Os. See Wilk. II. 28.

ducer, on the contrary, among the Israelites he is the only, the living, the one God manifest among his own people.

It is an important difference, that among the Egyptians the symbol appears to have referred merely to judging in its narrower sense, while the Urim and Thummim was a symbol of the judicial office in a broader sense, promising generally to the high priest divine assistance in difficult and important decisions, especially such as have reference to the weal and woe of the whole people.[1]

THE CHERUBIM AND THE SPHINXES.

The affinity of the Cherubim with the Egyptian Sphinxes is more doubtful, yet it is so only just so long as we consider the thing merely by itself, and leave out of the account the numerous other points of contact between the Pentateuch and Egypt. If these are taken into view, the similarity is sufficient to warrant here also such an alliance.

THE FIGURE AND SIGNIFICANCE OF THE SPHINXES.

We begin with some remarks upon the figure and significance of the Egyptian sphinxes. As respects the figure, it was the current belief, in all antiquity, that the sphinx was composed of the lion and a young female; and recently *Bähr*[2] has argued, on this supposition, against the affinity of the cherub with the sphinxes. This opinion has also been yet more confirmed by the scholars of the French expedition, who, while indeed *Herodotus*[3] speaks of the man-sphinx, assert[4] that all the sphinxes with human heads, which they saw, except one near the pyramids, had the head of a female. This is also in accordance with *Aelian*. On the contrary, the latest investigations of Egyptian antiquity, have come to the result, that the Egyptian sphinxes are *never* female, like those of the Greeks, but always have the head of a man and the body of a lion. *Wilkinson*[5] asserts this very confidently; as

---

[1] Dr Hengstenberg assumes through this discussion, that the wearing of the Urim and Thummim was little more than symbolical; but most English commentators believe that they afforded some miraculous aid in coming to a right decision. T.

[2] Th. 1. S. 342.
[3] B. 2. c. 175.
[4] See
[5] Vol. III. p. 23.

also *Rosellini*,[1] who remarks: with the exception of a very few cases, the sphinxes have a beard. It is consequently not true, as some affirm, led into error by the Greek and Roman sphinxes copied from those in Egypt, that these symbolic animals have the face of a female. They are rather of male sex, which accords with their symbolic import. The few exceptions are accounted for by supposing, that they symbolize a queen who reigned at the time. Each of these symbolic figures bears on the breast or some other part of the body, the name and title of the king whom they designate, and whose features the human head exhibits. The sphinxes without inscriptions, are the work of Grecian or Roman artists. Even before both these authors, *Minutoli*[2] had remarked: "The sphinxes have either bodies of lions with human faces, without however a trace of the female figure, or the heads of rams."

We will now speak of the import of the sphinxes. It is acknowledged that the Egyptian animal combinations, in general depending upon a symbolic significance, designate the union of different characteristic properties which, by each part, the animal made up will represent. So says *Jomard*:[3] "They have excelled not less in the combination of different figures of animals, in order to compose chimerical beings, expressing without doubt the reunion of the properties attributed to each of these figures." *Creuzer*[4] also remarks: "Upon this Egyptian coin of the time of the Emperor Adrian, we see the beardless sphinx with the lotus on its head. The front part of its body is covered with a veil down to the feet. Out of its breast there is leaping forth the inverted head of a crocodile, under its feet crawls a serpent, and upon its back a griffon appears with the wheel! There are, therefore, here the different attributes of the godhead; that of strength and wisdom, that of secret control, the idea of eternity and of a beneficent guardian angel, &c., united in this remarkable way; and this representation may be designated by the technical term *Pantheum*."

Now, therefore, the sphinx can designate nothing else than the union of strength and wisdom, and this import has also been at-

---

[1] II. 2. p. 177-8.
[2] S. 257.
[3] In the Descr. t. 1. p. 311.
[4] Vol. I. p. 499.

tributed to it from ancient times until the present, with no inconsiderable agreement.[1]

According to this whole view then, the sphinx symbolizes merely the union of the two designated qualities ;[2] whilst the possessor of these is not indicated by the symbol itself, but can be known only by the position in which the sphinx is found. If

---

[1] Thus Clemens, Alex. Strom. L. 5. c. 8. p. 671, says: "ἀλκῆς καὶ ῥύμης σύμβολον αὐτοῖς ὁ λέων.—Ἀλκῆς τε ἂν μετὰ συνέσεως ἡ σφίγξ, τὸ μὲν σῶμα πᾶν λέοντος, τὸ πρόσωπον δὲ ἀνθρώπου ἔχουσα. It is however granted, that it has not always this significance; on the contrary, in c. 5. of the same Vol. p. 664, its import is different. Synesius, De Regno, p. 7, designates the sphinx as the sacred symbol of the union of the virtues, the strength of the animal and the insight of man. Zoega, De Obeliscis, p. 598, says: Mens cum robore conjuncta primus et obvius Aeg. sphingis significatus. Champollion, Briefe, S. 229, gives a similar explanation: The monarch (Remeses Meiamun), adorned with all the insignia of royalty, sits upon a beautiful throne, which the golden images of justice and truth cover with their outstretched wings: the sphinx, a symbol both of wisdom and strength, and the lion, the emblem of courage, stand near the throne, and seem to be its guardians.

[2] *Mr Wilkinson*, in his last work, confirms the opinion expressed in the former one, with regard to the sphinx, and in effect, if his positions are correct, answers the objections of *Hengstenberg* to the view that the sphinx designates not qualities alone, but the king as the possessor of these qualities. I give a rather long extract, but trust it will not, from its bearing on the whole section, be deemed out of place. It will be recollected that the author of this volume had not seen this last series of *Mr Wilkinson*: "The most distinguished post among fabulous animals must be conceded to the sphinx. It was of three kinds,—the *Andro-sphinx*, with the head of a man, and the body of a lion, denoting the union of intellectual and physical power; the *Crio-sphinx*, with the head of a ram and the body of a lion; and the *Hieraco-sphinx*, with the same body and the head of a hawk. They were all types or representatives of the king. The two last were probably so figured in token of respect to the two deities whose heads they bore, Neph and Re; the other great deities, Amun, Khem, Pthah and Osiris, having human heads, and therefore all connected with the form of the Andro-sphinx. The king was not only represented under the mysterious figure of a sphinx, but also of a ram, and of a hawk; and this last had, moreover, the peculiar signification of 'Phrah,' or Pharaoh, '*the Sun*,' personified by the monarch. The inconsistency, therefore, of making the sphinx female, is sufficiently obvious.—When represented in the sculptures a deity is often seen presenting the sphinx with the sign of life, or other divine gifts usually vouchsafed by the gods to a king; as well as to the ram or hawk, when in the same capacity, as an emblem of a Pharaoh."—Vol. II. p. 200.

they are found, as they commonly are, at the entrance of a temple, where they form entire rows [1] on each side, they designate the union of these properties in the deity to whom the temple is dedicated. If they are found around the throne of the king, then the king is the possessor of these attributes.

On the contrary, *Rosellini* and *Wilkinson* assert, that the sphinx designates not merely qualites, but also the king as the possessor of them. But the defenders of this modern view have not attempted to substantiate its claims in opposition to the old theory, and we do not see how they can succeed in controverting the reasons which declare for the latter. How can the sphinx, in its usual position before the entrance of a temple, designate the king? How can the human face be understood to be personal, whilst the lion's body, and all those things which in many cases are added to it, as the hawk and vulture hovering over the sphinx, be symbolical? How can it be reconciled with this supposition, that besides the common sphinx or the Andro-sphinx, the Crio-sphinx, and the Hieraco-sphinx, the lion's body with the ram's or hawk's head, are found?[2] That which is adduced as positive proof for this theory, is anything but decisive. It rests upon the supposition that all sphinxes bear the name and title of a king. Allow that this is so, when the sphinx is intended to represent royal qualities, cannot the name and the title serve directly to designate the possessor of these symbolized qualities, not designated by the symbol itself?[3] But where the sphinx has a religious import, there the inscription may appropriately immortalize the name of the king who built the temple. Were it true, that the human faces of the sphinxes represent the countenances of the kings whose name they bear, it might be accounted for, by supposing that they considered the face of the king as the most noble representative of the human face.

THE CHERUBIM—THEIR FORM AND IMPORT.

We turn to the Cherubim. That this symbol, as such, aside

---

[1] See Descr. t. 2. p. 505 seq. Creuzer, I. S. 498.
[2] Wilk. Vol. III. p. 27.
[3] The crown also and other symbols of royalty, which according to Wilk. Vol. III. p. 362, are said to be often represented on the sphinxes, are for the same purpose.

from its significance, which includes a real, original, Israelitish element, did not spring up on Jewish ground, appears probable from the merely scattered notices of it which are found. We cannot, however, appropriate to ourselves the argument which *Bauer* has adduced in favour of its foreign origin, namely, that 'the cherubim was not first introduced by Moses, since the law speaks of it in a manner that it could not do, except on the supposition that it was already definitely known among the people :' for indeed, at the time in which the law was written down, cherubs with all the accompanying things, for which *Bauer*[1] argues in like manner, had already existed a long time,—a circumstance which could not fail to modify the record, and cause the thing to appear, in various ways, as if it were well known at the time of its introduction.

We are specially guided to the Egyptian origin of the cherubim, since of all the people with whom the Israelites in ancient times were closely connected, only among the Egyptians are compound animals found in history. "Among the Phoenician animal combinations," says *Bähr*,[2] "we only recollect Moloch." But the information that the image of Moloch had a bullock's head, is found in *R. Simon Haddarschan*, A. D. 1310!![3] And, in like manner, it is of no importance what is found in the same author[4] concerning compound animals among the Carthaginians.

But the real similarity of form between the Hebrew cherubim, and the Egyptian sphinxes, is of greater importance. Even in the cherub of Ezekiel, this agreement is still in a considerable degree perceivable. Two of the same elements, lion and man, are found here and in the sphinx. But it is generally agreed that the form of the cherubim in Ezekiel is not the original one, but that the prophet, as from his whole character cannot be supposed improbable, expanded variously the symbol.[5] In what the additions and changes consisted, is difficult to determine, since we possess only so very imperfect notices of the figure of the Mosaic cherubim.[6]

---

[1] Rel. des Alt. Test. Th. I. S. 300.   [2] I. S. 358.
[3] Compare Münter Relig. der Carthag. S. 9.
[4] S. 68.
[5] See, e. g. among the ancient writers, Witsius Egyptiaca, p. 158, among those of modern times, Bähr, S. 311 ff.
[6] Witsius remarks correctly, p. 155: Moses speaks of the form as only twofold, *quod passus habuerint alas sursum versus quodque suis*

But we can show, with great probability, from Ezekiel himself, that the changes have reference to just those things in which the cherubim of Ezekiel are unlike the Egyptian sphinxes. Thus, while the cherubim in Ezek. i. 10, appear to be made up of four elements, and have four faces, that of a man, an ox, a lion and an eagle; in Ez. xli. 18—20, only two faces, that of a man and of a lion, are ascribed to them. Now we may certainly, with *Lightfoot* and *Michaelis*,[1] assume that the two other faces are to be considered as existing, but not in sight,[2] an assumption which receives confirmation from Ez. i. 10, according to which the ox and the eagle were on the reverse side. But yet this at least remains in force, that in the cherubim of Ezekiel, the man and the lion were in front, and therefore when placed against the wall they only came in sight. This leads us to the result, that the change before spoken of by Ezekiel, consisted in his addition of the element of the ox and the eagle, just as also in the sphinxes, to the original and principal elements, the lion and man, in many cases others are also added.[3] Thus, the form of the cherubim is reduced almost to that of the sphinx. The only remaining difference of importance, namely, that the simple cherub yet has two faces, while the sphinx, although composed of two elements, has only one, is probably also to be set to the account of Ezekiel. That the Mosaic cherub had only *one* face has been rightly shown[4] from Exod. xxv. 20. "And their faces shall be towards one another; towards the mercy-seat shall the faces of the cherubim be."

As respects the significance of the cherubim, their real agreement in this particular with the Egyptian sphinxes cannot be doubted, and the difference and opposition respects not so much the import of the symbol, as rather the possessor of the qualities signified by them. "The cherub," remarks *Bähr*, who of all writers has comprehended most correctly and thoroughly the

alis obtexerint propitiatorium, dein quod facies habuerint ob versus sibi mutuo itemque conversas ad propitiatorium.

[1] Bibl. Heb. on this passage.

[2] Alias quatuor, quia hic duae tantum in plano apparebant. Duae itaque aliae facies concipi debent quasi parieti obversae et ab ea obscuratae. Latuit facies vitulina a sinistris et facies aquilina a tergo.

[3] See the passage cited from Creuzer, S. 159.

[4] See, e. g. Ges. Thesaurus, same word.

nature of this symbol, "is such a being as standing on the highest grade of created existence, and containing in itself the most perfect created life, is the best manifestation of God and the divine life. It is a representative of creation in its highest grade, an ideal creature. The vital powers communicated to the most elevated existences in the visible creation are collected and individualized in it." Accordingly the difference would perhaps consist only in this, that in the cherubim, the divine properties were only indirectly symbolized, so far as they came into view in the works of creation, whilst in the sphinx, directly, a difference which cannot be considered important.[1]

LEVITICUS, Chap. XVI. AZAZEL.

An Egyptian reference, it appears to us, must necessarily be acknowledged in the ceremony of the great atonement day. But in order to exhibit this reference, we must first substantiate our view of the meaning of the word עֲזָאזֵל, *Azazel*, which is, that it designates Satan. And this can only be seen at a right point of view, if we in the first place, in a general survey of the whole rite, point out definitely the position which the word Azazel takes in it.

First, in verses 1—10, the general outlines are given, and then follows in v. 11 seq. the explanation of separate points. It is of no small importance for the interpretation, that this arrangement, a knowledge of which has escaped most interpreters, be understood. Aaron first offers a bullock as a sin-offering for himself and his house. He then takes a fire-pan full of coals from the altar, with fragrant incense, and goes within the vail. There he

---

[1] The author has signally failed to establish any similarity, much less an identity between the Hebrew cherubim, and the Egyptian sphinxes. It is utterly incredible that Moses would have taken an idolatrous emblem and placed it in the most sacred part of the tabernacle; such a proceeding would have been an indirect sanction of Egyptian corruptions. On the contrary, the great course of the Levitical legislation seems directed to changing the habits, and breaking of the associations which the Israelites formed in Egypt. T.

puts the incense on the fire before the Lord, and "the cloud of the incense (the embodied prayer) covers the mercy-seat which is upon the testimony, that he die not." Aaron then takes of the blood of the bullock, and sprinkles it seven times before the mercy-seat. After he has thus completed the expiation for himself, he proceeds to the expiation for the people. He takes two he-goats for a sin-offering, לְחַטָּאת, Lehâtath, for the children of Israel, verse 5. These he places before the Lord at the door of the tabernacle of the congregation, verse 7. He casts lots upon them, one lot for the Lord, לַיהוָה, La Jehovah, and one lot for Azazel, לַעֲזָאזֵל, La Azazel, verse 8. The goat upon which the lot for the Lord, לַיהוָה, La Jehovah, fell, verse 9, he offers as a sin-offering, brings his blood within the vail, and does with it as with the blood of the bullock. In this way is the sanctuary purified from the defilements of the children of Israel, their transgressions and all their sins, so that the Lord, the holy one and pure, can continue to dwell there with them. After the expiation is completed, the second goat, the one on which the lot for Azazel, לַעֲזָאזֵל, La Azazel, fell, is brought forward, verse 10. He is first placed before the Lord to absolve him, לְכַפֵּר עָלָיו, Le kassep alaiv.[1] Then Aaron lays both his hands upon his head, and confesses over him the (forgiven) iniquities, transgressions and sins of the children of Israel, puts them upon his head, and gives him to a man to take away, in order that he may bear the sins of the people into a solitary land,[2] verse 22, into the desert, for Azazel, verse 10. Then Aaron offers a burnt-offering for himself, and one for the people.

Now, in respect to language, there can be no objection to interpreting Azazel as meaning Satan. The exposition below shows this conclusively.[3]

[1] Verse 10, with 16 and 18.

[2] אֶל־אֶרֶץ גְּזֵרָה, literally, in terram abscissam, sc. a terra habitata. The Seventy; εἰς γῆν ἄβατον. Vulgate: in terram solitariam.

[3] That the Hebrew root עָזַל, Azal, corresponds to the Arabic عَزَلَ, as was asserted by Bochart as early as his time, and afterwards by Schröder in Scheid and Groenewood, Lex. Hebr. II. 397, is now generally acknowledged. עֲזָאזֵל (for עֲזַלְזֵל) belongs to the form which repeats the second and third radicals. In reference to this form, Ewald in his smaller Grammar, § 333, remarks: "The form indeed also expresses general in-

But this explanation, as far as facts in the case are concerned, is in like manner exposed to no well grounded objections. The doctrinal significance of the symbolic action, so far as it has reference to Azazel, is this, that Satan, the enemy of the people of God, cannot harm those forgiven by God, but they, with sins forgiven of God, can go before him with a light heart, deride him and triumph over him.

The positive reasons, which favour this explanation and oppose every other, are the following:

1. The manner in which the phrase לַעֲזָאזֵל, for Azazel, is contrasted with לַיהוָה, for Jehovah, necessarily requires that Azazel should designate a personal existence, and if so, only Satan can be intended. 2. If by Azazel, Satan is not meant, there is no reason for the lots that were cast. We can then see no reason why the decision was referred to God, why the high priest did not simply assign one goat for a sin-offering, the other for sending away into the desert. The circumstance that lots are cast, implies that Jehovah is made the antagonist of a personal existence, with respect to which it is designed to exalt the unlimited power of Jehovah, and exclude all equality of this being with Jehovah. 3. Azazel, as a word of comparatively infrequent formation and only used here, is best fitted for the designation of Satan. In every other explanation, the question remains, why then (as it has every appearance of being) is the word formed for this occasion, and why is it never found except here?

tension, but the idea of continual, regular repetition, without interruption, is also especially expressed by the repetition of nearly the whole word." In reference to the meaning of the word we are referred to the Arabic. The word عزل signifies in that language, semovit, dimovit, removit, descivit; in the pass. remotus, depositus fuit; and the part. عازل means, a ceteris se sejungens. In like manner, معزول واعزل signify semotus, remotus, abdicatus. Accordingly two explanations of עֲזָאזֵל relating to Satan are furnished, either the apostate (from God) or the one entirely separate. It is in favour of the latter, 1. that the signification, descivit, is only a derived one, and 2. that it is appropriate to the abode in the desert. The goat is sent to Azazel, in the desert, in the divided land (terram abscissam.) How could he then be designated by a more appropriate name than the separate one?

4. By this explanation the third chapter of Zechariah comes into a relation with our passage, entirely like that in which chap. iv. of the same prophecy stands to Exod. chap. xxv. 31. Here as there, the Lord, Satan, and the high-priest, appear. Satan wishes by his accusations to destroy the favourable relations between the Lord and his people. The high-priest presents himself before the Lord not with a claim of purity, according to law, but laden with his own sins, and the sins of the people. Here Satan thinks to find the safest occasion for his attack, but he mistakes. Forgiveness baffles his designs; he is compelled to retire in confusion.[1] It is evident that the doctrinal import of both passages is substantially the same, and the one in Zechariah may be considered as the oldest commentary extant on the words of Moses. In substance we have the same scene also in the Apocalypse, xii. 10, 11: " The accuser of our brethren is cast down, who accuses them before our God day and night, and they overcome him by the blood of the Lamb."

5. The relation in which, according to our explanation, Satan is here placed to the desert, finds analogy in other passages of the Bible, where the deserted and waste places appear as peculiarly the abode of the evil spirit. See Matt. xii. 43, where the unclean spirit cast out from the man is represented as going through "dry places," Luke viii. 27, and Apocalypse xviii. 2, according to which the fallen Babylon is to be the dwelling of all unclean spirits. 6. To the reasons already given the Egyptian reference which the rite has according to this explanation, may be added—a reference which is so remarkable that no room can remain for the thought that it has arisen through false explanation.

Among the *objections* to this explanation, the one which is most important, and has exerted the most influence is this, that it gives a sense which stands in direct opposition to the spirit of the religion of Jehovah. It was this objection which made so many of the ancient theologians disinclined to interpret the passage as we have done.[2]

---

[1] Christol. Th. S. 33 seq.

[2] Deyling, e. g. who after he has been candid enough to remark, in the Obss. Sac. 1. p. 50: Lamed Jehovae et Azazeli prefixum casum eundem, nempe dativum notat, nec possunt ei significationes diversae in eodem commate attribui, yet, p. 51, shrinks back from the explanation of Azazel as meaning Satan, with these words: Quid fingi potest ineptius absurdi.

The objections which so many in modern times, even as late as *Bähr*, have cherished against this interpretation, proceed almost entirely from this point. Most of its opposers expressly declare themselves as of the same opinion with *Baumgarten-Crusius*, who in his Biblical Theology[1] says: " In fact, could an offering properly be made to the evil spirit, in the desert, which the common precepts of religion in the Mosaic law, as well as the significance of this ceremony, entirely oppose ? "

Now, were it really necessary to connect with the explanation of Azazel as meaning Satan, the assumption that sacrifice was offered to him, we should feel obliged to abandon it, notwithstanding all the reasons in its favour. Especially in the manner in which *Gesenius*[2] understands the passage, it presents an opposition to the vital being of the religion of Jehovah, so atrociously unjust, that whoever adopts this cannot think of assenting to that.

But nothing is easier than to show that this manner of understanding the explanation is entirely arbitrary. The following reasons prove that an offering made to Azazel cannot be supposed:

1. Both the goats were designated in verse 5 as a sin-offering. " And from the congregation of the children of Israel he shall take two goats for a sin-offering." That these goats were taken together as forming unitedly one sin-offering, wholly excludes the thought that one of them was brought as an offering to Jehovah, and the other as an offering to Azazel: and further, an offering which is given to a bad being, can indeed never be a sin-offering. The idea of a sin-offering implies holiness, hatred of sin in the one to whom the offering is made.[3]

usque, quam deum ex duobus hircis alterum sibi, alterum diabolo destinasse et offeri jussisse. Nonne Lev. xvii. 7, sacrificare dæmonibus expressis verbis vetat? Lund also gives a similar explanation, S. 1032.

[1] S. 294.

[2] In Robinson's Gesenius, p. 751, it is said: I render it (עֲזָאזֵל) without hesitation, the averter, the expiator, *averruncus ἀλεξίκακος*. By this name I suppose is to be understood originally some idol that was appeased with sacrifices; but afterwards, as the names of idols were often transferred to demons, it seem to denote an evil demon dwelling in the desert, and to be placated with victims, in accordance with this very ancient and also gentile rite.

[3] It is acknowledged that this reason would lose its force, if it were

2. Both the goats were first placed at the gate of the tabernacle of the congregation, before the Lord. To him therefore they both belong; and when afterwards one of them is sent to Azazel, this is done in accordance with the wish of Jehovah, and also without destroying the original relation, since the one sent to Azazel does not cease to belong to the Lord.

3. The casting of lots also shows that both these goats are to be considered as belonging to the Lord. The lot is never used in the Old Testament except as a means of obtaining the decision of Jehovah. So then, here also, Jehovah decides which goat is to be offered as a sin-offering, and which shall be sent to Azazel.[1]

4. The goat assigned to Azazel, before he is sent away, is absolved: "And the goat upon whom the lot falls for Azazel, shall

---

allowable, with Bähr, S. 679, to generalize the meaning of חַטָּאת, *Chatath*. It need not, he remarks, be taken in its most limited sense, as a sin-offering, but it may be translated in a general way, as the Seventy have done, by περὶ ἁμαρτίας; Aaron shall take the two goats *on account of sin*. But this generalizing, of which even the Seventy had no conception, we must consider as entirely arbitrary. The word חַטָּאת has everywhere only the two significations, sin and sin-offering, (compare Ges. Thes. s. v.,) and since the first here is not suitable, only the last can be understood. That this sense is the correct one here, can the less be doubted, since the word is so often used in the context itself with this meaning. It is especially required by the antithesis between חַטָּאת and עֹלָה, in verse 5. Who can doubt that in the connection with burnt-offering so frequently occurring חַטָּאת, must designate sin-offering? Just the same connection of לְחַטָּאת and לְעוֹלָה, we also have in verse 3.

[1] The last two reasons are stated even by Rabbi Bechai upon this passage, quoted in Mauritius, De Sortione Hebraeorum, p. 35: Uterque hircus iste erat oblatio domini, ad indicandum non debere nos aliter cogitare de utroque, quam soli deo benedicto esse oblatum, atque ideo sacerdos statim ab initio hujus operis duas res istas fecit: nimirum obtulit utrumque hircorum in oblationem dei et projiciebat sortes super illos: res enim illa, quae opera sortitionis dividitur, est portio, quae a domino venit, uti scriptum exstat: in sinu projicitur sors et a deo omnis ejus causa. Quodsi enim sacerdos ipse ore tenus sanctificasset eos dicens: hic est dei et hic est Asaselis, tunc utramque rem similem fecisset, quomodo autem non facere licet. Jam vero, cum medio sortis hoc factum sit, en deus ipse Asaseli hircum dedicat, atque ita ab ipso veniebat hircus ad eum, sicque deus ipse electionem faciebat, non nós.

be placed alive before the Lord in order to absolve him,[1] לְכַפֵּר עָלָיו, and then send him to Azazel in the desert." The act by which the second goat is, as it were, identified with the first, to transfer to the living the nature which the dead possessed, shows to what the phrase 'for a sin-offering' in verse 5 has reference, and what *Spencer* indeed perceived,—the two goats, says he, are as it were one goat,—that the duality of the goats rests only on the physical impossibility of making one example represent the different points to be exhibited. Had it been possible, in the circumstances, to restore life to the goat that was sacrificed, this would have been done. The two goats in this connection, stand in a relation entirely similar to that of the two birds in the purification of the leprous person in Lev. i. 4, of which the one let go was dipped in the blood of the one slain. As soon as the second goat is considered as an offering to Azazel, the connection between it and the first ceases, and it cannot be conceived why it was absolved before it was sent away.

5. According to verse 21, the already *forgiven* sins of Israel are laid on the head of the goat. These he bears to Azazel in the desert. But where there is already forgiveness of sins, there is no more offering.

6. The goat is sent alive into the desert. But in accordance with the view of the thing in the Old Testament, no animal offering is made without the shedding of blood.

Thus, therefore, this first and principal objection to the interpretation of Azazel by Satan, is to be considered as fully confuted.[2] What *Bähr* remarks: "Now if we understand Azazel as a

---

[1] The endeavour to give a different sense to these words is vain. The preposition עַל accompanying כָּפֵּר designates always and without exception the object of sin, (compare Bähr, S. 683,) and even in this same chapter כָּפֵּר with עַל is so used. Even Cocceius says that he cannot find that כָּפֵּר with עַל is used otherwise, nisi vel de personis pro quibus expiatio facta, vel de instrumentis cultus sacri altari et similibus.

[2] It is worth while to consider also what Schröder, De Azazeic Marb. 1725. S. 31, adduces for the intimate relation which the two goats sustain to each other: Notari et hoc imprimis meretur, ambos hircos in ipsa consecratione ita fuisse sibi mutuo implexos, ut neutrius ritus seorsim absolvendi, sed utriusque cerimoniae pariter inchoandae, alternis vicibus administrandae et junctim quasi consummandae unius piaculi sacra referre videantur. Uterque accipitur quasi unus, ad Aharonem adducitur, coram domino sistitur, utriusque sors ducitur, ... mactatur, ejusque san-

personal superhuman being, opposed to Jehovah, the text, verse 8, does not permit us to understand the phrase, for Azazel, in an entirely different sense from that, for Jehovah; on the other hand, it is necessary to recognise an offering in the second goat, as well as in the first, both before in verse 5 are particularly represented as appointed for a sin-offering,"[1]—will not easily lead any one into error. What *Bähr* here adduces as an argument against the interpretation approved by us, far more strongly opposes his own, and every other explanation, than that by Satan. We can, I think, at least, which is the first point insisted on, understand the ל in ליהוה and in לעזאזל, as in the same grammatical construction. According to our interpretation, one animal, at least in a certain sense, belongs to Jehovah, and the other to Azazel. The demand that both shall belong in precisely the same sense, as offerings to the one and to the other, is entirely inadmissible, since the contrary is expressly said. The goat which fell to the share of the Lord, is indeed, according to verse 9, offered to him as a sin-offering; the one which fell to Azazel is, according to verse 10, first absolved and then sent alive to him. The hypothesis of *Bähr* is not wholly without foundation. The symbol is intended to exhibit diversity, on the ground of a certain equality in the beginning. The design is to oppose the heathenish and peculiarly Egyptian view, which represents the evil principle as equally powerful, with equal right to be propitiated in like manner with the good being. With reference to this notion, two like things were first simply placed together, in order that the difference between both, and the dissimilarity of that which is to be done to them, may be presented in so much the clearer light.

---

guis spargitur; alter impositis cum prece manibus dimittitur: dum illius exta exemta super altari, caro cum pelle extra castra cremantur, hic in desertum locum abducitur sicque ambo una expediuntur. Praecedebat alias in sacrificiis piacularibus simplicibus, una tantum victima constantibus manuum impositio mactationem; quod inconveniens plane esset jugulato animali eo ritu peccata imponere: sed quod hoc sacrificium et mori et superstes esse deberet, unius hirci morte ac sanguine sparso reatus ante auferendus erat, quam alteri vivo imponeretur poena. Ita sane uterque hircus deo, ille mactatione, sparsione, incensione, combustione, hic omnia fidelis populi peccata portans, vindicatus est.

[1] S. 686.

Bähr[1] adduces a second objection: "Nowhere in the Mosaic ritual are Jehovah and the Devil placed together in a general way, much less then in such a manner, that lots are cast between the two, in order to determine their claims. This would have had, in the eyes of the people, an appearance of equality between the two beings." But the whole rite, according to our explanation, rather has the tendency to destroy the inclination existing among a people to believe in such an equality. The casting of lots, instead of being opposed to this tendency, is rather firmly established in its favour. This follows directly, if it is only settled, that according to the view of the Old Testament, the lot is under the direction of Jehovah. That the casting of lots here is not as a mediation between the two, so that it as an independant third agency decides to which of the two the one and to which the other shall fall, is clear from the fact, that both goats are represented as belonging to the Lord, before the lots are cast, by the phrase, for a sin-offering, in verse 5, and by the direction in verse 7, to place them before the Lord. The passage therefore by no means exhibits an equality, or even the appearance of it.

Ewald[2] refers to a third objection: "A bad demon, Azazel, which those later than the exile have first made out from the passage, cannot be found in the Pentateuch." But an explanation, which is demanded with absolute necessity by the laws of interpretation, cannot be disproved by such objections. They in any case have force only when the thing cannot be decided with certainty on exegetical grounds. And why is it said, that an account of Satan cannot be found in the Pentateuch? Because it was first notorious after the exile? But even *Ewald* allows that the book of Job was composed long before this time; and should it be asserted that the Satan of this book is still not possessed of the real attributes of Satan, every one will easily perceive that that which seems to favour this belongs only to the poetic drapery. It will vanish as soon as that only is understood, which is as clear as open day, namely, that the prologue bears, in the same degree, a poetical character, that the speeches do.

The hypothesis, that the knowledge of Satan does not appear among the Israelites until after the exile, has been evidently called forth by a motive external to the thing itself, by the feeling

---

[1] S. 687. [2] Gr. Gram. S. 243.

that this knowledge is of heathen origin, and consequently able to cast a shadow upon the truth of the account. But it is scarcely possible to conceive how it can be believed, that one, even with this object in view, is confined to Persian times. Is it not unaccountable, that it is not perceived, that just as much is accomplished by a reference to the Egyptian Typhon as to the Persian Ahriman? That this view is so firmly adhered to, appears to be explicable, only on the ground that at the time when this interest first arose, the Zendavesta was just in fashion, and that, as this lost popularity, the hypothesis already strengthened had become historical tradition, which was received without argument.

From a theological point of view, which, according to our belief, is the true and only scientific one, it will, from the nature of the case, be found almost impossible, that a dogma, which in the later period of the revelation holds so important a place, should not also at least be referred to in the statement of the first principles of that revelation. So far, therefore, from expelling it by force, where it does exist, we are rather inclined to search carefully for the traces of its existence. Besides, our passage is not the only one in the Pentateuch which contains intimations of the doctrine of a Satan. That such a doctrine is also prominent in Genesis iii. has been shown in recent times, among others, by *Schott*,[1] *Rosenmueller*,[2] *Hahn*,[3] and in the Christology.[4]

After exhibiting the positive reasons for the explanation of Azazel by Satan, and obviating the objections to it, we must now also subject to examination those among the various explanations that have been given, which are now current, whilst in reference to the rest we refer to *Bähr*.

According to *Ewald*,[5] Azazel designates "the unclean, the unholy (literally, the separate, the abhorred) sin." But this explanation must, on philological grounds, be considered as questionable.[6] It however appears much more untenable, when we exa-

---

[1] Theol. Dogmat. p. 128.
[2] Dogmat. S. 345.
[3] S. 109.
[4] I. 1. S. 27 ff.
[5] Gr. Gram. S. 243.
[6] The signification which Ewald gives to the word is quite unlike that of the root in the Arabic. No authority is found for the change. It stands entirely by itself. If it were allowed to proceed in this way, עזאזל could signify something very different still.

mine the context. According to this, what can be the meaning when it is said in verse 10, "to send it to Azazel, לַעֲזָאזֵל in the desert?" or in verse 26, "he who brings the goat to Azazel, לַעֲזָאזֵל?". In what sense can it be said that the goat was sent to sin?

Moreover, this explanation has indeed been adopted by no one except its originator, who has perhaps himself long ago abandoned it. There is another, to which the authority of *Tholuck*[1] among others has given more currency, and which is defended by *Bähr*:[2] "for complete removal." "As far as philology is concerned," says *Bähr*, very confidently, "there is at any rate no objection to it." But we cannot assent to this. The explanation is rather philologically entirely untenable.[3]

How little one can succeed with this in the context lies on the surface. Even in verse 8 we do not know how to dispose of it. "A lot for Jehovah, and a lot for complete removal:" this is not congruous. The lot is not to be carried away. Also the demand for similarity in the use of the prepositions in לַיהוָה and לַעֲזָאזֵל, for Jehovah and for Azazel, will then be grossly violated. We see, therefore, that we are compelled, at the outset, to modify the explanation with *Tholuck*, who translates: 'one lot for the animal devoted to God; the other lot for the animal destined for removal.' But the interpretation, thus modified, is not congruous, again, in verse 10: 'the goat on which the lot fell for Azazel.' There we cannot translate: 'for the *animal* destined for removal,' but 'for complete removal;' and just so, also, in the last words of the same verse: 'to send it, לַעֲזָאזֵל for complete removal, in the desert.' And if the ל in these last two cases can only be interpreted by *for* (denoting purpose), it is not proper to translate it in verse 8, as even the לַיהוָה demands by *for* (denoting possession). Also in verse 26, this explanation of Azazel is not suitable. It is there said: he who let go (or sent away) the goat, לַעֲזָאזֵל. If we here translate, 'for complete removal,' it it will neither be said for whom, to whom, or whither, the goat is

---
[1] The A. T. in the N. T. (Beit. zum Br. an die Hebr.), S. 80.
[2] S. 668.
[3] The forms like עֲזָאזֵל are only *adjectiva*, (compare Ewald Kl. Gram. § 333,) not *abstracta*, least of all *nomina actionis*, which cannot come from words originally *adjectiva*.

sent away. That the first (the individual to whom it is sent) is designated by לַעֲזָאזֵל is so entirely evident, that any one will scarcely be able to deny it without doing violence to his conscience as an interpreter.[1]

If it is now established that Satan is to be understood by the term Azazel, then an illusion to Egypt, in the whole rite, cannot be mistaken.

Among the great errors which necessarily arise as soon as man having attained to reflection is abandoned by insight into the depth of human sinfulness, which insight alone will explain the riddle of human life, is dualism, an error proportionally harmless, which in Egypt also took very deep root. "Every bad influence or power of nature, and generally the bad itself, in a physical or ethical respect," was there personified under the name of Typhon.[2]

The doctrine of a Typhon among the Egyptians, is as old as it is firmly established. Representations of him are found on numerous monuments as old as the time of the Pharaohs.[3] *Herodotus* speaks of Typhon in 2. 144, 56. and 3. 5. But *Plutarch* gives the most accurate and particular accounts, with indeed many incorrect additions[4]

The barren regions around Egypt generally belonged to Typhon.[5] The desert was especially assigned to him as his residence, whence he made his wasting inroads into the consecrated land. "He is," says *Creuzer*,[6] "the lover of the degenerate Nephthys, the hostile Lybian desert, and of the sea-shore,—there is the kingdom of Typhon; on the contrary, Egypt the blessed, the Nile-valley glittering with fresh crops, is the land of Isis." *Herodotus*[7] ascribes a similar dwelling to Typhon.[8]

---

[1] The לְ in לַעֲזָאזֵל in verse 8 and 10 can the less be explained by *for* (denoting purpose), and some other than a personal being be understood by Azazel, since לְ is used in other places to designate the person to whom a lot belongs. Compare Josh. xix. 1—"And the second lot came forth לְשִׁמְעוֹן to Simeon." Verse 10, "And the third lot came out for the children of Zebulon," לִבְנֵי זְבוּלֻן, and so also in other verses in the same chapter.

[2] Creuzer, Myth. I. S. 317.   [3] Compare Creuzer, S. 322 ff.
[4] Compare Jablonski, III. pp. 59, 60.
[5] Τῶν ἐσχάτων ἁπτόμενος, Plutarch in Jabl. p. 83.
[6] S. 269.   [7] B. 3. c. 5.
[8] Compare upon this passage, Bähr and Creuzer in Comm. Herod. p. 285.

In a strange but very natural alternation, the Egyptians sought sometimes to propitiate the god whom they hated, but feared, by offerings, and indeed by those which consisted of sacred animals. Sometimes, again, when they supposed that the power of the good gods was prevalent and sustained them against him, they allowed themselves in every species of mockery and abuse. "The obscured and broken power of Typhon," says *Plutarch*,[1] "even now, in the convulsions of death, they seek sometimes to propitiate by offerings, and endeavour to persuade him to favour them; but, at other times, on certain festival occasions, they scoff at and insult him. Then they cast mud at those who are of a red complexion, and throw down an ass from a precipice, as the Coptites do, because they suppose that Typhon was of the colour of the fox and the ass." The most important passage on the worship of Typhon is found on p. 380: "But when a great and troublesome heat prevails, which in excess either brings along with it destructive sickness or other strange or extraordinary misfortunes, the priests take some of the sacred animals, in profound silence, to a dark place. There they threaten them first and terrify them, and when the calamity continues they offer these animals in sacrifice there."[2]

Now the supposition of a reference to these *Typhonia sacra*, *Witsius* considers as a profanation.[3] But it is seen at once that the reference contended for by him is materially different from that adopted by us. The latter is a polemic one. In opposition to the Egyptian view which implied the necessity of yielding respect even to bad beings generally, if men would ensure themselves against them, it was intended by this rite to bring Israel to the deepest consciousness, that all trouble is the punishment of a just and holy God, whom they, through their sins, have offended, that they must reconcile themselves only with him; that when that is done and the forgiveness of sins is obtained, the bad being can harm them no farther.

How very natural and how entirely in accordance with circum-

[1] De Iside et Os. p. 362.
[2] Compare Comm. upon the passage in Schmidt, De Sacerdotibus et Sacrif. Aeg. p. 312 seq.
[3] Aeg. L. II. c. 9. p. 119: Num permisit suis deus, nedum ut jusserit genium aliquem averruncum agnoscere, quem sacratis placarent animantibus, aut quicquam facere abominationibus Aegyptiorum simile.

stances such a reference was, is evident from the facts contained in other passages of the Pentateuch, which show how severe a contest the religious principles of the Israelites had to undergo with the religious notions imbibed in Egypt. This is especially exhibited in the regulations in Leviticus xvii., following directly upon the law concerning the atonement day, which prove that the Egyptian idol worship yet continued to be practised among the Israelites. The same thing is also evident from the occurrences connected with the worship of the golden calf.

The assumption of a reference so specially polemic might indeed be supposed unnecessary, since in a religion which teaches generally the existence of a powerful bad being, the error here combated, the belief that this being possesses other than derived power, will naturally arise in those who have not found the right solution of the riddle of human life in the deeper knowledge of human sinfulness.

But yet the whole rite has too direct a reference to a prescribed practice of propitiating the bad being, and implies that formal offerings were made to him—such a thing as has never been the product of Israelitish soil, and could scarcely spring up there, since such an embodying of error contradicts fundamental principles among the Israelites respecting the being of Jehovah, which indeed allows the existence of no other power with itself. And finally, there exists here a peculiar trait, which, in our opinion, makes it certain that there is an Egyptian reference, namely, the circumstance that the goat was sent to Azazel into the desert. The special residence of Typhon was in the desert, according to the Egyptian doctrine, which is most intimately connected with the natural condition of the country. There, accordingly, is Azazel [1] placed in our passage, not in the belief that this was literally true, but merely symbolically.[2]

[1] Compare "Theologische Studien und Kritiken," Erstes Heft 1843, S. 191 and 2, and "Bibl. Repository" for July 1842, p. 116 seq.

[2] To the theory propounded and ably sustained in this section, there are several important objections, which deserve to be attentively considered. There are no names of angels in the Pentateuch, and the existence of evil angels, unless this passage be an exception, is nowhere mentioned in the Mosaic writings. If Azazel be the proper name of a demon supposed to reside in the wilderness, and if Leviticus xvi. 8 must be rendered, "Aaron shall cast lots upon the two goats, one lot for Jehovah, and the other for Azazel," it would follow that Moses taught one of the worst

NUMBERS, Chap. XIX.

In the law concerning the manner of purifying those who have defiled themselves with the dead, in Num. xix., it is said, verse 2, "Speak to the children of Israel, that they bring thee a red features of Demonolatry, that which consists in the worship, or, at least, the sacrificial propitiation of an evil being, from which the whole course of his legislation is abhorrent. The Septuagint, like our version, renders the word "scape-goat," ἀποπομπαῖος; Symmachus ἀπερχόμενος, and Aquila ἀπολελύμενος; the Vulgate similarly has *emissarius*, and most of the lexicographers derive עֲזָאזֵל *Azazel* from עֵז *ez*, "a goat," and אֵל *azal*, "to go away." To this received interpretation Gesenius makes two objections, first, that עֵז *ez* signifies only "a she-goat," and secondly, that the phrase "for the scape-goat," is a broken antithesis in relation to the preceding clause. On examining the passages where עֵז *ez* occurs, we can find no reason for limiting its gender, (see Gen. xxvii. 9, and Deut. xiv. 4,) and the cognate word in the other Semitic dialects is applied indifferently to goats, whether male or female. The harshness of the antithesis has been noticed by many commentators, and some of the Rabbins have proposed to render the passage, "one lot for the Lord, and the other lot for the desert." This however does not mend the matter; and, besides, we are driven to derive the signification of עֲזָאזֵל *Azazel*, from an Arabic plural of very remote affinity. A further objection to this rendering is, that it would lead to the conclusion that this sacrifice was only to be offered during the wanderings of the Israelites in the desert, but the whole current of Rabbinical tradition shows that it continued during the whole Jewish polity. Dr Hengstenberg justly remarks, that the later Jews, as well as the Christians and Mohammedans, speak of an evil angel named Azazel; but he ought to have mentioned, that this imaginary being belongs to the legends of Persian or Chaldean origin, which the Jews learned during the Babylonian captivity. According to the tale, Azazel was one of the Sinus, taken prisoner when the angels waged war against these imaginary beings; he was brought up among the conquerors, and educated in their knowledge, but when required by the Creator to worship Adam, he not only refused but headed a revolt in heaven; being conquered and banished, he received the name of Ebbo from his *despair*. In this legend there is nothing to identify Azazel with a demon of the desert, or with any fiction of Egyptian mythology, and therefore, instead of supporting Dr Hengstenberg's theory, it gives presumptive evidence against it.

But there is what we think a decisive proof that the Septuagint, the

heifer without spot, wherein is no blemish, and upon which never came yoke."

The inquiry whether an Egyptian reference is prominent here, must depend upon the significance of the *red colour* demanded by the law. For, that this is not without significance, we consider as evident without argument. "As repects the red colour," *Bähr* [1] correctly says, "this is nowhere else demanded for an animal offering or in general even any determinate colour, so much the less then can it be doubted that its determination in this case is intentional." That the colour here must have a significance, has at all times been generally acknowledged, although it has been declared difficult, and in some respects impossible to fully determine its import; as, for example, the old Rabbins said, that not even Solomon knew why the heifer must be of red, to the exclusion of all other colours.[2]

We maintain that the red colour of the heifer serves to characterize it as a sin-offering. We adduce the following arguments in proof of this assumption:

1. Isaiah i. 18 shows undeniably that the *red* colour in the symbolic language of the Scriptures denotes sin: "Though your sins be as scarlet, they shall be as white as snow; though they be red like crimson, they shall be as wool." The context, verse 15, "Your hands are full of blood," verse 21, "and now murderers," shows at once on what this significance rests, namely, on the fact that in the shedding of innocent blood their sin was consummated.

2. According to this interpretation, both the designated peculiarities of the beast for sacrifice grow up from one and the same root; as a sin-offering, it is at the same time a *female* and *red*. The answer to the question why a heifer must here be offered,

---

Vulgate, and the English version, have rightly interpreted the passage, namely, that an offering analogous to that of the scape-goat is elsewhere enjoined in the Levitical law. At the purification of a leper, two clean birds were offered, one of which was sacrificed, and the other let loose into the open field. T.

[1] Symb. 2. S. 498.

[2] Compare also Witsius, Aeg. 115: At quæ tandem causa dici potest cur, cum in cæteris sacrificiis omnibus sine colorum discrimine munda animantia rite offerrentur, solam hanc lustralem vaccam rubram esse necesse fuerit?

while in Lev. iv. 14 the rule is laid down that each sin-offering for the whole congregation shall be a bullock, lies manifestly in the phrase הִוא חַטָּאת, it is a sin-offering, literally, it is sin, in verse 9 and verse 17. Since sin in Hebrew is of the feminine gender, so must the animal also be which bears its image, which representing it shall atone for it.

3. According to this explanation, the red colour of the heifer corresponds accurately with the scarlet, with which and cedar wood and hyssop her ashes are to be mingled. That also this designates sin, is evident from Isa. i. 18, already quoted, which must be considered as an approved interpretation.[1] *Bähr*[2] exerts himself in vain to show that in Hebrew the scarlet is the symbol of life. He has not adduced in favour of it the semblance of a proof. Let it not be said that the scarlet cannot, on account of its union with cedar and hyssop, be a symbol of sin. This connection, which occurs once besides in the directions for purifying the leprous person, in Lev. xiv. 4, may be explained as follows: The key for the interpretation of cedar and hyssop, which are not to be separated from one another, as *Bähr*[3] has done, but must be considered in connection, as they never appear singly, is furnished by 1 Kings v. 13, (iv. 33): "From the cedar upon Lebanon, even to the hyssop that springeth out of the wall." The cedar, as the loftiest among created things,—hence the cedars in Scripture are the cedars of God, Ps. lxxx. 11, (10),—symbolizes his elevation and majesty; the hyssop, on the contrary, as the least, his lowliness and condescension, which David celebrates in Ps. viii.[4] In the cedar and the hyssop, both the divine qualities are represented which are exercised in the atonement and forgiveness of sin; his majesty, which gives the right and power,—and his lowliness and compassionate love, which ensures the will. The scarlet represents the object with reference to which both these divine qualities are exercised, the occasion for which they are displayed.[5]

---

[1] The שְׁנִי תוֹלַעַת in Num. xix. is in Isaiah separated: שָׁנִים is in the first clause, and תּוֹלָע in the second.

[2] Symbol. 1. S. 334 ff.

[3] II. p. 503. [4] Compare Ps. xviii. 36.

[5] Grotius was substantially in the right way of explaining this rite, when he remarked upon Lev. xiv.: Superbiam cedrus significat, vermiculus, sive coccinum peccatum, et hyssopus oppositam virtutem, ταπεινο-

4. The reference of the red colour to sin, is in accordance with the spirit of the whole rite, described in Num. xix. Every thing in it points to the fact, that the consciousness of sin unfolds itself in death, the image and recompense of sin.[1] The whole has the remembrance of sins, ἀνάμνησις ἁμαρτιῶν, Heb. x. 3, for its object. Since the sin-offering here represents sin, and is designed to awaken the consciousness of the odiousness of sin for itself, it cannot be slain in the holy place like all other offerings, but this must rather be done out of the camp. While in other cases of sin-offering for the people, the blood was sprinkled seven times before the vail,[2] it was here from without the camp, sprinkled only in the direction of the vail.[3] The whole animal was burned, and not even a part of it was laid on the altar, as in the case of other sin-offerings for the congregation. The ceremony, notwithstanding its importance, was not performed by the high-priest himself, who must not defile himself, but by the oldest of his sons; and even he performed only that which must necessarily be done by a priest; all the rest was executed by persons who were not priests. All the persons employed were defiled, even the water of purification polluted the clean person. The clean man who performed the purification was, in consequence of doing this, impure until evening, and must then wash his garments and bathe himself; according to verse 21, every person who touched the water of purification was unclean.

ροσύνην. He erred only in making the sinner, instead of God, the possessor of the attributes represented by cedar and hyssop. Bähr says, Th. 2. S. 503: "Purifying power is ascribed to the hyssop in Ps. li. 9. But why? it is asked, and this question cannot be answered from the passage itself, but from the 'locus classicus' to which David the same as expressly refers. If *it* is correctly understood, this verse of Ps. li. also appears in its true light. It is the condescending love and pity of God in which David takes refuge, when he desires to be purged with hyssop.

[1] This appears so much the more as such, when we take into account the immediate occasion of this law. "Occasionem praebente," remarks Deyling, Obss. Sac. p. 73, " pollutorum multitudine in castris Israelitarum qui ex cadaveribus seditiosorum cum Korah tumultum contra Mosem excitaret, contaminati erant." Yet, in this case, the general import of death is only shown in a particular conspicuous manner. That, according to the Israelitish view, death generally is considered as the image and recompense of sin, is shown by Gen. ii. 17 and iii. 19.

[2] Lev. iv. 17.   [3] Bähr. S. 501.

THE RED COLOUR DESIGNATES SIN.

These are the reasons which declare in favour of our interpretation. But the following objection is raised against it. It can scarcely be conceived how that by which sin is to be removed can itself be characterized as sin. "Indeed all sin-offerings are themselves considered as something most holy after death, so that they can be eaten only by holy persons, by priests." Every thought of sin is here especially excluded by the phrase, "a perfect one in which is no blemish, and on which yoke never came."

The most simple and natural answer to this objection is this: If the heifer could be called *sin*, (the word חַטָּאת means literally only this, not sin-offering,) its colour could as well, at least, symbolize the same thing. When the symbol, thus interpreted, is explained as inappropriate, the *name* is also, and the way is closed against its justification. Farther, the same antithesis which is considered as inadmissable in the qualifications of the heifer, and which it is attempted to exclude, are seen everywhere throughout the whole rite, so that nothing is gained, if it is forcibly excluded here. As the purifying power which exists in the ashes of the offering corresponds with the declaration, "a perfect one, and in which is no blemish," and is founded on this quality; so the fact that all who come in contact with the animal and his ashes are defiled, is in accordance with the character of sin expressed by the gender and colour.

If we go back to the idea of substitution, which lies at the basis of all sin-offerings, the twofold character which is carried through the whole rite is explained. The substitution at once requires two things: original purity and imputed impurity, or natural sinlessness and assumed sinfulness. The union of both appears most conspicuous in the antitype of all sin-offerings, in Him whom, when he knew no sin, God made to be sin for us.[1]

---

[1] Compare Deyling. Obss. Sac. p. 78 : " Hæc enim vacca, quæ תְּמִימָה, ab omni macula esse debebat immunis, ob suscepta tamen inquinamenta populi immundissima facta est, quid aliud significavit, quam Christum. Hunc enim μὴ γνόντα ἁμαρτίαν deus ὑπὲρ ἡμῶν ἁμαρτίαν ἐποίησεν, ἵνα ἡμεῖς γινώμεθα δικαιοσύνη θεοῦ ἐν αὐτῷ," 2 Cor. v. 21. The twofold nature with belongs to sin-offerings generally, and specially to this one, is explained with substantial correctness by Spencer, p. 503 : " E legis usa factum est, ut animalia omnia ad peccatum et immunditiem tellendam seposita, puritatem quidem offerentibus, maximam autem immunditiem sibi ipsis conciliarent : prout aqua ad manus a sordibus purgandas usurpata lavanti quidem

It might be further objected, that it is inadmissable to understand here, that in the gender and colour of the animal sin is signified, while in other sin-offerings the quality common to them with this is *not* symbolized in this way. But this objection is entirely without force, since the feminine gender and red colour are peculiar to this case. But only in accordance with our view can an appropriate explanation of the peculiarity of this case be given. Since sin was here made so specially prominent a thing, and was even symbolized by gender and colour, as is done in no other case, it is clear that this uncleanness was the greatest of all, that the lawgiver aimed at awakening a just abhorrence of death, and accordingly of sin, whose type and penalty it is. In it is also shown, in the most striking manner, that we are dead through trespasses and sins, νεκροὶ τοῖς παραπτώμασι καὶ ταῖς ἁμαρτίαις.[1]

If it be now established, that the red heifer was a type of sin, we have a remarkable parallel from Egyptian antiquity. "In the symbolic colours, as arranged by the Egyptians," says *Drumann*, in the passage before quoted, "black was the colour of death and mourning, for slaughter and its author the red colour was chosen." *Herodotus*[2] says, the animals designated for sacrifice were among the Egyptians accurately examined beforehand, and if only one black hair was found on the bullock, it was proved unsuitable for offering. What *Plutarch*[3] says in his book on Isis and Osiris, performs the office of a commentary on this passage. We see from it, that the animals offered must be throughout entirely *red:* " The Egyptians, since they suppose that Typhon is of a red complexion, devote to him red bullocks, and they in-

munditiem affert, dum interim puritatis propriæ jacturam patitur. Ille, cui hircum piacularem dimittendi provincia demandata est et sacerdos qui juvencum pro expiatione combussit, immundi facti sunt, nec iis ad sanctuarium aditus concessus, donec vestes et corpora abluissent ; eo quod populi immunditiæ in animalia illa, prout corporis sordes in aquam purgatricem transire atque adhærere crederentur." Pfeiffer expresses himself still more definitely, Dubia Vex. p. 290 : " Polluebat mundos, quia imputative erat piaculum sive catharma, præfigurans Christum, pro nobis factum; κατάραν. Gal. iii. 13 ; 2 Cor. v. 21. Mundabat vero ῥαντισμός aquæ, ejus cinere et quasi pulverisato sanguine mistæ pollutos, designans ῥαντισμὸν sanguinis Christi nos ab omnibus peccatis mundantis et expiantis."

[1] Eph. ii. 1, 5 ; Col. ii. 13. [2] B. 2, c. 38. [3] P. 363, A.

stitute so close an inspection of them, that they consider the animal unfit for sacrifice if a single black or white hair is found on him." Besides, says *Plutarch*, the Egyptians celebrated certain feast days, on which they, in order to revile and disgrace Typhon, abused men who had red hair. *Diodorus*,[1] of Sicily, says, in ancient times the Egyptians offered men, who like Typhon had red hair, at the tomb of Osiris.

Now, the choice of red colour to designate the evil and the base is not certainly arbitrary. It depends in all probability among the Egyptians, as among the Hebrews, upon the fact that red is the colour of blood.[2] Thence it might be supposed that both of these nations came, independently of one another, to one and the same symbolic designation. With reference to this, it is proper to remark further, that these two are the only nations among whom red is found as a fixed and nationally recognised designation of evil, and that the connection of the colour with the thing designated is a looser one, than, for example, in the case of white as the colour of innocence, and black as the colour of mourning, then also, it may be added, that among both these nations this symbolic view obtains influence directly upon the offering of sacrifices, among the Israelites only in particular cases, but among the Egyptians generally. If we take this into consideration, a dependence of one of these nations upon the other will appear very probable, and then we can decide for ourselves whether the origin of the symbolic designation was not among the Egyptians.

Finally, it is evident from the foregoing remarks, that the Egyptian reference in Num. xix. by no means respects the whole rite, but is a very partial one; it is limited to the identity of the symbolic import of the red colour, to which may perhaps also be added, that the colour has an influence in the choice of the

---

[1] 1. 88.

[2] According to Bähr, Symbol. Th. 2. S. 234, Typhon has the red colour, "as the personified burning heat, which dries up the fertilizing Nile, and scorches every thing." But no proof for this derivation of the red colour is adduced. We could quote in our favour Goulianof, who in the Archéologie Eg. Leipz. 1839, t. 3. p. 89 seq. has a separate section entitled: Etude des allegories de la couleur rouge, in which it is attempted to show, that red as the colour of blood is the colour of impiety. Compare the section, p. 422, seq.: Etude des allég. attaches a la couleur pourpre ou écarlate. But we do not consider l ·ority.

victim.[1] There is no direct authority for finding, with **Spencer**,[2] who has followed *Thomas Aquinas* and *Du Voisin*, in the choice of the heifer instead of the bullock, which on other occasions was taken, a reference, and indeed a hostile one, to an Egyptian custom,—he supposes the designation of the heifer for an offering of purification is a practical derision of the Egyptian notion of the sacredness of the cow,—since the choice of the heifer is sufficiently explained by the reasons already given, without such a reference. Yet it may be remarked, that the position taken by us, by no means excludes the reference claimed by *Spencer*, but, on the other hand, both may very easily be reconciled. If the heifer was chosen instead of the bullock commonly offered, in order to designate it as impersonated sin, there would even in this be found the strongest opposition to the Egyptian notion of the sacredness of the cow.

LAWS WITH REFERENCE TO FOOD.

The Egyptians and the Israelites stand alone among the nations of antiquity, in reference to the great care which they bestowed upon the selection of food. Among both, regulations of this kind had extensive influence. Through these laws, some of the most important means of subsistence were either withdrawn, or at least made odious, as, for example, fish, which could not be

---

[1] Witsius, Aeg. p. 115, seeks to destroy the connection between the red bullock which was sacrificed by the Egyptians and the red heifer, by the following remarks: Aegyptii rufos boves immolabant non quod pretiosiores eos aut diis suis gratiores esse existimarent, sed ex odio et contemptu. Dictabant enim θύσιμον οὐ φίλον εἶναι θεοῖς. (Compare Schmidt, De Sacerdotibus et Sacrif. Aeg. Bähr, Symbol. Th. 2, S. 237.) But if the significance of the red colour of the heifer is correctly determined, this remark serves rather to bring both nearer each other.

[2] This author, p. 486, after he has referred to passages by which it is proved that the cow is considered sacred among the Egyptians, says: Cum itaque eo dementiae et impietatis prolapsi essent Aeg., ut vaccam tanto cultu studioque honorarent: deus vaccam multa cum cerimonia mactari voluit et lixivium ex illius ceneribus ad populi immunditias expurgandas confici; ut Aeg. vanitatem sugillaret et per hanc disciplinam, cum Aegypti more sensuque pugnantem, Israelite ad cultus illius vaccini contemptum atque odium sensim perducerentur.

eaten by the priests,[1] and the leguminous fruits.[2] How much the regulations which had reference to food influenced them in life, is best shown by the passages collected by *Spencer*.[3]

This fact indeed leads us to conjecture, that the Israelitish laws respecting food were not without an allusion to Egyptian customs. If no such thing is supposed, the coincidence perceived between the two nations appears very remarkable. That the admission of such a reference detracts from the dignity of the Israelitish law, no one should affirm. This depends wholly upon the manner in which the reference is understood. That a distinction of food originated very anciently, is indeed certain without argument, since the different nature of animals, in very many respects, speaks a language of signs, clear without reasoning to the allegorizing mind of antiquity. Thus, we find, even in the time of the flood,[4] the distinction made between the clean and unclean beasts and birds. But that a beginning merely was made so anciently, these same passages show, since there is not a trace of a distinction between the clean and unclean wild beasts found in them. Now in Egypt from these first elements a complete system was formed. The Mosaic code of laws found a people which was accustomed to a distinction of food of extensive application. In these circumstances it was natural,—which, in case the Israelites yet occupied the position of the patriarchs, would have been entirely unnatural,—that the laws of diet had reference, not merely to individual things, but that they extended into the whole province concerned, even to its furthest limits, and arranged all its parts with respect to the fundamental idea of the Israelitish religion. The fear of too great minuteness could not here have had any place, since the laws were made for a people accustomed to law, and its advantages and blessings would not be allowed to remain unenjoyed. Besides, if the ground had been left unoccupied, it would have been immediately seized upon, or rather retained in possession by the opposer, whom it was important to expel from the borders of the Israelitish jurisdiction in which he had already so strongly intrenched himself.

[1] See Herod. 2, 37. Plut. De Isid. et Os. p. 363.
[2] Larcher zu Herod. 2. S. 252 ff.
[3] Page 130. See also the wonderful passage of Porphyry, De Abstinentia, B. 4, c. 7.
[4] Gen. vii, 2, 3; viii, 20.

Not the existence alone of certain dietetic rules is common to the Egyptians and Israelites, but they also both agree in this, that these regulations have in them a religious-ethical significance. In respect to those of the Israelites, this could be denied, and a mere dietetic object asserted only in a time, which through its peculiar impiety has lost the key to those phenomena which take root on religious ground. From the reception of dietetic reasons merely, the designation of animals not to be eaten as unclean, an abomination, a terror, is not accounted for, neither is the founding of the prohibition, on the declaration that Israel " is a consecrated people to the Lord its God," nor this command, " its dead body you shall not touch." This permission, " To the stranger which is in thy gates mayest thou give it, that he may eat it, or thou mayest sell it to a stranger," is also explainable only on the supposition that the uncleanness was founded on symbolic reasons, which applied only to the Israelites. We have in Deut. xxiii. 18 (19), as good as an express declaration of the reason of the prohibition of certain kinds of food : " Thou shalt not bring the hire of a harlot and the price of a dog, i. e. (as appears from ver. 17 [18,]) of licentious men, into the house of the Lord." From which we see that the dog and other animals placed on an equality with it, as the representatives of moral uncleanness, were unclean. Indeed, in accordance with the general character of the law, it cannot be supposed to have a dietetic object. Moses would fall entirely below his station, if he here for the time acted as a mere guardian of health by appealing to the fears of the people.[1]

That also among the Egyptians the prohibitions of food rest on religious-moral grounds, cannot be doubted. They abstain from that food which stands in any supposed relation to Typhon, the evil principle ; and the reason of the hatred against certain animals lies, among them, above all in this, that they are considered the representatives and the physical manifestation of Typhon, as Typhoically infected. Thus they abstain, according to *Plutarch*,[2] from fish, because they come out of the sea, which belongs to the dominion of Typhon. The swine was hated by them,

---

[1] Besides, even Spencer argued against the dietetic view : "deum animalia nonnulla inter impura imposuisse, quae veterum gula non tantum salubria sed mensarum suarum delitias habuit," e. g. the hare.

[2] De Isid. p. 363.

on account of its filthy habits, as the incarnation of the unclean spirit. " In general," says *Plutarch*, " they consider all hurtful plants and animals, as well as all unfortunate events, as the acts of Typhon."[1] To the religious significance, a moral was joined. The representatives of Typhon, in the animal kingdom, were considered at the same time as symbols of the men devoted to him. " The guilty person," remarks *Champollion*,[2] " appears under the figure of huge swine, upon which is written, in great letters, ' gormandizing and gluttony,' without doubt the capital crime of the culprit, perhaps of a glutton of that time."

But together with this agreement between the Egyptian and the Israelitish regulations in respect to food, there is a very important difference, which is adapted to meet all apprehensions which might arise from a supposed too near contact of the two, and which fully excludes the supposition of a crude transferring of a heathenish institution. Among the Egyptians, the separation between the rational and irrational creation was removed,[3]

---

[1] Compare upon the relation in which unclean animals are placed to Typhon, Jablonski Panth. Aeg. 3. p. 67, 8.

[2] Briefe, S. 153.

[3] The notions of the Egyptians with regard to animals, were, many of them, strange and exceedingly ridiculous. Many of them were looked upon as deities, and worshipped, throughout the country. Others were mere emblems of the gods. Some were honoured as good, and others were execrated as bad. The same animal was venerated in one province, and served up, as a delicacy of the table, in another. Keepers, of both sexes, were appointed to take charge of the sacred animals, and a revenue was provided for the maintenance both of the keepers and the animals. This employment was considered particularly honourable, and was executed by persons of the first caste. While living, animals were treated with all the respect which belongs to the most honoured human beings ; and although they could neither understand nor enjoy them, were provided with all the luxuries and surrounded by all the comforts which wealth can bestow ; and when they died, they were lamented and embalmed as if they were most dear friends. Different authors have attempted to account for these facts in different ways. After enumerating several theories, *Wilkinson* (Manners and Customs, Second Series, Vol. II. p. 108) says : " It is therefore evident, that neither the benefits derived by man from the habits of certain animals, nor the reputed reasons for their peculiar choice as emblems of the gods, were sufficient to account for the reverence paid to many of those they held sacred. Some, no doubt, may have been indebted to the first-mentioned cause ; and, however little connection appears to subsist between these animals and the

and accordingly the uncleanness of animals was to them something indwelling and physical; a swine and a man given to excess, were entirely in a like manner the creatures of Typhon. The eating of the flesh of animals belonging to Typhon, introduced with it a Typhonic element into the one eating. Entirely otherwise was it, according to the divine law. At the very commencement of the Pentateuch, the limit between the rational and brute creation is strongly drawn. Man only has the image of God, and therefore he alone can properly be the subject of cleanness and uncleanness; and when mention is there made of these qualities in the animal kingdom, this can be only as a symbol and representative of that which belongs to the reasoning creation. On Jewish ground only, such laws respecting food could find place, and notwithstanding their formal abrogation, they will for substance always exist.

THE INSTITUTION OF THE HOLY WOMEN.

An Egyptian reference is undeniable in the Israelitish institution of the holy women. The first and principal passage upon it is in Exod. xxxviii. 8, "And he made the laver of brass, and its foot of brass, of the mirrors of the female servants who served at the gate of the tabernacle of the congregation." That the insti-

---

gods of whom they were the types, we may believe that the ox, cow, sheep, dog, cat, vulture, hawk, Ibis, and some others, were chosen from their utility to man. We may also see sufficient reasons for making some others sacred, in order to prevent their being killed for food, because their flesh was unwholesome, as was the case with certain fish of the Nile,—a precaution which extended to some of the vegetables of the country. But this will not account for the choice they made in many instances; for why should not the camel and horse have been selected for the first, and many other common animals and reptiles for the last mentioned reason? There was, as Porphyry observes, some other hidden motive, independent of these; and whether it was, as Plutarch supposes, founded on rational grounds, (with a view to promote the welfare of the community,) on accidental or imaginary analogy, or on mere caprice, it is equally difficult to discover it, or satisfactorily to account for the selection of certain animals, as the exclusive types of particular deities."

tution did not probably end with the Mosaic period, but rather continued through the whole period of the kings, we see from 1 Sam. ii. 22, where, among the great crimes of the sons of Eli, it is mentioned that they defiled the women which served at the gate of the tabernacle.

An inquiry concerning the nature of this institution was instituted in the Contributions, and we will insert what was there said here.

The service before the door of the tabernacle of the congregation, is designated as the employment of these women. צָבָא signifies military service. Figuratively it stands, therefore, for the *militia sacra* of the priests and Levites, Num. iv. 23, 35, 43. viii. 25. Their leader and standard-bearer is the God of Israel. In addition to the sacred host composed of men, there appears in our passage a corresponding one consisting of women; and the manner in which it is spoken of, shows that it was a general, important, and formally organized institution. The expression in the passages referred to, does not imply, that they had external service at the tabernacle—only by an inapposite reference to the German use of the word service (Dienen), has this idea been found in it—and it must be altogether doubtful whether they were so employed. Neither the law nor history give any information of the service of the women at the tabernacle in this sense.

That the ancient Jews did not understand that any such occupations were implied in our passage, that it, on the contrary, has reference to spiritual service, to offices which have direct reference to the worship of God which the women were occupied with at the sanctuary, is shown by the paraphrase of the Alexandrian translators, who substitute for ' service,' ' fasting,' ἐκ τῶν κατόπ-τρων τῶν νηστευσασῶν, ἃι ἐνήστευσαν, as well as by that of Onkelos, who, in remarkable agreement with these, translates the same word by ' to pray.' Aben-Ezra understands it in the same way: " They came daily to the tabernacle to pray, and to hear the words of the law." But of special importance for understanding what this service was, is the third passage upon the institution of the holy women, which shows that it continued even to the time of Christ. It is found in Luke ii. 37, where it is said of Anna, " Who departed not from the temple, but served God with *fastings* and *prayers* night and day." The relation of this passage to Exod. xxxviii. 7, is the more distinct if we compare it with the translation of the Seventy and of Onkelos. If we take these into the account, we shall also find a reference to the Jewish institution in 1 Tim. v. 5, " Now she that is a widow indeed, and desolate, trusteth in God, and continueth in supplications and prayers night and day," a reference which implies that the service of the women was not performed with the hands but with the heart.

This institution had a strictly ascetic character. This is evident from the fact—in connection with Exod. xxv. 1, where Moses is required to take from the Israelites free-will offerings for the construction of the sanctuary, " from every one whose heart moves him shall ye take my offering,"[1]—that the article which the holy women gave was their looking-glasses, their means of pleasing the world. This giving up of the use of the mirror is of the same nature as the leaving of the hair to grow in the case of the Nazarites, by which they gave a practical demonstration that they, for the time in which this was done, renounced the world, in which the cutting of the hair belongs to the proprieties of social life, so that they might serve God only. The new use to which Moses devoted the mirrors, also indicated that the offering of them had this significance. This gives, in addition to the negative, the positive reason. Not for the world, but for God, ought we to adorn ourselves, and seek to please him alone.[2]

That women of rank devoted themselves to the Lord, is evident indeed from the nature of the case,—where such a way is once opened, it will be trodden by more in proportion of the higher than of the lower order of people—and it is also especially evident from the mention which is made of the mirror. Metal mirrors were, as even the fact that they were offered shows, an article of luxury, and they are represented as such also in the third chapter of Isaiah.

That the institution has an Egyptian reference, is very probable without argument, from the circumstance that it was, in all probability, not introduced by Moses by a law, but was found by him as an already existing institution. It evidently arose of itself, from the Israelitish manner of life; and since this stood under manifest Egyptian influences, we should expect to find an analo-

---

[1] Compare Ex. xxxviii. 24, seq. and Num. vii.   [2] 1 Peter iii. 3, 4.

gous Egyptian institution, after which the Israelitish one was, in form, copied, whilst the spirit of both institutions must necessarily be as different as the service of the Holy One of Israel, from the natural religion of the Egyptians.

This expectation is accordingly entirely realized. Among classical writers, *Herodotus* first mentions the holy women among the Egyptians. He [1] says, " Concerning the two oracles, namely, among the Greeks and in Lybia, the Egyptians gave me the following account: The priests of Jupiter at Thebes said that two holy women (literally priestesses) were carried away from Thebes by the Phoenicians, and they had learned that one of them was sold in Lybia, and the other in Greece. And these women were the first founders of the oracles among these people." Further, it is said: " If the Phoenicians really carried away the holy women," and: " As was natural, she who ministered at Thebes in the temple of Jupiter was mindful of him in the place to which she came." [2] Besides, *Herodotus* also [3] alludes to the institution of the holy women in Egypt in other places. " In the temple (of Belus at Babylon) there stands a great couch beautifully spread, and near it is placed a table of gold. But there is no image there, and no mortal passes the night there, except sometimes one native-born woman, whoever, as the Chaldeans say, the god chooses from all who are his priests. These same Chaldeans relate also, but I do not believe them, that the god comes sometimes into the temple and sleeps upon the bed, just as the Egyptians relate of Thebes, for there also a woman sleeps in the temple of the Theban Jupiter. Both these women, they say, never have intercourse with man. So also at Patara in Lycia, there is a chief priestess of the god when he is there, for there is not always an oracle at this place, but when he is there, she is shut up at night with him in the temple."

Diodorus [4] of Sicily, speaks of "the concubines of Jupiter," that is, of Amon. *Strabo* [5] says: " But to Jupiter, whom they most honour, a very beautiful and noble young woman is devoted, whom they call the Grecian Pallas: but this one has intercourse with whatever men she wishes until she arrives at the age of

---

[1] B. 2. c. 54.
[2] B 1. c. 181, 2.
[3] B. 17. 1171.
[4] B. 2. c. 56.
[5] B. 1. 47.

womanhood. After that she is married. But before her marriage there is a lamentation made for her. What *Strabo* here says of the impurity of the young women devoted to Amon, rests without doubt upon the misunderstanding of the expression, "the concubines of Amon." *Herodotus* gives us a contrary account: "These women are said never to have intercourse with a man," and in another place, he says that among the Egyptians impurity is excluded from the circuit of the holy places, in which these women had their abode.[1]

The monuments confirm the accounts of classical writers.[2] The data which they furnish are found collected in *Wilkinson*,[3] where there is also an engraving[4] of the holy women given, and in *Rosellini*,[5] according to whom these young women bore the title of "bride of God." See also *Minutoli's*[6] Travels, where it is said in the innermost part of the temple at Carnac, "near the king and the priests, maidens are also seen represented."

The characteristic peculiarities in which the Israelitish agrees with the Egyptian institution of the holy women, are the following: 1. Among the Israelites, as among the Egyptians, the holy women, with all the respect which they enjoy, still are not priest-

---

[1] The declaration of Strabo concerning the impurity of the holy women is confuted also by Rosellini, I. 1. p. 216, and Wilkinson, Vol. I. p. 259.

[2] Mr *Wilkinson*, in his Manners and Customs, Second Series, I. p. 203, says of the sacred women among the Egyptians : "That certain women, of the first families of the country, were devoted to the service of the god of Thebes, is perfectly true, as I have had occasion already to remark ; and they were the same whom Herodotus mentions under the name of γυναῖκας ἱρητας, or 'sacred women, consecrated to the Theban Jove.' The statement of Diodorus, that their sepulchres were distant from the tomb of Osymandyas ten stadia, or little more than 6000 feet, agrees perfectly with the position of those where the Queens and princesses were buried, in the Necropolis of Thebes ; and is highly satisfactory, from its confirming the opinion formed from the sculptures respecting the office they held. For though we are unable to ascertain the exact duties they performed, it is evident that they assisted in the most important ceremonies of the temple, in company with the monarch himself, holding the sacred emblems which were the badge of their office ; and the importance of the post is sufficiently evinced by the fact that the wives and daughters of the noblest families of the country, of the high-priests, and of the kings themselves, were proud to enjoy the honour it conferred."

[3] Vol. I. p. 258 seq.

[4] P. 260.

[5] I. 1. p. 216.

[6] S. 181.

esses; among both the priesthood belongs only to the men. What Herodotus mentions in B. 2. c. 35, as a distinguishing peculiarity of the Egyptians, "A woman never performs the office of a priest for a god or goddess,"[1] applies also accurately *mutatis mutandis*, to the Israelites.

2. That the holy women among the Israelites had no external service in the tabernacle of testimony, that their service was rather a spiritual one, we have already seen. Just so is it among the Egyptians. That their holy women were not, as *Bähr*[2] supposes, servants of the priests, (hierodulen) is sufficiently proved by the quotations from *Herodotus*.[3] He says, indeed, that they *served* the temple of Jupiter at Thebes.[4] But that their service, just as in Ex. xxxviii., is to be understood as spiritual service, the account shows, since these Egyptian women are supposed to have founded the oracles of Greece and Lybia. If they served Jupiter in these countries by foretelling future events, they were also employed in a similar manner in their father-land.

3. That also among the Israelites, noble women especially were devoted to the service of the temple, was previously shown. Just so was it among the Egyptians. According to *Strabo*,[5] the most beautiful and the most noble maidens were devoted to Jupiter or Amon. *Wilkinson* says, whilst speaking of the tombs of the holy women described by *Diodorus*, which are now seen at Thebes in a valley 3000 feet behind the ruins of Medeenet Haboo: "The sculptures show that they were women of the highest rank, since all the occupants of these tombs were either the wives or daughters of kings." *Rosellini*[6] says: "We shall find in the sequel, also, other examples of royal young maidens devoted to Amon, from which it may be inferred, that it was a custom in the earliest period of the Pharaohs to place by this rite some of the king's daughters in a nearer relation to religion."

4. That the holy women among the Israelites were always unmarried, either young women or widows, has been shown in the

---

[1] Ἱρᾶται γυνὴ μὲν οὐδεμία οὔτε ἔρσενος θεοῦ οὔτε θηλέης, ἄνδρες δὲ πάντων τε καὶ πασέων.

[2] Zu Herod. B. 2. c. 54.   [3] B. 2. c. 54-56.

[4] Ὥσπερ ἦν οἶκός, ἀμφιπολεύουσαν ἐν Θήβῃσι ἱρὸν Διός, ἔνθα ἀπίκετο, ἐνθαῦτα μνήμην αὐτοῦ ἔχειν.

[5] Εὐειδεστάτη καὶ γένους λαμπροτάτου παρθένος.

[6] P. 217.

Contributions.[1] Just so also is it with the holy women among the Egyptians. According to *Herodotus*[2] the brides of Amon were excluded from all intercourse with men.[3] According to *Strabo* the most beautiful and noble young women were devoted to Jupiter, and when they wished to marry, there was previously a great lamentation made for them as for one dead.[4]

THE NAZARITES.

From the institution of the holy women we turn to that of the Nazarites. We must naturally expect an Egyptian reference more or less distinct here also. For the institution of the Nazarites originated, not by the appointment of the lawgiver, but it is implied, in Num. chap. vi., as an existing institution, and is there only sanctioned.

But if we examine the matter more closely, we perceive indications of Egyptian influence, yet it is less conspicuous here than in the institution of the holy women. For the institution in general, Egypt furnishes no parallel. An Egyptian reference can be pointed out for only a single feature of the system, the leaving of the hair to grow, and that is one which has no connection with religion, but with the customs of the people. Finally, the single allusion to Egypt, although truly worthy of notice, is still not so characteristic that we could with full certainty assert its existence.

It is necessary for our purpose, that we first determine the significance of leaving the hair unshorn by the Nazarite. We begin with an examination of the view of *Bahr*.[5] The obligation of the Nazarite, he asserts, to let the hair grow freely, has its basis in

---

[1] Th. III. S. 142-3.   [2] B. 1. c. 182.

[3] Καὶ γὰρ δὴ ἐκεῖθι κοιμᾶται ἐν τῷ τοῦ Διὸς τοῦ Θεβαιέος γυνή· ἀμφότεραι δὲ αὖται γέλονται ἀνδρῶν οὐδάμων ἐς ὁμιλίην φοιτᾶν.

[4] Πρὶν δὲ δοθῆναι, πένθος αὐτῆς ἄγεται μετὰ τὸν τῆς παλλακείας καιρόν. This lamentation, on leaving this community, agrees remarkably with the mourning of the daughter of Jephtha when she entered it. In both cases it depends upon the view of the exclusiveness of the relation.

[5] Symbol. Th. 2. S. 432.

the idea of holiness. Among the orientals, and especially among the Hebrews, the hair of the head is the same as the products of the earth, the grass of the field, and the growth of the trees. Especially in accordance with this is the naming of the vine in the year of jubilee, נָזִיר (nazyr), in Lev. xxv. 5, since they prune it not this year, but allow its leaves and branches to grow freely. From this it is evident, that the growth of the hair, according to oriental view, signifies grass, shoots, blossoms of men. But in so far as the Hebrew looked upon men as distinctively moral beings, the human blossoms and shoots represent holiness.

This view is by no means new; but it is discarded by all judicious investigators, as mere mystical refinement. The following reasons are especially decisive against it.[1]

1. The proofs which are brought for the position, that according to oriental and especially Israelitish views, the growth of the hair is a symbol for the thriving condition of man, are very weak. The one derived from Lev. chap. xxv. is the only one which is worth the trouble of a closer examination. It is there said of the sabbatical year, in verse 5: "The grain which groweth of its own accord thou shalt not reap, and the grapes of thy undressed vines (nazarites) thou shalt not gather, a year of rest is it for the land," after that it had been said before in verse 4, "Thy field thou shalt not sow, and thy vineyard thou shalt not prune." Then in v. 11, concerning the year of jubilee: "You shall not sow, neither reap that which groweth of itself, neither gather its nazarites."[2] It is not entirely certain, that there is a special reference in these passages to the leaving of the hair to grow in the case of the Nazarites.

The general idea of separation, which lies at the basis of the whole institution of the Nazarites, might here also apply. As the Nazarites were separated from the world, so was the vine from the

---

[1] Compare e. g. Carpzov. Appar. ad Antiq. p. 153: Ut eos taceam, qui mysticam commenti rationem, nutritionem capillamenti symbolum instituunt nutritionis interioris, quo Abarbanel in h. l. et Gregorius, L. II. Moral. c. 26, tendit.

[2] Besides the establishment of the law in chap. vi. these passages also, in which before the giving of the law concerning the Nazarites allusion is made to them, show that the lawgiver found it as an existing institution.

use of man in the sabbatical year and the year of jubilee. But if we suppose a reference to the unshorn hair of the Nazarites, which the 'not gathering' and 'not pruning' in verses 4 and 5 favour, yet at any rate the point of comparison is only with respect to the separation. That the unpruned vine is not better, but worse, is decidedly against the opinion of *Bähr*. It shoots out in wood, and an injury is done to its true growth.[1] This is decisive against the opinion that the growth of the hair among the Israelites is a symbol of prosperity, namely, that it belongs to propriety among the Israelites to go with shorn hair, whereas, according to this view, long hair must have been considered an ornament, as among most nations of antiquity.[2]

2. The fundamental idea in the institution of the Nazarite is that of separation from the world, with its enjoyments, which oppose holiness, and its corrupting influences. This negative point of separation, involves the positive one of sanctification, the separate person is at the same time holy to the Lord,—since the world stands in opposition to the Lord, every renunciation of it is at the same time a union with the Lord, and the separation is here made directly for the sake of the Lord. That the idea of separation lies at the foundation, the name, by which the significance of the institution must be expressed, indicates.[3] נָזִיר (nazyr) means *the separate one*. Equally in favour of this idea is Num. vi. 2: "The vow of a Nazarite is for a separating to the Lord." This fundamental idea of the institution must be traceable in all of its separate points. That especially the command to leave the hair unshorn rests upon it, we have even the express explanation of the lawgiver. It is said in verse 5, "All the days of the vow of his separation, no razor shall come upon

---

[1] John xv. 2.

[2] Carpzov. p. 153: Communis inter priscos Judaeos mos ita tulit ut tonsis incederent capillis, secus ac Graeci veteres Romani, Galli aut Germani, qui comati erant. Compare, in reference to the consideration in which long hair was held among these nations, the collections by Lampe in the Miscell. Gröning. t. 4, p. 209, seq.

[3] Carpzov. p. 151: Haud dubia נָזִיר est a נָזַר, separavit, abstraxit, continuit se a re aliqua et propterea segregatum, separatum notat.— Satis omnino praesidio huic interpretationi est ex sede hujus instituti primaria, Num. vi. 2, ubi votam Nasaraei dicitur ad separandum se domino.

his head : until the days be fulfilled in which he separateth himself unto the Lord, he shall be holy ; he shall let the hair of his head grow." The separation is here given as a reason for allowing the hair to grow. Even the hair of the Nazarite is in verses 9 and 18 named נֵזֶר, *separation*, but with the accompanying idea of designation. Now, according to the view of *Bähr*, the idea of separation is entirely lost. The negative idea, which, as has been alleged, must form the foundation upon which the positive is supported, falls entirely away. Thereby then this element of the institution of the Nazarite will be entirely separated from both the others in which the negative idea, as can be demonstrated and is allowed, prevails.

At the same time with the view of *Bähr*, that which *Winer* (after the authority of *Lampe*,) has proposed, falls to the ground.[1] "The head of the Nazarite with its natural ornament was regarded as specially devoted, and the touching of it with a razor is consequently a profanation of that which belongs to Jehovah." The negative idea, according to this view, is also robbed of its just right. Long hair cannot, according to the notions of the Israelites, be considered as "a natural ornament."

The proof for the interpretation of the rite claimed by us, is given in the confutation of other views. We believe that long hair is a symbol of separation from the world. It belongs, as we have already seen, to the Israelitish ideas of propriety to go with shorn head,[2] and he who left his hair to grow, furnished by this act a practical confession that he renounced the world, and abandoned all intercourse with men. That also, on other occasions, those who considered themselves as separated from men suffered their hair to grow, is shown by Deut. xxi. 12, where, concerning the captive which an Israelite determined to marry, it is said : "And thou shalt bring her into thine house, and she shall shear her head and pare her nails." By shearing her head and paring her nails she enters again into human society.[3]

---

[1] In dem Reallexicon, II. 1, S. 165.

[2] Geier, De Hebr. Luctu, p. 203, correctly says : Israelitarum populum comatum haudquaquam fuisse vel inde colligi potest, quod comam alere proprium esset Nazaraeorum, adeo ut hi ipsi ab aliis popularibus facile internoscerentur ex coma.

[3] This passage shows very distinctly with what justice Bähr asserts, S. 437 : It was the Israelitish custom in mourning, not to allow the hair to

If the significance of leaving the hair unshorn is determined, the Egyptian reference in this rite lies on the surface. Indeed it must appear remarkable that the Israelites agree with the Egyptians, almost against the whole of the rest of the world, in considering short hair as belonging to social propriety.[1] Indeed, this agreement is explained most easily by the long-continued residence of the Israelites in Egypt. But it is a point of more importance, that among the Egyptians not less than among the Israelites, the temporary withdrawing from the world, the going out of society, was symbolized by leaving the hair to grow. We see this from Gen. xli. 14, according to which the captives in Egypt left their hair unshorn, and also from *Herodotus*, 2. 36: "The priests of the gods wear, in other lands, long hair; but in Egypt they cut it off; among other nations it is the custom to shear the beard when a relative dies. But when any of their friends die, the Egyptians leave the hair which was before cut, to grow both on the head and chin."

Whilst the proof that the leaving of the hair to grow, among the Nazarites, was a sign of separation, shows on the one hand that the rite stood in an external relation to Egyptian customs, it serves, on the other hand, for confuting the hypothesis of *Spencer*, concerning the heathenish origin of the whole rite. The cases in which the heathen devoted the hair of the head and the beard to their divinities, appears from this point of view as entirely different.

Our inquiries concerning the Egyptian references in the religious institutions of the books of Moses, are finished. It only remains now, in a last chapter, to collect together those things for which, until now, no suitable place has been found.

---

be long, but to cut it. The cutting of it must indeed be different from shaving, calvitium facere. Only the latter was the appropriate condition in mourning. Comp. Geier, De Hebr. Luctu. c. 8. § 6 and 7.

[1] Compare remarks upon Gen xli. 14, where we have shown that cutting the hair was considered as a distinguishing peculiarity of the Egyptians.

CHAPTER VII.

MISCELLANEOUS PASSAGES.

THE GENEALOGICAL TABLE IN GEN. X.

It has often been asserted that the genealogical table in Gen. x. cannot be from Moses; since so extended a knowledge of nations lies far beyond the geographical horizon of the Mosaic age. This hypothesis must now be considered as exploded. The new discoveries and investigations in Egypt have shown that they maintained, even from the most ancient times, a vigorous commerce with other nations, and sometimes with very distant nations. The proofs are found in *Creuzer*,[1] *Heeren*,[2] in my Contributions,[3] and in *Wilkinson*.[4] This last author, among other things, remarks, that the strongest proof for the commerce of the Egyptians with distant nations of Asia, is furnished by the materials out of which many of the articles in use in civil and domestic life, found in the tombs of Thebes, which belong to the 18th or 19th dynasty, are made in Egypt; for example, the vessels of wood, which are commonly made of foreign wood, and not seldom of the mahogany of India.

But not merely in general do the investigations in Egyptian antiquities favour the belief that Moses was the author of the account in this tenth chapter of Genesis. On the Egyptian monuments, those especially which represent the conquests of the ancient Pharaohs over foreign nations, (conquests which certainly were oftener achieved in imagination than in reality, as indeed the almost regular recurrence of these representations under nearly all the ancient Pharaohs shows, so that nothing can be more erroneous than the present popular way of relying upon them,

---

[1] Symb. Th. I. S. 319 ff.
[2] Th. 2, S. 451 ff.
[3] S. 275, 321 ff., 376 ff., 571 ff.
[4] Vol. 1. p. 164.

without inquiry, as sources of historical truth,) not a few names have been found which correspond with those contained in the chapter before us. We will here speak only of those where the agreement is perfectly certain. It must be allowed that far more still could be effected if our knowledge of hieroglyphics were not so very imperfect.[1]

Among the sons of Japheth, in verse 2, Meshech and Tiras are mentioned in close connection. Among the Asiatic nations which are represented on the monuments as engaged in war with the Egyptians, the Toersha also appear, according to *Wilkinson*.[2] They are shown, indeed, among the nations who are said to have been conquered by the third Remeses. Their identity with Tiras is the less doubtful, since another nation, the Mashoash, is named along with them. These last *Wilkinson*[3] designates as "another Asiatic nation who resemble the former in their general features and the shape of their beards." The agreement between Meshech and Tiras on the one side, and Mashoash and Toersha on the other, is the less exposed to suspicion since *Wilkinson* did not think to place both in connection, as indeed in general, the present attempt at comparing the names of the people represented on the monuments with those found in Gen. x., is the first.

Among the sons of Japheth, in the same verse, Javan, the Ionians or Greeks, is mentioned. According to *Rosellini*,[4] the Uoinim, the Ionians are found among others, in a symbolic painting, representing king Menephthah I., the 12th king of the 18th Dynasty, as in the sight of Amon-re he slays one individual of each of the conquered nations. These[5] same people were also mentioned on the monuments which belong to Thothmes V.[6]

Among the sons of Gomer, the son of Japhet, consequently as a Japhetic nation, Riphat is mentioned in verse 3, probably identical with the Pouônt or Pount, who are represented on the monuments as engaged in war with the Egyptians as early as the time of Amun-m-gori II., which the more recent chronologers place at about the year 1680 B. C.[7]

---

[1] Wilkinson, Vol. I. 377.
[2] Wilkinson, Vol. I. 378.
[3] Wilk., Vol. I. p. 379.
[4] Vol. III. 1. p. 425.
[5] Vol. III. 1. p. 426.
[6] P. 210.
[7] See Wilk. 1. 374.

Among the sons of Ham in verse 5, Cush is first mentioned. The Cush, according to *Wilkinson*,[1] are represented among the African people who are conquered by the monarchs of the eighteenth or nineteenth dynasty. " These," (the Cush,) he remarks, " were long at war with the Egyptians; and a part of their country, which was reduced at a very remote period by the arms of the Pharaohs, was obliged to pay an annual tribute to the conquerors."[2] According to *Rosellini*,[3] the victory of king Horus over the same people is represented on a monument at Selsilis. According to the same author,[4] they appear in the painting already referred to, among the nations conquered by Menephthah I. Eleven separate Cushite tribes are there mentioned in agreement with verse 7, according to which Cush is not the name of a separate tribe, but of several tribes belonging to one general family.

As the second son of Ham, the second Hamitish head of a family, Mizraim is mentioned. This name was, as the dual form signifies, originally the name of the land. The division of the land into the upper and lower regions to which it refers, appears on the monuments even in the most ancient times. In proof of this see *Wilkinson*[5] and *Champollion's* Letters,[6] where an inscription is quoted: " I give thee the upper and the lower Egypt, in order that you may rule over them as king."

According to verse 13, Mizraim was the progenitor among other nations, of the Lahabim and Naphtuhim. It serves for a confirmation of the statement, that the Lybians (the Lehabim) are an offshoot from the Egyptians, that they even to the time of the Ptolemies were considered a part of the Egyptians. *Champollion*[7] affirms, that he found Niphaiat (= Naphtuchim) on the monuments as a name of Lybian nations.

The Canaanites and Amorites (called Asmaori) are represented on the Egyptian monuments with Lemanon[8] (the people of Lebanon) and Ascalon.[9] The land Canaan is specifically named

---

[1] Vol. I. p. 387.
[2] III. 1. p. 277 seq.
[3] Vol. II. p. 73.
[4] See also Champollion Briefe, S. 105.
[5] P. 430.
[6] S. 140. [7] S. 124.
[8] *Wilkinson*, Vol. I. p. 62, says: "The common custom of substituting *m* for *b* in Coptic, and the representation of a mountainous and woody country in which the chariots could not pass, convince me that this is intended for mount Lobanon."
[9] Wilk. Vol. I. 385.

among the inscriptions upon a representation of the triumph of Menephtha I., together with the region of Nahareina or Mesopotamia and Singara or Sinear.[1] In reference to a representation of a campaign of Osirei, the father of Remeses the Great, *Wilkinson*[2] says: " The country of Lemanon is shown by the artist to have been mountainous, inaccessible to chariots, and abounding in lofty trees, which the affrighted mountaineers are engaged in felling, in order to impede the advance of the invading army. The Egyptian monarch, having taken by assault the fortified towns on the frontier, advances with the light infantry in pursuit of the fugitives who had escaped and taken refuge in the woods, and sending a herald to offer terms on condition of their surrender, the chiefs are induced to trust to his clemency and return to their allegiance, as are those of Canana, whose strongholds yield in like manner to the arms of the conqueror." It is readily seen from these representations with what justice an argument against the Pentateuch has been derived from the knowledge of Canana which its author exhibits.

" The sons of Shem," it is said in verse 22, " are Elam and *Asshur* and Arphaxad and *Lud* and Aram."

It is in the highest degree probable that Asshur appears on the monuments under the name Shari. That the Shari, who especially under the reign of Osirei and his son Remeses the Great, are represented as engaged in war with the Egyptians, are the Assyrians, is indicated not only by the name but by the similarity of dress between them and the captives of Tirhaka.[3]

The Ludim act a conspicuous part on the Egyptian monuments. In a representation of a triumph of Menephthah I. five foreign nations are found, the Romenen, the Scios, the people Ots from the land of Omar, the Tohen and the Sceto. All of these, with the exception of Ots, are represented in the inscriptions as belonging to the land of Ludim. And of the whole expedition it is repeatedly said, that it was directed against the people of the land of Ludim, which is in accordance with the book of Genesis, in which likewise Lud is not represented as a single tribe but as an entire nation. Since in these same inscrip-

---

[1] See Ros. III. 1. p. 437, also upon Canana, p. 341.
[2] Vol. I. p. 387.
[3] Wilk. I. p. 375-6. Compare also Champollion, S. 105.

tions the land of Canana is also named and the region of Nahareina and Singara, just as in Genesis Lud is closely connected with Aram, *Rosellini*[1] argues that the land Ludim lay in the neighbourhood of Canaan and Mesopotamia, and he asserts that it must be sought in the western part of Asia.

ABRAHAM AND SARAH IN EGYPT, GEN. xii.

In Gen. xii. 14, 15 it is said: " And it came to pass, that when Abraham came into Egypt, the Egyptians beheld the woman that she was very fair. The princes of Pharaoh also saw her and commended her before Pharaoh, and the woman was taken into Pharaoh's house."

Sarah must therefore have been unveiled.[2] The monuments show that, according to Egyptian customs, she could only so appear in public. " We find from the monuments," says *Taylor*,[3] " that the Egyptian women, in the reign of the Pharaohs, exposed their faces, and were permitted to enjoy as much liberty as the ladies of modern Europe. But this custom was changed after the conquest of the country by the Persians."

The recognition which Sarah's beauty finds is more easily ex-

---

[1] III. 1. p. 437-8.
[2] A passage from *Gliddon's* Ancient Egypt, p. 48, is worthy of insertion here, not only from the light which it throws upon this section and the one contained on pp. 25-6, but also from its general interest in relation to the state of society among the ancient Egyptians : " There was no *Salic* law in Egypt ; and in a country where *females* were admitted to a full participation in all legitimate privileges with man—where women were queens in their own right—royal priestesses from their birth ; and otherwise treated as females are, in all civilized and Christian countries, there were none of those social restrictions that elsewhere enslaved the minds, or constrained the persons of the gentler sex. We have the most positive and incontrovertible evidence, in a series of monuments coeval with Egyptian events for 2500 years, to prove that the female sex in Egypt was honoured, civilized, educated, and as free as among ourselves ; and this is the most unanswerable proof of the high civilization of that ancient people. This is the strongest point of distinction between the Egyptian social system of ancient times, and that of any other eastern nation. Even among the Hebrews, the Jewish female was never placed in relation to man, in the same high position as her more happy and privileged sister enjoyed in Egypt."
[3] P. 4.

plained, if we take into the account that the Egyptian women, although not so dark as the Nubians and Ethiopians, were yet of a browner tinge than the Asiatics. On the monuments the women of high rank, in compliment to them, were commonly represented with fairer complexions than their attendants.[1]

That Pharaoh is immediately thereupon ready to take Sarah into his harem, appears not to be consistent with Herodotus, B. 2, c. 92, according to which each Egyptian had only one wife.[2] But that *Herodotus* speaks only of the common practice among them, and that polygamy was there allowed by law, is shown by what *Diodorus*[3] says : " Among the Egyptians the priests marry only one woman, but the rest of the men, each one as many as he chooses." That polygamy was infrequent among the Egyptians, is evident from numerous representations of domestic life on the monuments.[4] But with their wives the noble Egyptians had also other inmates of the harem, which were sometimes merely servants and sometimes also concubines ; " most of them appear to have been foreigners, either taken in war or brought to Egypt to be sold as slaves."[5] Of this class are the women at Medeenet Haboo, attending upon Remeses, and not the wives of the monarch. The concubines were members of the family, and were in rank next to the wives and children of their lord. Without doubt Sarah was intended for such a station. Among the gifts which Abraham received from Pharaoh, male and female slaves are mentioned, in chap. xii. 16. " Domestic slavery," says *Taylor,*[6] " seems to have been established in Egypt from the earliest

---

[1] Ibid. p. 4. The passage to which Hengstenberg refers is as follows: An aggravation of Abraham's alarm arose from the complexion of his wife: "Thou art a fair woman." Though the Egyptian ladies were not so dark as the Nubians and Ethiopians, they were of a browner tinge than the Syrians and Arabians: we also find on the monuments, that ladies of high rank are usually represented in lighter tints than their attendants, though we occasionally find some as dark as that which we have copied ; but there is ample evidence that a fair complexion was deemed a high recommendation in the age of the Pharaohs. This circumstance, so fully confirmed by the monuments, is recorded in no history but the book of Genesis, and it is a remarkable confirmation of the veracity of the Pentateuch.

[2] This is clearly the meaning of the passage, and Bähr is entirely wrong in making it mean the opposite.

[3] 1. 80.   [4] Wilk. Vol. II. p. 62.   [5] Ibid. 64.   [6] P. 7.

ages, and we find from the monuments that the mistress of a mansion was very rigid in enforcing her authority over the female domestics. We see these unfortunate beings trembling and cringing before their superiors, beaten with rods by the overseers, and sometimes threatened with a formidable whip wielded by the lady of the mansion herself. Hagar was one of the female slaves obtained by Abraham at this time." See upon slavery among the Egyptians, *Wilkinson* :¹—" The Ethiopians were obliged to supply the Egyptians with slaves, which the Egyptians sometimes exacted even from the conquered countries of Asia."

GENESIS xiii. 10.

In Gen. xiii. 10, the author says the plain of the Jordan was everywhere well watered, " as the garden of the Lord (Paradise), like the land of Egypt." Less wonderful is it here that the author understands the natural condition of Egypt, than that just this same land presents itself to him directly as a means of comparison.²

---

¹ Vol. I. p. 388.
² There is no ancient nation in which horticulture received any thing like the same attention that it did in Egypt; the garden seems to have been an object of greater care than the house; in almost every representation of a banquet, we find that flowers were regarded as the chief ornaments, and fruits as the principal delicacies. While the operations of the farmer were confined to the brief seasons of sowing and harvest, the cares of the horticulturist appear to have been incessant. From the total disregard of perspective in the paintings and bas-reliefs, the representations of Egyptian gardens are very confused, and at first suggest very few ideas of beauty. A closer examination proves that their pleasure-grounds were laid out in what used to be called the Dutch style, which was so fashionable in England about a century ago. The flower-beds are square and formal ; the raised terraces run in straight lines ; arbours of trellis-work occur at definite intervals, covered with vines and other creepers, which it is difficult to identify. Some of the ponds are stored with water-fowl, and others with fish. Vegetables are depicted in great variety and abundance. It is indeed impossible to look at any representation of an Egyptian garden, without feeling some sympathy for the complaints and murmurings of the Israelites in the desert. " The children of Israel also wept again and said, Who shall give us flesh to eat ? We remember the fish, which we did eat in Egypt freely ; the cucumbers, and the melons, and the onions, and the garlick ; but now our soul is

EXODUS xx. 25.

In Exod. xx. 25, it is said, "And if thou wilt make me an altar of stone, thou shalt not build it of hewn stone; for if thou lift up thy tool upon it, thou hast polluted it." The preparation of hewn stone is represented in a tomb at Thebes—some workmen stand there smoothing the surfaces of a stone with chisels of different forms; others are examining to see whether it is perfectly square. The great skill of the Egyptians in the preparation of hewn stone, is one of the principal causes of the durability of the Egyptian monuments.[1]

THE FESTIVAL OF THE GOLDEN CALF, &C. EXOD. xxxii. AND LEV. xvii. 7.

A succession of allusions to Egypt are found in the 32d chapter of Exodus. That the representation of Jehovah under the image of the golden calf is only explainable on the supposition of Egyptian influence, and that it stands in connection with the worship of Apis,[2] has been fully discussed in the Contribu-

dried away, there is nothing at all besides this manna before our eyes." (Numb. xi. 4—6.)

This attachment to gardens is frequently made the subject of poetical allusions in the Song of Solomon, which, though it has a much more high and holy signification, as both Jewish and Christian commentators unanimously agree, yet was primarily designed as an epithalamium on his marriage with a beautiful Egyptian princess, the daughter of the reigning Pharaoh. "A garden inclosed is my sister, my spouse; a spring shut up, a fountain sealed. Thy plants are an orchard of pomegranates, with pleasant fruits; camphire, with spikenard; spikenard and saffron; calamus and cinnamon, with all trees of frankincense; myrrh and aloes, with all the chief spices; a fountain of gardens, a well of living waters, and streams from Lebanon." (Cantic. iv. 12—15.) T.

[1] Rosellini, II. 2. p. 159.
[2] *Wilkinson* connects it with the worship of the Mnevis of Heliopolis. After speaking of the worship of the sacred animals in general, he says: "The Hebrew legislator felt the necessity of preventing the Jews from falling into this, the most gross practice of which idolatry was guilty. The worship of the golden calf, a representation of the Mnevis of Heliopolis, was a proof how their minds had become imbued with the superstitions they had beheld in Egypt, which the mixed 'multitude had practised

tions.¹ In the same work, it was also shown that striking analogy is found in the descriptions of the feasts of the gods among the Egyptians, for the manner in which the festival of the golden calf was celebrated by the Israelites, as exhibited in the following passages: verse 6—"And the people sat down to eat and to drink and rose up to *play*." Verse 17 : " And when Joshua heard the noise of the people as they shouted, he said unto Moses, There is a noise of war in the camp." Verse 18, where Moses says : " The noise of song I hear." And in verse 19 : " And he saw the calf and the dancing." The most ancient popular rites of the Egyptians were, according to *Creuzer*,² of the nature of orgies, and the fundamental character of their religion was Bacchanalian. Sensual songs were sung, with the accompaniment of noisy instruments. Of the yearly journey to Bubastis, *Herodotus*³ says : " Throughout the whole journey, some of the women strike the cymbal, whilst men play the flute, and the rest of the women and men sing and clap with their hands ; and when they, in their journey, come near a town, they bring the boat near the shore, and conduct as follows : some of the women do as I have already described, some jeer at the women of the town, with loud voices, and some dance," while others commit other unseemly acts. Especially is it said concerning the feast of Apis,⁴ " But when Cambyses came to Memphis, Apis (whom the Greeks call Epaphos) was shown to the Egyptians, and as he appeared, the Egyptians forthwith put on their most costly garments and exulted." ⁵

Just as here, in a manner throughout inimitable by one of later times, the circumstances, tendencies and feelings of the people, who had grown up under Egyptian influences, are exhibited with incontrovertible truth. So are they, also, in the passage Lev. xvii. 7, already explained at large in a former work.⁶ It is there said, in reference to the rebellious Israelites: " They shall no longer offer their sacrifices to he-goats (שְׂעִירִם), after which they

there.'" Second Series, Vol. II. p. 96-7. But it is of little consequence which is referred to. The allusion is sufficiently plain in either case.

¹ Th. 2. S. 155 ff.   ² Symbol. I. S. 448, 9.
³ B. 2. c. 60.   ⁴ B. 3. c. 27.

⁵ See also upon the sacred dance among the Egyptians, Wilkinson, II. p. 340.

· Beiträgen, Th. 2. S. 118 ff.

have lusted." The opposition which exists between a he-goat and a god, was removed in the Egyptian religion and in it only. "The he-goat, and also Pan, were, in the language of Egypt, named Mendes," says *Herodotus*,[1] and almost all the Greeks follow him. This identity of names between the god and the he-goat, is explained by the pantheistic element in the Egyptian conception of the world. The he-goat was not barely a symbol of Mendes, for whom the Greeks, looking away from the other great differences, because of the form of the he-goat and his wantonness, substituted Pan, but the physical presentation, the incarnation of this god, and was therefore considered holy and as worthy of divine honour. The service of the he-goat, as a deity, was very anciently performed in Egypt, and he was the participant of very high honour among them,[2] so that we must necessarily expect the idolatrous inclination of the Israelites, awakened after a short slumber, to be also directed specially to this deity.

We turn back to Exodus xxxii. Aaron demands, according to verse 2, of the children of Israel, the golden rings which are in the ears of their wives, their sons, and their daughters, in order to fashion from them the calf. "The golden ornaments found in Egypt," says *Wilkinson*,[3] " consists of rings, bracelets, armlets, necklaces, ear-rings, and numerous trinkets belonging to the toilet; many of these are of the times of Osirtasen I. and Thothmes III., contemporaries of Joseph and Moses." The same author[4] shows that ear-rings were commonly worn in Egypt. Rings of gold were so common in Egypt, according to *Rosellini*,[5] that they took to a certain extent the place of coin, and many times were used in trade.

According to verse 20, Moses took the calf that they made and burnt it, and beat it,[6] (namely, the elements of the calf, externally

---

[1] B. 2. c. 46.
[3] Wilk., Vol. III. p. 225.
[5] Vol. II. p. 280.
[2] Compare Creuzer, Th. III. S. 325.
[4] Vol. III. p. 371-1.
[6] In *Wilkinson*, Vol. III. p. 220-1, it is said: "A strong evidence of the skill of the Egyptians in working metals, and of the early advancement they made in this art, is derived from their success in the management of different alloys; which, as *M. Goguet* observes, is further argued from the casting of the golden calf, and still more from Moses being able to burn the metal and reduce it to powder; a secret which he could only have learned in Egypt. It is said in Exodus that 'Moses took the calf

gold and internally wood, which had escaped the fire) until it was fine as powder. In Deut. ix. 21, Moses says of the same transaction: "And burned it with fire, and beat it, grinding it thoroughly, until it was as fine as dust." *Wilkinson*[1] says, certain persons were employed in the towns of Egypt, to pound various substances, in large stone mortars, with heavy metal pestles. When the substance was well pounded, it was taken out and passed through a sieve, and the larger particles were again returned to the mortar, until the whole was sufficiently fine.

In verse 32, Moses asks of God: "And now if thou wilt, forgive their sin; and if not, blot me, I pray thee, out of thy book which thou hast written." These words imply the customary employment of lists and rolls, which have existed in scarcely any other land so generally as they did in Egypt. The monuments often exhibit this frequency. Thus there is represented in a tomb at Gurnab a levying of Egyptian soldiers. The men, conducted by their commander, go before a scribe in order to be enrolled.[2]

PROHIBITION OF MARRIAGE BETWEEN NEAR RELATIVES, LEV. XVIII.

The law concerning unlawful intercourse, in Lev. xviii., in which marriages between near relatives occupies the first place, is in verse 3 accompanied by the words: "After the doings of the land of Egypt wherein ye dwelt, shall ye not do." Truly, among no

---

which they had made, and burned it in the fire and ground it to powder, and strewed it upon the water, and made the children of Israel drink of it;' an operation which, according to the French *savant*, 'is known by all who work in metals to be very difficult.' 'Commentators' heads,' he adds, 'have been much perplexed to explain how Moses burnt and reduced the gold to powder. Many have offered vain and improbable conjectures, but an experienced chemist has removed every difficulty upon the subject, and has suggested this simple process. In the place of tartaric acid, which we employ, the Hebrew legislator used natron, which is common in the east. What follows, respecting his making the Israelites drink this powder, proves that he was perfectly acquainted with the whole effect of the operation. He wished to increase the punishment of their disobedience, and nothing could have been more suitable; for gold reduced, and made into a draught, in the manner I have mentioned, has a most disagreeable taste.'"

[1] Vol. III. p. 181, and Drawing.
[2] Rosellini. II. 3. p. 210. Compare also Herod. B. 2. c. 177.

people of antiquity was the moral feeling, with reference to marriage among relatives, so blunted, as among the Egyptians. The marriage with the sister, so strongly forbidden by Moses, was considered among them as unconditionally allowable. *Diodorus*[1] says: "It is, contrary to the common custom, lawful among the Egyptians to marry a sister, since such a union, in the case of Isis, was so fortunate in its consequences." *Pausanias*[2] says of Philadelphus, who married his sister by birth: "He in this did that which was by no means lawful among the Macedonians, but entirely in accordance with the law of the Egyptians, over whom he ruled." *Philo*[3] relates of the Egyptian lawgiver, that he gave permission to all to marry their sisters, those who are sisters by birth, not less than step-sisters, those of like age and older, not less than the younger. "By the sculptures in Upper and Lower Egypt," remarks *Wilkinson*,[4] "it is fully authenticated, that this law was in force in the earliest times."

DEFILEMENT WITH ANIMALS, LEV. xviii. 23, EXOD. xxii. 18, &c.

The prohibition of defilement with animals is in the Pentateuch so often repeated and so vigorously enforced, (see Lev. xviii. 23: Neither shalt thou lie with any beast to defile thyself therewith, neither shall any woman stand before a beast to lie down thereto; it is confusion, תֶּבֶל),[5] that we are involuntarily driven to the supposition that the author has a very special reason for enjoining the prohibition of this so unnatural and infrequent a crime, and that he takes into account an immorality which ruled among those by whom the Israelites had been previously surrounded, which was introduced among them through a pseudo-religious motive, and had acquired an influence which it could never have exerted without that sanction. We should the more expect to find such a vile practice among the Egyptians, the further erroneous views of the position of animals in the whole creation, and the changing of the proper relation of animals to human beings, was carried. That this enormity really existed among the Egyptians, *Herodotus*[6] shows: "In this same province (the Mendesian) the following

[1] B. 1. c. 27.
[2] Att. 1. 7.
[3] De Special Legg. p. 780.
[4] Vol. II. p. 63.
[5] See also Exod. xxii. 18, Lev. xx. 15, Deut. xxvii. 21.
[6] 2. 46.

prodigy happened in my time : ἐγένετο δ' ἐν τῷ νομῷ τούτῳ ἐπ' ἐμεῦ τοῦτο τὸ τέρας· γυναικὶ τράγος ἐμίσγετο ἀναφανδόν. τοῦτο ἐς ἐπίδειξιν ἀνθρώπων ἀπίκετο."[1] That the occurrence which *Herodotus* here mentions was not a single one, is evident from the declarations of other writers.[2]

The reference of the Mosaic law on this subject to the irregularities connected with the worship of the goat among the Egyptians, appear the more certain, since this worship of the goat among the Israelites, according to the passage in Lev. xvii. 7, already discussed, was during the passage through the desert yet very prevalent.

We are still more confirmed in our belief of an Egyptian reference in this prohibition of defilement with animals, from its being comprised in the number of those which in Lev. xviii. 3 are introduced by the words : "After the doings of the land of Egypt, wherein ye dwelt, shall ye not do."

LEVITICUS xxiv. 10—12.

The account of " the son of the Israelitish woman whose father was an Egyptian," in Lev. xxiv. 10—12, transfers us, and in a manner peculiar and inimitable by a later writer, into the very heart of things as they must have existed at the time of the departure of the people from Egypt. If any narrative carries the proof of its authenticity along with it, this does. The name of the mother and her father are given, and the name of the tribe of the latter is also stated. That the father is an Egyptian and the mother an Israelite, is entirely in accordance with the common relation of the Egyptians to the Israelites, while the opposite case, an Israelitish father and an Egyptian mother, is hardly supposable. It is entirely natural that in the son of an Egyptian father, the

---

[1] Bähr says upon this passage : Mendetis in urbe hircos mulieribus se miscere Pindarus quoque cecinerat (v. Strabo 17, p. 1154), ex quo alii repetierunt laudati a Schneidero ad Pindari fragm. p. 122. ed. Heyn. t. 3. et Bocharto, Hieroz. 2, 53. Idem facinus de Thuiitis alii retulerunt, v. Clem. Al. p. 27. Ac turpissimi hujus amoris causam a religione repetendam esse, qua ductae mulieres Pani s. hirco, ejus symbolo, se permiserint, in dubium vocari nequit. The passage of Pindar quoted reads :

Μένδητα παρὰ κρημνὸν θαλάσσας, ἔσχατον
Νείλου κέρας, αἰγιβάται ὅθι τράγοι γυναιξὶ μίσγονται.

[2] See the preceding note.

heathenish blood should show itself, so that he curses the God of Israel.

NUMBERS xi. 4.

In Num. xi. 4. it is said: "The mixed multitude that was with them fell a lusting, and the children of Israel wept again, and said, who shall give us flesh to eat?" Verse 5: "We remember the fish, which we did eat in Egypt freely; the cucumbers, and the melons, and the grass (helbeh,) and the onions, and the garlic."

This passage is especially important, in respect to the connection of the Pentateuch with Egypt. All the things named in it certainly existed in Egypt in great abundance, and most of them were distinguished for their excellence; and among those means of subsistence, which ancient Egypt produced in great abundance, which were generally in favour with the whole people, and specially with them, there is no one omitted. Among those named, one is found, the grass (helbeh), which is so entirely peculiar to Egypt, that interpreters down to the latest times have erred in reference to it, since they fail to derive the explanation from accurate knowledge of Egypt. These peculiarities can appear natural to us, in this connection, only on the supposition that Moses is the author of the Pentateuch, but on that hypothesis they are entirely in accordance with the circumstances of the case.

We begin with that product, the naming of which is especially worthy of notice, and suited to convince us of the author's knowledge of Egypt.

THE GRASS (*helbeh*), חָצִיר.

The current opinion, as it is found, for example, in *Rosenmueller* upon this passage, and in *Gesenius's* Thesaurus, same word, is this: חָצִיר means here, leek, which on account of its grasslike appearance takes this name.

But this opinion is entirely without foundation. Appeal cannot be made to the authority of the ancient translators.[1] For who can give us security, that they, supposing that all herbage

---

[1] Septuagint, πράσα, Vulgate, porri.

used for fodder is excluded, and looking around among the productions which serve men for food, for one that at least furnishes an external similarity to grass, have not merely guessed at the one they have taken?

But the correct view is arrived at through a different counter-argument. The חָצִיר has etymologically the meaning of food for cattle—it is originally not grass, but pasturage, fodder,[1] and so also according to common use.[2] The first criterion for the correctness of the interpretation is, therefore, that the article of food which is identified with חָצִיר must be appropriately food for beasts, so that man goes, as it were, to the same table with them. Now if such an article of food could by no means be found, we should be warranted in giving up this criterion, which is entirely wanting in the leek.

But among the wonders of the natural history of Egypt, it is mentioned by travellers that the common people there eat, with special relish, a kind of grass similar to clover. The impression which the sight of this makes on those who have travelled much, is very graphically described by *Mayr*:[3] "A great heap of clover was thrown before the beasts, and a smaller pile of clover, like fodder, was placed before the master of the house and his companions. The quadrupeds and the bipeds ate with equal greediness, and the pile of the latter was all gone before the former had finished theirs—this plant is very similar to clover, except that it has more pointed leaves and whitish blossoms. Enormous quantities are eaten by the inhabitants, and it is not unpalatable. I was afterwards, when hungry, in a situation to lay myself down upon the fields where it grows, and *graze* with pleasure."

Raffenau Delile gives a more scientific description:[4] "The fenu-grec (trigonella foenum Graecum, Linn.) is an annual plant, known in Egypt under the name of Helbeh; it very much resembles clover. The people of the country find the young fresh shoots, before blossoming, a very delicious food."

---

[1] See Gesenius, loc. cit.
[2] E. g. 1 Kings xviii. 5, Job xl. 15, and other passages. Compare Gesenius.
[3] Reise nach Aegypten u. s. w. S. 226.
[4] Hist. des Plantes cultiv. en Egypte, § 2; Du Trèfle d'Egypte et de Fenu-grec, cultivés comme fourages, in the Description, t. 19, p. 59.

But the most particular and best account is found in *Sonnini*.[1] From him we make a somewhat copious extract, since it clearly shows us how the emigrating Egyptians and the Israelites could, among other things, also look back longingly to the *grass* of Egypt: "Although this helbeh of the Egyptians is a nourishing food for the numerous beasts who cover the plains of the Delta; although horses, oxen, and the buffaloes eat it with equal relish, it appears not to be destined especially for the sustenance of animals, since the *barsim* furnishes an aliment better even and more abundant. But that which will appear very extraordinary is, that in this singularly fertile country, the Egyptians themselves eat the fenu-grec so much that it can properly be called the food of *men*. In the month of November, they cry, "Green helbeh for sale," in the streets of the towns. It is tied up in large bunches, which the inhabitants eagerly purchase at a low price, and which they eat with an incredible greediness, without any species of seasoning. They pretend that this singular diet is an excellent stomachic, a specific against worms and dysentery; in fine, a preservative against a great number of maladies. Finally, the Egyptians regard this plant as endowed with so many good qualities that it is, in their estimation, a true panacea. *Prosper Alpinus* has entered into long details upon its use in medicine. After so many excellent properties, real or supposed, it is not astonishing that the Egyptians hold the fern-grec in so great estimation, that, according to one of their proverbs, "Fortunate are the feet which tread the earth on which grows the hebeh."

Besides those named, *von Schubert*[2] may be compared. He says: "The kinds of clover whose young shoots and leaves we saw eaten in many ways by the Egyptians, were the helbeh (trig. foenum, Gr.) and the *gilban* (Lathyrus sativus)."

---

[1] Voyage dans la haute et basse Egypte, Tom. I. p. 379, seq.
[2] Reise, Th. II. S. 107.

THE FISH.

The fact that fish were placed first in the narrative,[1] and also the phrase, "which we ate in Egypt *freely*," indicate that they were very numerous. And it is so well known that almost incredible numbers exist in Egypt, that we need not quote all the

---

[1] We make the following extract from its interest, in connection with several other passages in the Pentateuch and Isaiah, as well as the one under discussion: "Fishing is one of the employments most frequently depicted on the monuments. It is combined with fowling by amateur sportsmen, and even with the chase of the crocodile and the hippopotamus; but is also pursued as a regular trade by an entire caste. It is recorded as a fearful aggravation of the first plague of Egypt, that 'the fish that was in the river died,' (Exod. vii. 21). The first great complaints of the Israelites, when they murmured against Moses in the desert, was, 'We remember the fish that we did eat in Egypt freely,' (Numbers xi. 5.) And this abundance of fish was still further increased by the ponds, sluices, and artificial lakes which were constructed for the propagation of the finny tribe. Hence Isaiah, in denouncing divine vengeance against the Egyptians, dwells particularly on the ruin which would fall upon those who derived their subsistence from the animals and plants of the Nile: 'And the waters shall fail from the sea, and the river shall be wasted and dried up. And they shall turn the rivers far away; and the brooks of defence shall be emptied and dried up: the reeds and flags shall wither. The paper reeds by the brooks, by the mouth of the brooks, and every thing sown by the brooks, shall wither, be driven away, and be no more. The fishers also shall mourn, and all they that cast angle into the brooks shall lament, and they that spread nets upon the waters shall languish. Moreover, they that work in fine flax, and they that weave net works, shall be confounded. And they shall be broken in the purposes thereof, all that make sluices and ponds for fish,' (Isaiah xix. 5—10). Although the Nile, and the artificial lakes, were constantly swept with nets, we are unable to discover any proof of the Egyptians having ever fished in the open sea; and indeed there is reason to believe that the fishes of the sea were, from religious motives, regarded with abhorrence. The supply has not failed in modern times; the right of fishery on the canals and lakes is annually farmed out by the government to certain individuals, who pay very large sums for the privilege. 'The small village of Agalteh at Thebes,' says *Mr Wilkinson*, 'pays annually 1500 piastres (about £21.) to government for the fish of its canal.' *M. Michaud*, in his delightful Letters, gives an account of the fisheries on the lake Menzaleh, too interesting to be omitted. 'The waters of Menzaleh abound in fish; the Arabs say that the varieties of ⸺ lake exceed the number of days in the year. Al-

separate proofs of the fact. We only refer to *Oedmann*,[1] *Mayr*,[2] *Bähr*,[3] *Taylor*,[4] and *Wilkinson*.[5] But it should, perhaps, be particularly mentioned; that, according to *Herodotus*, a part of the inhabitants of the marshes of the Delta, shepherds, who probably were not of Egyptian origin, and were hated[6] by the cultivators of the soil, lived entirely on fish.[7]

THE CUCUMBER.

Upon the cucumber, also, we need not delay long. It is known that they exist in Egypt, and of peculiar excellence. They are large, of fine flavour, and very much eaten.[8]

though this may be deemed an exaggeration, it is certain that whatever be the number of their species, the fishes of this lake multiply infinitely.'
—' On the monuments the fishermen appear as a class inferior to the agricultural population, and we know historically that they formed one of the lowest castes. This was also the case in Palestine, and hence when Christ chose two of this class to become apostles, he announces to them that they were for the future to be engaged in a more honourable occupation. ' Now as he walked by the sea of Galilee, he saw Simon and Andrew his brother casting a net into the sea, for they were fishers. And Jesus said unto them, Come ye after me, and I will make you to become fishers of men. And straightway they forsook their nets and followed him.' "—*Taylor*, p. 62, seq.

[1] Verm. Samml. 1. S. 136. Radzivil says there: "We saw, to-day, about a hundred fishermen lying in the turbid waters of the Nile, and catching fish with their hands. Some of them came up with three fish— one in each hand and one in the mouth. The fish were an ell long, and of different kinds."

[2] Mayr, S. 188.   [3] Zu Herodotus, I. S. 658.
[4] P. 62 seq.   [5] Vol. III. p. 63.
[6] See Bähr, l. c. S. 687 : Heeren, S. 150.

[7] Minutoli stands entirely alone in his assertion, S. 406 : " In fish the Nile is poor, as well in respect to numbers as in variety of species, of which there are not many." Were this correct, we should despair of ever finding truth in history. But we will not trouble ourselves about that in anticipation.

[8] Compare the passage from Prosper Alpinus, which has already been quoted by Rosenmueller ; Forskal, Flora, p. 169; Description, t. 19, p. 109 ; De Sacy upon Abdallatiph, p. 125 ; and Abdallatiph himself, p. 34 ; Hartmann, Aeg. S. 180.

THE MELONS, אֲבַטִּחִים.

The melons are of very great importance to Egypt. The following passages from *Sonnini*,[1] best show how they could become objects of general longing in the desert, where "the souls of the people were dry," verse 6. But the species of fruit which, by its pulp and its refreshing water, best serves to moderate the internal heat which the climate generates, is the *pastek* or water-melon (cucurbita citrullus).[2] The markets are filled with them, and they sell at so very small a price, that the poor as well as the rich can refresh themselves with their watery and sweet juice. They are a healthful nourishment, and useful in the climate where the heat makes the blood boil, and gives sharpness to the humours."[3]

ONIONS.

The onions of Egypt are also far renowned and much praised. They are often represented in the sculptures.[4] According to *Arvieux*,[5] they are sweet and large, and taste better than those of Smyrna. *Hasselquist*[6] protests that there are in the whole world none better. *Herodotus* shows that they were, in antiquity, frequently an article of diet of the people, and a common food of those who laboured upon the pyramids.[7] In what estimation they are now held, we see from *Sonnini:*[8] "This species of vegetable is yet extraordinarily common in this country: it is the aliment of the more ordinary of the people, and almost the only food of the lowest class. Onions, cooked or raw, are sold in the streets and markets for almost nothing. These onions have not the tartness of those of Europe; they are sweet; they sting not the mouth unpleasantly; and they do not produce weeping in those who cut them."

[1] Th. 3. S. 101.
[2] Aegyptiis battich Forsk., p. 75.
[3] See also Sonnini, p. 109; Abdallatiph, p. 35; De Sacy, p. 127 and 8.
[4] Wilk. II. p. 373.
[5] Hartmann, S. 180.
[6] P. 562.
[7] B. 2. c. 125.
[8] Tom. II. S. 66, 67.

THE GARLIC.

Finally, the garlic, just as here, is spoken of by *Herodotus*, in connection with the onion, as a principal article of food, especially of the poorest classes.[1] *Pliny*[2] also speaks of the two in connection. *Dioscorides* describes the garlic among the plants of Egypt; and *Rosellini*[3] thinks he has discovered it upon a painting in Beni Hassan. It is not now produced in Egypt;[4] just as also other plants very abundant in Egypt in former times, especially the papyrus-plant, are now either entirely or almost entirely extinct.[5]

NUMBERS xvii. 2.

According to Num. xvii. 2, Moses takes from each one of the twelve princes of the tribes of Israel a rod, and writes their name thereon. "The name of each person," *Wilkinson*[6] remarks, "was frequently written on his stick, instances of which I have seen in those found at Thebes."

[1] " Among the lower orders, vegetables constituted a very great part of their ordinary food, and they gladly availed themselves of the variety and abundance of esculent roots growing spontaneously, in the lands irrigated by the rising Nile, as soon as its waters had subsided; some of which were eaten in a crude state, and others roasted in the ashes, boiled or stewed: their chief allment, and that of their children, consisting of milk and cheese, roots, liguminous, cucurbitaceous, and other plants, and ordinary fruits of the country. *Herodotus* describes the food of the workmen who built the Pyramids, to have been the ' *raphanus* or *figl*, onions, and garlic;' yet if these were among the number they used, and perhaps the solo provisions supplied at the government expense, we are not to suppose they were limited to them: and it is probable that lentils, of which it is inferred from Strabo they had an abundance on this occasion, may be reckoned as part, or even the chief article, of their food."—*Wilk*. II. 370.

[2] Hist. Nat. 19. 6: allium cepasque inter deos in Jurejurando habent Aegyptii.

[3] Vol. II. 1. S. 383. [4] Sonnini, p. 68.

[5] What Michaud says, tom. 8, p. 56, concerning the manner of living among the Fellahs in the Delta, may be compared with this whole passage: " Rien n'égale la sobriété de ce peuple: il soutient sa vie avec quelques *herbes*, des concombres, des oignons, un mauvais pain de dourah ou lentilles.

[6] Vol. III. p. 388.

DEUTERONOMY vi. 9; AND xi. 20.

The passages, Deut. chap. vi. 9: "And thou shall write them (the divine commands) upon the posts of thy house, and on thy gates," and xi. 20, imply that the custom of giving to houses inscriptions, was quite common among the people with whom the Israelites dwelt.[1] According to the monuments, the name of the owner of a house among the Egyptians was not unfrequently written upon the lintels of the doors.[2] "Besides the owner's name," says *Wilkinson*,[3] "they sometimes wrote a lucky sentence over the entrance of the house for a favourable omen, and the lintels and imposts of the doors in the royal mansions were often covered with hieroglyphics, containing the ovals and titles of the monarch."

THE DISEASES OF EGYPT SEVERE. DEUT. vii. 15; xxviii. 27, 35, 60; EXOD. xv. 26.

In Deut. vii. 15, it is said, "And the Lord will remove from thee all sickness, and will put none of the evil diseases of Egypt, which thou knowest, upon thee." A similar expression is also found in Exod. xv. 26, "If thou wilt diligently hearken to the voice of the Lord thy God, and will do that which is right in his sight, and will give ear to his commandments, and keep all his statutes, I will put none of these diseases upon thee, which I have brought upon the Egyptians, for I the Lord am He who healeth thee." In Deut. xxviii. 60, it is said, "And the Lord will bring again upon thee all the diseases of Egypt, of which thou wast afraid, and they shall cleave to thee." In verses 27 and 35 of the same chapter, erring Israel is threatened with the infliction of a sickness peculiarly Egyptian, concerning which we have already in another connection made investigation.

All of these scattered passages agree in this, that Egypt, in reference to diseases, is a very peculiar land, and is visited by them in a very special degree. The accounts of all those who have

[1] See Boitr. Th. 2. S. 459.
[2] See engraving in Wilk. Vol. II. 102.
[3] Vol. II. p. 123-4, and concerning the inscriptions on the gates of the gardens, p. 144.

made the diseases of Egypt an object of particular attention, show that the author is right in this. *Wagner*,[1] in his natural history of man, calls Egypt "a great focus of the diseases in universal history." *De Chabrol*, in his "inquiry concerning the customs of the modern inhabitants of Egypt," of the most important diseases, says, "With an almost equable temperature, and with an always serene sky, Egypt can have only a small number of diseases, but they are for the most part terrible."[2]

The same author then speaks of single maladies, the plague, which is almost never wanting in Cairo, and particularly in Alexandria, the dysentery of which he says: "This disease causes great destruction among them, and especially attacks the children, which it carries off in a frightful manner;" the diseases of the eyes, with which one at least out of five individuals is afflicted, the small-pox which in Egypt is frightful, and rages far worse than in Europe, &c.

In the "observations upon several diseases which attacked the soldiers of the French army," four seasons of the year are made[3] with reference to healthfulness. The first comprises the time of the inundation. "I name," says the author, "this first season of the year, which continues about three months, the *damp* season; it may be considered as the winter of the country. The west wind, which then blows, increases the dampness of the atmosphere, which at evening and especially in the morning is full of mist. The consequence is a coolness, which is uncomfortable and detrimental to animal secretions. In this season of the year diseases of the eyes, the hospital fever, diarrhoea and catarrhal pains prevail."[4] "The *third* season of the year," says the same author further, "which I will give the name of the *sick* season, since it is destructive to the health of the inhabitants and especially of strangers, begins about the first of March and continues generally until about the end of May. The south wind takes the place of the east wind, which had prevailed during the earlier part of the year. These south winds are first light, but they increase gradu-

---

[1] Th. II. S. 270.   [2] Description, t. 7, p. 43, seq. § 8.

[3] In the Descr. t. 13, p. 216, seq.

[4] Of this same time says Abdallatiph, p. 4. De Sacy: During this season of the year unhealthful evaporations prevail; the air is bad—putrid diseases, caused by bilious and phlegmy humours, rage among the inhabitants.

ally—they afterwards decrease in the same way—and indeed to such a degree, that during a period of about fifty days, from which they have taken the name chamsin, they are very violent and hot, and hence would become insupportable, if they blew without cessation. At this season of the year, wounds heal with difficulty, and are easily seized with mortification. Sicknesses of all kinds take an unusual character, and require the greatest carefulness on the part of the physician, and in general all living beings are more or less affected."[1]

CULTIVATION OF THE LAND IN EGYPT AND PALESTINE, DEUT. xi. 10, 11.

In Deut. xi. 10, 11, it is said : "For the land whither thou goest in to possess it, is not as the land of Egypt, from whence ye came out, where thou sowedst thy seed, and wateredst it with thy foot as a garden of herbs : but the land whither ye go to possess it, is a land of hills and valleys, and drinketh water of the rain of heaven." These verses furnish occasion for the following remarks :

1. The supposition that Egypt is without rain, lies at the foundation of this passage. Against the correctness of this implication, the accounts of modern travellers cannot be adduced in argument, according to whom, especially in Lower Egypt, it certainly sometimes rains : for these rains are yet proportionally so seldom, and, what is the principal thing to which reference is made in this immediate connection, they have so little influence in fertilizing the earth, that the classical writers are accustomed to speak of Egypt as if it never rained there. *Herodotus*[2] says perfectly plainly, "it rains not in their land."[3] Collections concern-

---

[1] Compare also upon the diseases of Egypt, Prosper Alpinus, De Medicina Aeg. ed. Friedreich, t. 1. p. 95, seq. : De morbis Aegyptiis peculiaribus eorumque causis ; and Hartmann, Aegypt. S. 54 ff, where blindness is designated as the most to be feared of any of them. Volney found among 100 persons who met him, oftentimes twenty entirely blind, ten blind with one eye, and twenty others whose eyes were either red or festered or diseased in some other way.

[2] B. 2. c. 14.

[3] Compare Diod. 1. 41. Plinius Panegyr. c. 30 : Aegyptus alendis augendisque seminibus ita gloriata est, ut nihil imbribus coeloque deberet. Mela names Aeg. expers imbrium. Lucilius in Seneca, Nat. Quaest. IV. 2 : Nemo aratorum aspicit coelum, and Tibullus : nec pluvio supplicat herba Jovi.

ing rain in Egypt are given by *Faber*,[1] *Nordmeier*,[2] and *Hartmann*.[3]

2. The author in designating Canaan, in opposition to Egypt, as a land of mountains and valleys, places in the flatness of country of Egypt the cause of absence of rain, and that he in this way proves himself acquainted with the natural condition of Egypt, no man can deny.[4]

3. It appears at first view remarkable that the author represents it as a superiority of Canaan over Egypt, that it is subject to rain, and is not watered by a river. If we compare what *Herodotus*[5] says of the inhabitants of the region below Memphis, the thing will assume quite another phasis. "For now indeed these people obtain the fruits of their land with far less trouble and labour than other people, even than the other Egyptians. They need not trouble themselves to turn up furrows with the plough, nor to dig with the hoe, nor with any other kind of labour, which men bestow upon the earth, but the river comes of its own accord upon their land, and waters it, and having done this, it leaves it again, and then each one sows his ground." The great facility of cultivation in Egypt is also asserted by *Rosellini*.[6] But if we examine the affair more minutely, it appears that the author is perfectly right, and that the error, if it is altogether an error, falls rather on the side of *Herodotus*[7] and those who take him as authority.

---

[1] Zu den Beob. a. d. Orient, B. 1. S. 4 ff. 2. S. 347 ff.
[2] In the Calend. Aeg. p. 11 and 20.   [3] S. 197.
[4] Vossius upon Mela L. 1. c. 9, § 1. ed. Tzschuck. III. 1. p. 247, says: Quaerit vero causum Aristobulus apud Strabonem 1. 15. (p. 476 s. 692.) quare, cum in Syene imbres cadant, intermedia tantum loca pluvia omnino careant. Quaestio haec ibi proponitur, sed non solvitur. Ratio tamen est manifesta, quia nempe illa Aegypti pars, ubi nullae cadunt pluviae, plana, humilis, sicca, arenosa ac calida est admodum, utpote torridae zonae vicina. Vapores itaque, qui a terra arida egrediuntur, cum rari admodum et tenues sint, aut noctu decidunt in rorem mutati, aut toti ab aestu consumuntur, priusquam in pluviam abeant. At vero tractus Syeniticus, quia excelsus et montosus est, necessario pluviis abundat. Ubi enim montes, ibi nivium et aquarum lapsus perpetui.
[5] B. 2. c. 14.   [6] II. 1. p. 288.
[7] Bähr upon Herodotus says: Herodoteis similia proferunt Diod. 1. 36, Columella II. 25, Athenaeus V. 8. Sed recentioris aetatis scriptores si audias, vix ulla invenitur terra, quae quo fructus ferat magis hominum opera indigeat quam Aegyptus. Quae cum ita sint, nisi erroris patrem

First, it is to be remarked, that *Herodotus* particularly designates only those labours as unnecessary for the Egyptians, which in other lands precede seed-sowing. But in Egypt, the burdensome labour, the watering, begins not until after the seed is sown, and this circumstance is made very particularly prominent in our passage. That irrigation is really a very laborious employment, is confirmed by many witnesses. "*Forskål*," says *Oedmann*,[1] "has shown that the cultivation of the land in Egypt requires more toil than one would imagine. The watering must be often repeated, and for that purpose the land is intersected by canals. These canals must be cleared out yearly, and sustained by hedges, &c. planted on their banks. And in *Shaw*,[2] it can also be seen with what indescribable pains the water must be conducted through the numerous little channels, to furnish sustenance for the productions of the land, to say nothing of the various machines which are drawn by buffaloes, and are used for carrying up the water to the gardens, after the canals and cisterns are dry." The difficulty of cultivation in Egypt, *Girard*[3] also asserts. A single 'Feddan Doorah'[4] sometimes requires, according to him, a hundred days' work of watering. *Prokesch*[5] says: "The watering is indispensably necessary, and must be performed at stated intervals. It is the custom to water the fields in winter once in fourteen days; in the spring, if the dew falls sufficiently, once in twelve days; but in the summer once in eight days." The same author describes[6] the various machines for irrigation. Finally, *Michaud*[7] says: "The labour of tillage is not that which most occupies the agricultural population here; for the land is easy to cultivate. The great difficulty is to water the fields; even the most robust of the Fellahs are employed to raise the water and perform the irrigation."

Further, it must not be overlooked, that *Herodotus* speaks only

---

historiae incusare velis, ejus verba non ad omnem Aegyptum erunt referenda, sed ad unam modo alteramve ejus partem, eximia agrorum fertilitate insignem.

[1] Verm. Beitr. 1. S. 126.   [2] Page 172.
[3] In the Descr. t. 17, p. 56.
[4] The *Feddan*, the most common measure of land in Egypt, was a few years ago equal to about an English acre. It is now less than an acre.
[5] In den Erinnerung. Th. 2. S. 135.   [6] S. 137.
[7] Correspondence from the East, Vol. VIII. p. 54.

of a single region of Egypt, of that which enjoys the blessings of the Nile in the fullest measure. He explicitly contrasts the inhabitants of the region below Memphis with the rest of the Egyptians. But our passage has particularly in view that part of Egypt which was inhabited by the Israelites. This lay upon the borders of the desert, and the blessings of the Nile could be appropriated to them only by means of the greatest exertions.

Finally, it is to be considered that the Canaan of which the author speaks is in a manner an *ideal* land. It was never what it might have been, since the bond of allegiance, in consequence of which God had promised to give the land its rain in its season, was always far from being perfectly complied with.

4. That our passage is spoken in opposition to the boasting of the Egyptians, who looked down with proud pity upon all other lands, since these had no Nile, is probable from a comparison of *Herodotus*, 2. 13, which has a striking relation to our passage: " For when they heard that in all the country of the Greeks the land is watered by rain, and not by rivers, as in Egypt, they said, 'the Greeks, disappointed in their brightest hopes, will sometimes suffer severe famine;' which means, if God at some time shall not send rain, but drought, then famine will press upon them, for they can obtain water only from God." The phrase, 'only from God,' which seems so terrible to the Egyptians, is here represented as a mark of favour to the people, which has God for its friend, and to which the eyes of the Lord its God are directed from the beginning until the end of the year, verse 12.

5. The words, " Where thou sowedst thy seed and wateredst it with thy foot as a garden of herbs," shows at least that the author was acquainted with the manner of irrigation in Egypt, and is most easily explained on the supposition that he was acquainted with the manner of life among the Egyptians by personal observation. At the first view, these words appear without doubt to have reference to an Egyptian watering machine described by *Philo*,[1] with which they carried the water from the Nile and its canals into the fields. This machine, a wheel for raising water turned by the foot, is even now in use in Egypt. Nevertheless, since the au-

---

[1] De Confusione Ling. p. 255.

thority of *Diodorus*, for the newness of the invention of this machine, scarcely sufficient of itself, (he mentions [1] that it was invented by Archimedes,) is confirmed by the circumstance that this machine is not represented in the sculptures,[2] whilst the machine, now most common for irrigation, the *shadûf*, is found even on very ancient monuments,[3] it is most natural to refer the words rather to the carrying of the water in which the foot has the most to do.[4] This process we find also represented on the Egyptian monuments.[5] Two men are there employed in watering a piece of cultivated land. They bear upon their shoulders a yoke with straps at each end, to which earthen vessels are fastened. They fill these with water from a neighbouring shadûf or from a pool, and carry it to the field. Another stands there with a bundle of herbs which he appears to have just collected, by which the phrase, 'like an herb-garden,' is very naturally suggested.

6. The whole passage transfers us, in a manner inimitable by a 'modern writer, to the time in which the Israelites were stationed midway between Egypt and Canaan, yet full of the advantages which they had enjoyed in the former land, and in want of a counterpoise to the longing desire for that which they had lost.

[1] I. 34. 5. 37.
[2] Wilk. II. p. 5.
[3] Wilk. I. p. 53. II. p. 4. Ros. II. 1. p. 385.
[4] This does not reach the point, since the passage in question does not seem to refer to the mode of distributing, but of supplying the water. "Possibly," says *Dr Robinson*, 1. 542, "in more ancient times the water-wheel may have been smaller, and turned not by oxen, but by men pressing upon it with the foot, in the same way that water is still often drawn from wells in Palestine, as we afterwards saw. *Niebuhr* describes one such machine in Cairo, where it was called *Sâkieh tedûr bir rijl*, 'a watering machine that turns by the foot,' a view of which he also subjoins." The testimony in regard to the severity of the labour of irrigation is uniform. *Lane*, Modern Egyptians, Vol. II. p. 24, speaking of the raising of water by the Shadûf, says, "The operation is extremely laborious." *Dr Robinson*, p. 541, also remarks: "The *Shadûf* has a toilsome occupation. His instrument is exactly the well-sweep of New England in miniature, supported by a cross-piece resting on two upright posts of wood or mud. His bucket is of leather or wicker-work. Two of these instruments are usually fixed side by side, and the men keep time at their work, raising the water five or six feet. Where the banks are higher, two, three, and even four couples are thus employed, one above another."
[5] See the engraving from Beni Hassan in Wilk. II. p. 137, and the descrip. in Ros. II. 1. p. 382-3.

DEUTERONOMY xvii. 16.

Among the precepts for the king, Deut. chap. xvii. it is said, verse 16 : "Only he shall not multiply horses to himself, nor cause the people to return to Egypt, so that he may multiply horses ; for the Lord hath said to you, Ye shall not return back again that way." It was shown in the Contributions,[1] that the apprehension here spoken of, that the love of horses in the king could finally cause the whole people to return to Egypt, was entirely natural in Moses' time, when a uniting of the band just now severed appears not impossible, when the people from the most trivial cause uttered their longing for Egypt, or even their determination to return,[2] but not natural in the period of Solomon and the later kings. Indeed, such a thing could not even have been in Joshua's time, when the people had come to a full consciousness of their national independence, and every thought on the possibility of a re-union with the Egyptians was obliterated. In same place it was also remarked, that Egypt also appears in this passage as the only country in which horses were raised, while indeed, in the age of Solomon, Palestine was to a certain extent distinguished for the same thing, so that it could no longer be supposed that a king who wished to be the possessor of many horses must go to Egypt.

KIND TREATMENT OF THE ISRAELITES BY INDIVIDUAL EGYPTIANS.
DEUT. xxiii. 8, (7.)

In the arrangement concerning those who are to be received into the congregation, and those who are to be excluded, in Deut. xxiii. 8, (7), it is said, "Thou shalt not abhor an Egyptian, because thou wast a stranger in his land." This passage implies that the Israelites received in some respects better treatment from individuals of the Egyptians separately, than from the State, so that the Israelites had cause for grateful regard to them in turn ; since the phrase, "For thou wast a stranger in his land," is not a sufficient reason for the command, "Thou shalt not abhor an Egyptian," unless it means that the Egyptians performed the

---

[1] Th. 3. S. 247-8.
[2] See Exod. xiv. 11. Num. xi. 5, seq. ; xxi. 5, 7.

offices of hospitality to the Israelites, and earned for themselves the claim of reciprocity. In accurate agreement with this, we read in Exodus that God gave the Israelites, as they were departing, favour with the Egyptians, turned their hearts to them in love and compassion, so that they gave them rich presents for their journey. The agreement is so nice a circumstance between passages so entirely disconnected, is worthy of notice, as also the contents of each passage by itself. It is natural in a representation drawn from acquaintance with the actual condition of things, that the contradictions which real life always furnishes, should come in for a share; a *mythic* representation, on the contrary, would certainly avoid this apparent contradiction, and would here leave to the Egyptians only hatred and hostility and a correspondent relation of the Israelites to them.

DEUTERONOMY xxiii. 12, 13.

The precepts upon the not defiling of the camp, &c., in Deut. xxiii. 12, 13, reminds us of what *Herodotus*[1] says of the Egyptians: "They εὐμαρίῃ χρίωνται in houses, and eat without, in the streets; for they think that things which are unseemly, but necessary, must be done in secret; but what is not unseemly, before all the world."[2] If a custom of this kind had been established among the Egyptians, from among whom the Israelites came, it could not be violated by the Israelites without offending against decorum, and the law comes in with its mandates to obviate this difficulty.

THRESHING WITH OXEN, DEUT. XXV. 4.

In Deut. xxv. 4, it is forbidden to muzzle the ox when he treadeth out the corn. Both ancient writers[3] and the monuments show that oxen were used in Egypt for threshing.[4] *Champol-*

---

[1] B. 2. c. 35.
[2] Compare Bähr concerning the varying custom among the Greeks, S. 557.
[3] See Bähr upon Herodotus. I. p. 508.
[4] *Wilkinson*, in his 2d Ser., Vol. I. p. 85, seq. gives engravings and a description of this same scene at Elethya. His interpretat ⋅ler-oglyphics differs, however, a little from the one in the text from Gliddon: "Thresh for yourselves, (twice repeat⋅ for yourselves, (twice,) measures for yoursel⋅

lion says,[1] in describing the subterranean apartment at Elkab (Elethya), which belongs to the reign of Remeses Meiamun : " Among other things I have myself seen there the treading out or the threshing of the sheafs of grain by oxen ; and over the engraving may be read, in almost entirely phonetic characters, the song which the overseer sings while threshing:

> " Tread ye out for yourselves,
> Tread ye out for yourselves,
>   O oxen !
> Tread ye out for yourselves,
> Tread ye out for yourselves,
>   the straw ;
> For men, who are your masters,
>   the grain."

Of this same representation at Elethya, *Rosellini*[2] says : " They make a great heap of ears in the midst of the threshing-floor, and cause them to be trodden out by six oxen, which are kept in constant motion by a man who goes behind with a whip." In regard to the signification of the hieroglyphics, *Rosellini* agrees with *Champollion*.

DEUTERONOMY xxviii. 56.

In Deut. xxviii. 56, the " tender and delicate woman " is mentioned, " who would not adventure to set the sole of her foot upon the ground for delicateness and tenderness." Here also we are reminded of the state of things in Egypt. The luxury of the Egyptian women exceeded that of all other nations.[3]

ters." The same author also remarks, that similar songs may be found on the sculptured tombs of Upper Egypt.—In this same connection, it is said, that wheat and barley were abundantly cultivated in every part of Egypt, and that the former was harvested in about five and the latter in about four months after sowing. Compare Exod. ix. 31, 32, from which it appears that the plague did not smite the wheat, because it was later ; and also p. 119 of this volume. In Gen. xli. 22, we read, " seven ears came up in one stalk." Among the kinds of wheat in Egypt, according to *Wilkinson*, " the seven-eared quality " may be mentioned. " It was cropped a *little* below the ear ;" hence the Israelites could obtain straw or stubble for their brick, from the fields, when it was not furnished by their task-masters.

[1] Briefe, S.   [2] II. 1. p. 308.   [3] Taylor, p. 173, 4.

DEUTERONOMY v. 15; iv. 20; vi. 20, seq.; vii. 8, &c.

In umerous passages of Deuteronomy, the Israelites are admonished to keep the law, by reminding them of their sad condition in Egypt, and the favour shown in bringing them out—a motive which implies that the consciousness of this condition and this favour was yet entirely fresh and lively. In Deut. v. 15, after it had been said that the rest of the Sabbath shall be granted to the servant, it is added: "And remember that thou wast a servant in the land of Egypt, and that the Lord thy God brought thee out thence." In the same verse is the duty of keeping the Sabbath holy, founded on the deliverance from Egypt. In chap. xxiv. 18, after the order not to pervert the right judgment of the stranger, or the fatherless, or take the widow's garment in pledge, it is said : "But thou shalt remember that thou wast a bondman in Egypt, and the Lord thy God redeemed thee thence : therefore I command thee to do this thing."[1] Similar references are found indeed in the earlier books.[2] That they are especially numerous in Deuteronomy, is explained from the preponderance of the admonitory element in the book; from the fact that it, more than the remaining books, (which present the law in its bare objectivity,) appeals to the heart of the Israelites, in order to bring the law nearer to it, which was one principal design of the book.

We have reached the limit of our inquiry. *V. Bohlen*, in his Introduction to Genesis,[3] supposes that the knowledge of Egypt which is found in the Pentateuch, can be wholly explained from the intercourse between the Israelites and the Egyptians in the age of Solomon. But those Egyptian references with which he was acquainted, filled scarcely half a page;[4] and indeed, in order to explain these from later circumstances, he was obliged to labour by availing himself of a number of "mistakes and inaccuracies" with reference to Egypt, to bring counter-arguments for the later age of the narrator, and for his position out of Egypt.

---

[1] Compare chap. iv. 20; vi. 20, seq.; vii. 8; xv. 15; xvi. 12; xxiv. 22.
[2] See Exod. xxii. 20; Lev. xix. 34.   [3] S. 41.
[4] S. 54.

We have proved that these pretended "mistakes and inaccuracies" are just so many proofs of the ignorance of him who alleged them. We have also shown that the Egyptian references of the Pentateuch are beyond comparison more numerous and direct than was hitherto supposed.[1] The unprejudiced critic henceforth will be obliged to recognise in the connection of the Pentateuch with Egypt, one of the most powerful arguments for its credibility and for its composition by Moses.

[1] In Exod. xxv. 12, seq., among other directions with regard to the construction of the ark, it is said, " And thou shalt cast four rings of gold for it, and put them in the four corners thereof: and two rings shall be in the one side of it, and two rings in the other side of it. And thou shalt make staves of shittim-wood, and overlay them with gold. And thou shalt put the staves into the rings by the sides of the ark, that the ark may be borne with them." And it is seen from 1 Chron. xv. 2, 15, that " the Levites bare the ark on their shoulders." The similarity between this construction of the ark and the manner of moving it, and the procession of shrines among the Egyptians, is too striking to be passed unnoticed. " One of the most important ceremonies," says *Wilkinson*, " was ' the procession of shrines,' which is mentioned in the Rosetta Stone, and is frequently represented on the walls of the temples. The shrines were of two kinds: the one a sort of canopy; the other an ark or sacred boat, which may be termed the great shrine. This was carried with grand pomp by the priests, a certain number being selected for that duty, who, supporting it on their shoulders by means of long staves, passing through metal rings at the side of the sledge on which it stood, brought it into the temple, where it was placed upon a stand or table, in order that the prescribed ceremonies might be performed before it. The stand was also carried in the procession by another set of priests, following the shrine, by means of similar staves; a method usually adopted for transporting large statues and sacred emblems, too heavy or too important to be borne by one person."

APPENDIX.

MANETHO AND THE HYCSOS.

I. MANETHO.

THE prevailing opinion is, that *Manetho*[1] was the chief of the priests in Heliopolis, who were the most distinguished for learning of any in Egypt, and wrote under the patronage of king Ptolemy

[1] The reasonings of our author upon the trustworthiness of Manetho, and the existence of the Hycsos, seem to us to partake somewhat of the nature of special pleading. He may be right, but we are not yet prepared to discard the testimony of those who are best qualified to judge in this matter. It is true, it must be very pleasant for those engaged in deciphering hieroglyphics, to find their results verified by an ancient author; but can it be supposed that such men as *Sir J. G. Wilkinson, Champollion, Rosellini,* and other Egyptian archæologists, are all deceived by this feeling? Their belief, as far as known, is uniform. *Wilkinson* (Vol. I. p. 38) says: "From the preceding extracts of Manetho, as from other passages in his work, it appears reasonable to conclude that Egypt was at one time invaded and occupied by a powerful Asiatic people, who held the country in subjection; and viceroys being appointed to govern it, these obtained the title of Pastor or Shepherd Kings. I have already shown there is authority for believing this event to have taken place in the early periods of Egyptian history, previous to the era of Osirtasen the First." He also says (p. 23): "I am, therefore, of opinion, that the irruption of the Pastors was anterior to the erection of any building now extant in Egypt, and long before the accession of the seventeenth dynasty." Although Hengstenberg has given us the view of *Rosellini,* we cannot forbear to quote a few lines from *Mr Gliddon,* who is supposed to agree in opinion with that author. We do it the more readily, as the passage shows the imperfect state in which Manetho is handed down to us, and thus answers some of the objections of our author. "This great work (of Manetho) has been lost; and the re-discovery of one copy of Manetho would be the most de-

Philadelphus, by the aid of the writings found in the sanctuaries of the temples.[1]

But there are several strong objections to this opinion : 1. In the specification of the gods and demi-gods who ruled Egypt,[2] ac-

sirable and satisfactory event that could be conceived in *Egyptian*, and we may add, in universal history and chronology. As the work of an Egyptian, testifying the glory of his nation, it was probably conscientiously prepared ; although he may have allowed national pride to give a too partial colouring to his narration, and possibly an exaggerated view of his country's antiquity. But we can no longer be harsh in our criticisms, seeing that to his sixteenth dynasty *he is confirmed by the sculptures*, while every new step of discovery that is made in hieroglyphics, gives some new confirmatory light in support of Manetho's *earlier* arrangement. Again, because we have only mutilated extracts of his original; one, a fragment preserved by Josephus, which seems to have been copied, verbatim, from Manetho's work ; another is an abstract in the chronology of Syncellus, who did not even see the original book himself, but embodied in his compilation the extracts he found in Julius Africanus and Eusebius. Within the last few years, the discovery of an Armenian version of Eusebius, has added some better readings to those we formerly possessed. These writers, Josephus, Eusebius, and Julius Africanus, differ so much from each other in the several portions of Manetho's history, of which they present the extracts, that, in their time, either great errors had crept into the then-existing copies of Manetho, or one or more of them were corrupted by design ; especially in the instance of Eusebius, who evidently suppressed some parts, and mutilated others, to make Manetho, by a pious fraud, conform to his own peculiar and contracted system of cosmogony." The absence of all indications of the Hycsos on the monuments is accounted for, as is seen, by *Wilkinson*, from the antiquity of their irruption. If (as *Rosellini* supposes,) they ruled Lower Egypt, while the seventeenth dynasty of Theban kings reigned in Upper Egypt, it is not certain that monuments of them may not yet be found. It is also not strange that no mention is made of the Hycsos in the Bible ; for the lineage of the Pharoahs, under whom they lived, would be of little consequence to the Jews. T.

[1] See e. g. Heeren, Ideen Aeg. S. 426.

[2] According to ancient writers, the Egyptians claimed to have been ruled first by the gods or Auritae and then by the demi-gods or Mestraeans, who were succeeded by Menes, the first human king. But *Wilkinson* says, there are positive grounds for the conviction that no Egyptian deity was supposed to have lived on the earth ; even the story of Osiris's rule in this world was purely allegorical and intimately connected with the most profound and curious mystery of their religion. It is probable that the earliest government of the country was a hierarchy, and the succession of the different gods to the sovereignty of the country would then be explained

cording to *Manetho*, before men, a remarkable ignorance of Egyptian divinity is exhibited, a strange mingling of Greek and Egyptian names of deities,—Mars, Apollo, and Ammon, are found as demi-gods, and Jupiter Ammon is divided into two divine persons, &c. From these facts, upon which *Jablonski*[1] as long ago as his time, and after him and copying from him *Meiners*[2] commented, *Rosellini*[3] has justly argued that this list was drawn up by one entirely unacquainted with Egyptian affairs. But when he proceeds further: The list cannot *therefore* be taken from the books of *Manetho*, this *therefore* is well founded only on the supposition that *Rosellini's* prejudice in favour of *Manetho* is just. Until further proofs are adduced, we are perfectly satisfied that that which is an argument against the *part* is also against the *whole*, since every trace of a later interpolation of this part, while the whole existed without it, is wanting.

2. In the notices of *Manetho* upon the Hycsos, preserved in *Josephus*,[4] it is said of the first king of the Hycsos: "But since he found in the Saïtic nome a very convenient city, which lay on the east side of the Bubastic channel," &c. This geographical designation involves an evident contradiction. A city could not be situated at the same time in the Saïtic nome and east of the Bubastic arm of the Nile. For the Saïtic nome lay in the western part of the Delta; the Bubastic channel, on the other hand, is the same

---

by that of the respective colleges of priests. "The Egyptians justly ridiculed the Greeks for pretending to derive their origin from deities. They showed Hecatæus and Herodotus a series of three hundred and forty-five high-priests, each of whom, they observed, was 'a man, son of a man,' but in no instance the descendant of a god: thus censuring the folly of Hecatæus, who claimed a deity as his sixteenth ancestor. Such is the meaning of the expression in Herodotus, 'a piromis, son of a piromis:' and it is singular that the historian should not have understood the signification of the word rômi, (man, or piròmi, the man,) as the sense alone suffices to point it out."—*Wilkinson*, Vol. L p. 17.

[1] Panth. Aeg. Proll. p. 67, seq. In reference to these things this author says: Totus animi pendeo, ancepsque haereo quodnam de scriptoris hujus, aut diligentia, aut peritia, aut accuratione, aut bona denique fide judicium ferre debeam, and therefore was in the best way, with their help, to perceive the indications of the truth.

[2] Religionsgesch. der ältesten Völker, besonders der Aegypter, S. 122.

[3] Vol. I. 1. p. 12.

[4] Contr. Ap. 1. 14: Εὑρὼν δὲ ἐν νομῷ τῷ Σαΐτῃ πόλιν ἐπικαιροτάτην, κειμένην μὲν πρὸς ἀνατολὴν τοῦ Βουβαστίτου ποταμοῦ κ. τ. λ.

with the Pelusiac, the most eastern of all. *Lakemacher*,[1] in order to avoid this difficulty, wishes for—' in the Saïtic nome,' to read—' in the Sethroitic nome.' So *Ed. Bernhard*. This is very well if it is only first shown that *Manetho* was a native Egyptian who lived in the time of Ptolemy Philadelphus. In the meantime, however, we intend to make use of this argument to show the opposite.

Others suppose that by Saïs is not meant the nome known in the west, but another much more easterly, commonly called Tanis, from which *Herodotus* borrowed his designation of Saïtic arm of the Nile, while his other accounts have reference to the western Saïs.[2] But the passage of *Herodotus*[3] spoken of, can be of no service to *Manetho*. It is granted that it is very probable that the Tanitic arm of the Nile is called in it the Saïtic, as even *Strabo*[4] seems to have admitted, who in the words, "the Tanitic arm of the Nile, which some call the Saïtic," by 'some' probably means *Herodotus*. But the attempt to explain this renaming of the Tanitic arm of the Nile by supposing that Tanis is called Saïs, is most improbable. Either *Herodotus* made a mistake in writing, or what is more probable, he designates as the Saïtic, the arm of the Nile which bounds the Saïtic nome on the East. But if Tanis had been called Saïs, a city over the Bubastic channel could not lie in the Tanitio-Saïtic nome. The Egyptian nomes were small, and one being on this side of the Bubastic Nile-arm, could the less extend over it, since the land on the two sides of this channel was carefully divided, and that beyond it was not considered as belonging to Egypt proper.[5] Besides, we know the names of the nomes in the region without the Pelusiac arm of the Nile.[6] Let any one judge whether so great ignorance of the geography of his native land can be accounted for in a noble Egyptian of the time of Ptolemy Philadelphus.

3. In the account concerning the Hycsos it is said : "But their whole nation were called Hycsos, i. e. shepherd-kings. For *Hyc* signifies in the sacred tongue, a king, but *sos* means shepherd,

---

[1] Obs. Phil. 6. 323.
[2] B. 2. c. 17.
[3] Mannert. alt. Geog. 10. 1. p. 562.
[4] B. 17. p. 802.
[5] Compare Champollion, L'Eg. s. l. Phar. 2. p. 269.
[6] Compare Cellarius. Not. Orbis Ant. ed. Schwarz II. p. 799. Champollion, 2. p. 277, seq.

and shepherds in the common dialect, and from these two is the word Hycsos compounded."[1] There is nowhere else any trace found of the co-existence of a sacred and common dialect in Egypt, as is here implied. The author, in his great ignorance of Egyptian affairs, puts in the place of a difference between sacred and common *writing*, the difference between the sacred and common language. The unfortunate attempt of *Latronne* in *Champollion's* " Précis "[2] to justify *Manetho* for this distinction between the sacred and common language, shows only to what violence the prejudice in favour of Manetho leads. If we look critically at this *one* circumstance, the gross ignorance of the author, which is revealed in this expression in regard to the Egyptian language, we shall have sufficient ground for freeing ourselves from this prejudice. Moreover, some suspicion with regard to the author's knowledge of Egyptian language, arises also from the fact that Hyc, which according to one declaration must mean king, and according to another captive—no slight difference—is found elsewhere neither in the one or the other signification.[3]

4. *Manetho* refers his notices as to their original source, to certain columns in the Seriadic land, engraved in the sacred dialect, and with sacred letters by Thoth, the first Hermes, whose contents were translated before the deluge, from the sacred dialect into the Greek language, and written upon papyrus, were deposited by *Agathodämon* the son of the second Hermes, the father of That, in the sanctuaries of the temples of Egypt.[4]

The prominent doubt which arises here is, how an Egyptian of

---

[1] Ἐκαλεῖτο δὲ τὸ σύμπαν αὐτῶν ἔθνος ὑκσώς, τοῦτο δέ ἐστι βασιλεῖς ποιμένες. Τὸ γὰρ ὑκ καθ' ἱερὰν γλῶσσαν βασιλέα σημαίνει, τὸ δὲ σως ποιμήν ἐστι καὶ ποιμένες κατὰ τὴν κοινὴν διάλεκτον καὶ οὕτω συντιθέμενον γίνεται ὑκσώς.

[2] P. 407.

[3] "In linguae Copticae monumentis omnibus," says Jablonski Von. Aeg., Opusc. 1. p. 357, concerning *Hyc* in the sense of king, " quae ad manus nostras pervenere, vocis istius vestigia nulla occurrunt." The same author remarks that the meaning *captive* is just as little capable of proof, p. 362.

[4] Ἐκ τῶν ἐν τῇ Σηριαδικῇ γῇ κειμένων στηλῶν ἱερᾷ φησι διαλέκτῳ ἢ ἱερογραφικοῖς γράμμασι κεχαρακτηρισμένων ὑπὸ Θῶθ τοῦ πρώτου Ἑρμοῦ, ἢ ἑρμηνευθεισῶν μετὰ τὸν κατακλυσμὸν ἐκ τῆς ἱερᾶς διαλέκτου εἰς τὴν Ἑλληνίδα φωνὴν γράμμασιν ἱερογλυφικοῖς, ἢ ἀποτεθέντων ἐν βίβλοις ὑπὸ τοῦ Ἀγαθοδαίμονος, υἱοῦ τοῦ δευτέρου Ἑρμοῦ, πατρὸς δὲ τοῦ Τὰτ ἐν τοῖς ἀδύτοις τῶν ἱερῶν Αἰγύπτου. Syncelli Chronographia, p. 40, ed. Goar. t. 1. p. 72. ed. Bonn.

high rank of the time of Ptolemy Philadelphus could believe that even in the most remote antiquity, there could be any necessity of Greek translations in his own land, and that these translations were deposited in the archives of the temples. Zoega endeavours to avoid this doubt, which he sees very much endangers the reputation of *Manetho*, by a change of the text. According to him, *Manetho* must have written, instead of "in the Greek language," " in the common dialect."[1] But the change is of little advantage to *Manetho*, for had he written as Zoega supposes he did, he would here again merit the reproach of making a distinction between the sacred and common dialect, an error which he indeed fell into in another place. Further, the change proposed is an unwarranted one ; such a one is allowed only in a writer of established reputation. Finally, why should the translation from the sacred dialect into the common one be mentioned ? It should evidently have been specified how the author obtained his knowledge of Greek. This writer even claims for the writing, in its Greek form, divine authority. All such attempts for the vindication of *Manetho*, (to which also that of *Heyne*[2] belongs, who sets down without argument all of that which *Syncellus* copies from the preface of *Manetho* as spurious,) would have been spared, if the attention had been directed not to particular things merely, but if, on the other hand, all which is related had been taken at once into view.

A second suspicion arises from the mentioning of columns in the Seriadic land. A Jewish fable, of similarity which cannot be mistaken, is furnished by *Josephus*.[3] Traditions of certain Egyptian columns are found even at a very early period, but in the form in which it is found in *Manetho*, it is of Jewish origin. This is clear, since in it as in Josephus, information is given in reference to the flood. On account of the impending flood they were erected. But of the flood, original Egyptian tradition knows

---

[1] He says, De Obeliscis, p. 36 : Scripsisse Manethonem εἰς τὴν κοινὴν φωνὴν ν. εἰς τὴν κοινὴν διάλεκτον quovis certarem pignore : at Graecis compilatoribus ἡ κοινὴ φωνὴ erat ἡ ἕλληνις.

[2] In der Gött. Comm. Vol. V. Hist. p. 103.

[3] Arch. 1. c. 2. § 3 : Οἱ ἀπὸ Σήθου σοφίαν τὴν περὶ τὰ οὐράνια ᾗ τὴν τούτων διακόσμησιν ἐπενόησαν· ὑπὲρ δὲ τοῦ μὴ διαφυγεῖν τοὺς ἀνθρώπους τὰ εὑρημένα, προειρηκότος ἀφανισμὸν Ἀδάμου τῶν ὅλων ἔσεσθαι — — στήλας δύο ποιησάμενοι, τὴν μὲν ἐκ πλίνθου, τὴν δ' ἑτέραν ἐκ λίθων, ἀμφοτέραις ἐνέγραψαν τὰ εὑρημένα — — μένει δ' ἄχρι τοῦ δεῦρο κατὰ γῆν τὴν Σιριάδα.

nothing at all, as generally in all heathen antiquity no single reference to it unconnected with Jewish influence appears, so that it is wretchedly uncritical to make use of these heathenish notices in confirmation or deprecation of the Mosaic history. Before they are made use of, some one account of the deluge in heathen writers should be referred to, of an earlier date than that of this composition.

Now it is granted that a possibility remains, even if we allow that this tradition is of Jewish origin, that an Egyptian writer as early as the time of Ptolemy Philadelphus could avail himself of this, but it is not probable ; for the whole Jewish system of tradition of this kind appears to belong specially to a later time.

That the Seriadic land is Utopian is shown by the fact that all attempts to discover it have been vain ;[1] but upon this we do not wish to lay any great stress. It serves, however, for the counteraction of the current prepossession in favour of the true historical character of *Manetho's* work, but it does not make it entirely impossible that the author lived as early as the reign of Philadelphus. So the Hycsos-city Avaris is just as vainly sought as the Seriadic Land. *Champollion*,[2] following the example of *Larcher*, seeks to show that Avaris is Heroöpolis ; but he does this merely by a comparison of what *Manetho* says of the position of Avaris, with the situation of Heroöpolis. No other writer mentions an Egyptian city Avaris ; and that the author had need to fear the control of geographers he himself betrays, since he takes refuge in a region not very accessible to them, and hints that the name Avaris belongs not to common language, but bears a higher character, has a mystical significance."[3]

5. The striking coincidence of that which *Manetho* relates concerning the Jews, with the declarations of such writers as *Chāremon, Lysimachus, Apion,* and *Apollonius Molo,* who all of them lived under the Roman dominion, render it improbable that he wrote as early as the age of Philadelphus. If the parallel narratives are compared with each other, it will be found improbable, if

[1] Compare Zoega, p. 36.
[2] Eg. s. l. Phar. 2. p. 87, seq.
[3] In one passage, καλουμένην ἀπό τινος ἀρχαίας θεολογίας Ἄυαριν. In a second, ἔστι δὲ ἡ πόλις κατὰ τὴν θεολογίαν ἄνωθεν, Τυφώνιος.

not directly impossible, that some centuries should elapse between the times of their composition; and the more so as the traces of Egyptio-Greek persecution against Jews, upon which these accounts are founded, cannot be referred to in the period of the Ptolemies, and especially of the more ancient Ptolemies. This persecution, on the contrary, meets us first in the time of the Romans. For the third book of the Maccabees evidently belongs to this latter period, and transfers its circumstances to the time of the Ptolemies.[1] Moreover, this persecution against the Jews, in the time of the earlier Ptolemies, is not only not demonstrable from history, but it could scarcely have existence in it. *Philo* and *Josephus* both show, in numerous passages, that the head-quarters of this persecution was Alexandria; that it grew out of the jealousy which the Egyptian inhabitants of that place cherished against those of Jewish origin; and that the Egyptians drew the Greeks and Romans into a partnership of their aversion.[2] Now the circumstances which called forth the persecution in Alexandria, did not exist there at all under the first Ptolemies. The inhabitants consisted originally only of Greeks and Jews. Upon the latter, both Alexander and Ptolemy Lagus bestowed great favours, and administered justice to them equally with the Greeks.[3] Not until later, did the Egyptians come in among them by degrees; and were, as intruders, subjected to great degradation; as for example, they were punished for crime in a far more severe manner than the Greeks and the Jews, who were on the same footing with the Greeks.[4] The position of these Egyptian

---

[1] Dähne, (Darstellung der Jüdisch-Alex. Religionsphil. I. S. 25,) it is allowed, supposes that the most important facts of the narrative must be considered as worthy of confidence; but the opposite was long ago proved; and besides, it is perfectly clear to every one who reads the book, and has sufficient knowledge of the world not to start with the presumption that every thing which claims to be history, must at least have a historical basis.

[2] In proof of this, see Philo in Flaccum, p. 969, 71, 76, De Legatione ad Cajum, p. 1615, 16, and Josephus contr. Apion, B. 2. c. 3, may be compared.

[3] Josephus contr. Ap. 2. 4. Arch. B. 12. 1.

[4] Compare Philo in Flaccum, p. 976 : Τῶν μαστίγων εἰσὶ διαφοραὶ διακεκριμέναι κατὰ τὴν πόλιν πρὸς τὰ τῶν τύπτεσθαι μελλόντων ἀξιώματα· τοὺς μὲν γὰρ Αἰγυπτίους ἑτέραις αἰκίζεσθαι συμβέβηκε, ᾗ πρὸς ἑτέρων, τοὺς δὲ Ἀλεξανδρέας σπάθαις ᾗ ὑπὸ σπαθηφόρων Ἀλεξανδρέων. Among those called Alex-

inhabitants of Alexandria were so low, that many entirely abjured their Egyptian origin. Thus *Josephus*[1] relates of Apion, that he was born in an oäsis of Egypt; but ashamed of his Egyptian origin, he pretended to be an Alexandrian. The most important passage concerning this whole matter, and that which best serves for the confirmation of our hypothesis, namely, that first in later times the causes were in operation which called forth such representations as those of *Manetho*, is found in *Josephus*, and is extant only in Latin.[2]

These objections lie against the hypothesis that *Manetho*, as a native Egyptian of high rank, wrote under Ptolemy Philadelphus, and show that he or the individual who appropriated his name, (which was perhaps an honoured one,) belonged to a far later period. In favour of the correctness of the commonly received opinion, we have only the author's own testimony. But how such authority can be allowed for this purpose, is inconceivable, when it is considered, that the same individual who claims to have lived in the time of Ptolemy Philadelphus, and professes to be an Egyptian high-priest, at the same time assures us that his *original* sources of information are those fabulous columns, and his secondary source the contents of a Greek translation made even before the flood, and laid up in the archives of the temple. How can any confidence be placed in the word of a man who is convicted of such palpable falsehoods in so important a matter?

andrians, the Jews belong, according to him. They were beaten with the ἐλευθεριωτέραις and πολιτικωτέραις μάστιξιν.

[1] Contr. Ap. 2. 3.
[2] Contr. Ap. 2. 6. "Any one who searches," he says, "will find that such citizens as Apion were the authors of sedition in Alexandria."— Donec enim Graeci fuere et Macedones hanc civitatem tenentes, nullam seditionem adversus nos gessere, sed antiquis cessere solennitatibus. Cum vero multitudo Aegyptiorum crevisset inter eos, propter confusiones temporum, etiam hoc opus semper est additum. Nostrum vero genus permansit purum. Ipsi igitur molestiae hujus fuere principium, nequaquam populo Macedonicam habente constantiam, neque prudentiam Graecam, sed cunctis scilicet utentibus malis moribus Aegyptiorum et antiquis inimicitiis adversum nos exercentibus. E diverso namque factum est, quod nobis improperare praesumunt. Nam cum plurimi corum non opportune jus ejus civitatis obtineant, peregrinos vocant eos, qui hoc privilegium ad omnes impetrasse noscuntur. Nam Aegyptiis neque regum quisquam videtur jus civitatis fuisse largitus neque nunc quilibet imperatorum.

The suspicion of deception increases when we recollect that we strictly have not to do with a writer of history, but with one of that class least of all to be trusted, among whom literary deception has always been the order of the day. With an almost natural confusion it is now very commonly overlooked, although perfectly clear, that *Manetho's* work has not properly a historical design ; that it was not his main object to give history ; but this rather serves him as a foundation for his peculiar structure. According to his own declaration in his letter to Ptolemy Philadelphus,[1] his writings comprise the answer to the question put to him by Ptolemy, (I will leave it for others to inquire whether this question is in accordance with the manner of thinking of a king,) upon the things which shall come to pass in the world, περὶ τῶν μελλόντων τῷ κόσμῳ γίγνεσθαι, as also the inscriptions on those pillars mentioned by *Josephus*, of which those of *Manetho* are a copy, were not of a historical but theological character ; they were said to preserve the hidden wisdom of the fathers for their posterity. Whence, we simply remark, *Manetho* took that which was of subordinate importance to him, his history, we have not so much as his declaration : he has not himself even referred back to the temple archives, as his friends and admirers assert, though they do it inconsiderately,—since *Josephus*, setting them the example of transferring that which belongs to prediction to history, furnishes then no confirmation in this error. If *Manetho* had done this, it would not contribute at all to the advantage of his credibility, but would rather be a detriment to it. For how could the assertion that he drew from the archives, according to the miserable and current manner, so little to the honour of our critical age, be isolated ; how could it be separated from the absurdities with which

---

[1] This letter is given entire, as found in the Latin version of the Chronographia of Syncellus, p. 73.

" Ad Ptolemaeum Philadelphum Manethonis Sebennytae epistola :

Ptolemaeo Philadelpho regi magno Augusto Manetho sacerdos et sacrorum per Aegyptum penetralium notarius, genere Sebennyta, urbe Heliopoli, domino meo Ptolemaeo salutem.

De rebus omnibus nobis tuo iussu, rex magne, propositis attente cogitandum est. Hac de causa interroganti tibi de iis quae mundo accident, quaeque ex libris ab primogenitore tuo ter magno Mercurio conscriptis mihi sunt nota, prout imperasti, cuncta manifestabuntur. Vale mihi, domine mi rex."

this assertion is so closely united? How inappropriate this is, *Zoega* felt; he thinks it necessary to defend *Manetho* against the opinion, that he affirms that he received his historical facts from the same source from which his prophecies are derived. He could, *Zoega* supposes, have very probably received his history from other fountains.[1] This we willingly grant; but must yet remark, that we could not expect that great care and conscientiousness would be exercised in the choice and use of his historical sources by one who, in the specification of those from which his prophecies are taken, so plainly shows himself a vain boaster, and one who, since his object, 'ex professo,' is to retail prophecies, is a boaster by profession.

Further, the suspicion of deception is also intimated, in that it is the same Ptolemy Philadelphus at whose suggestion the book is said to be composed; precisely the one among all princes to whom it would first occur to an impostor to dedicate his work. The passages of ancient authors, which show that the exertions of Ptolemy Philadelphus with regard to learning, and especially in reference to the increase of the Alexandrian Library, were very much praised, are found collected in *Hody*[2] and *Stahr*.[3] The many unauthenticated stories which are fastened upon the fact that Ptolemy Philadelphus took a strong interest in learning, go so far that he at last was even made out to be an author.[4] Ptolemy has by degrees become expressly a mythic personage.

Let not the striking analogy, which, as soon as we recognise in the claims of *Manetho* mere pretension, we have in the writings of the Pseudo-Aristeas, be overlooked. As *Manetho* professes to be a high-priest of the time of Ptolemy Philadelphus, so *Aristeas* claims to be a noble officer at the court of the same king. There is certainly nothing more absurd than to attempt, in the manner of a base *Juste milieu* in criticism, to obtain from the work of *Aristeas* also a share of historical truth; as, for example, *Parthey*[5] supposes that *Aristeas's* statement in regard to the seventy-two learned men is to be reduced to a half or a fourth! The only

[1] " Etiam ad hoc attendendum," he says, " quod ipse ex Hermeticis stelis futurorum cognitionem se hausisse scribit, non regum historias, quas ex aliis monumentis congerere *potuit*."
[2] De Biblicorum Textibus originalibus.
[3] Aristotelia, Th. 2. S. 61 ff.   [4] Stahr, S. 63.
[5] Das Alexandrnische Museum, Berlin, 1838, S. 58.

proper course is, on the other hand, to seek to destroy the last thread of the tissue of lies, and acknowledge that the circumstance, that the translation of the Books of Moses was made in obedience to the command of Ptolemy Philadelphus, cannot be considered as even furnishing a historical basis for the fiction. The whole reference in which the Alexandrian translation is placed to the Egyptian king, belongs to the vanity of the Jews, which has called forth so many similar fictions. The choice of Philadelphus in preference to others was caused by the fact that the name of this king had become classical for the time in this department, and the Alexandrian translation is the simple product of the wants of the Jews at Alexandria. What *Parthey*[1] says: "As Ptolemy Philadelphus, influenced by his curiosity in reference to historical subjects in general, summoned seventy-two interpreters for the translation of the Jewish religious books, so he caused the ancient Egyptian chronicles to be translated by the learned high-priest and temple-scribe, *Manetho*, from the hieroglyphic writing into Greek," is true, but in an entirely different sense from that of the author, namely, in that he did the one as little as the other ; but *Manetho* and *Aristeas*, in every respect a ' par nobile fratrum,' for similar reasons had recourse to him.

If any doubt yet remains in regard to rejecting the testimony which one so confirmed in falsehood as *Manetho* gives of himself, it may yet be considered, that we have under the name of *Manetho* also another work, the Apotelesmatica, and that the author of this work also, who in the declaration of his sources of information agrees[2] so accurately with our author, dedicates his book to Ptolemy Philadelphus, and makes mention of his wife Arsinoë, but this statement of his sources is now almost unanimously declared to be false, and indeed on much more trivial grounds than those on which we have relied in the rejection of his testimony for himself, in the work under discussion.[3]

[1] P. 165.

[2] He asserts, in B. 5. v. 1, 2, that he has derived his information ἐξ ἀδύτων ἱερῶν βίβλοιν, ᾗ κρυφίμων στηλῶν, ἃς ηὕρατο πάνσοφος Ερμῆς.

[3] So according to Zoega, p. 255, the author of the Apotelesmatica is a " man minime Aegyptius, Manethonis nomen sat impudenter mentitus," and forsooth because he " omnia ea, quae ad funerum curam pertinent Aegyptiis patrio ritu sanctissime obeunda, adspernatur." Compare also Meiners, l. c. S. 122 ff.

The testimony of other writers which substantiates *Manetho's* account of himself, is not in existence. There is no mention made of him by any writer who preceded the time of the Roman dominion. It is of little consequence, that one so credulous and uncritical, and so entirely governed by interest as *Josephus*, and who even transfers[1] writers evidently Jewish to the Gentiles, gives credit to his testimony of himself, and does not even express a suspicion of forgery. It is only necessary that the object of the quotations which *Josephus* gives from *Manetho* be taken into view. Greek writers have called in question the antiquity of the Jewish nation. *Josephus* wishes to confute their testimony from the Egyptians and Phoenicians, nations who are much more worthy of confidence in historical matters than the Greeks. It is plain that it was for the interest of *Josephus* to magnify the trustworthiness of *Manetho*.

But special importance is attached to the contents of the work, which are said to perfectly substantiate the claim which the author makes for the honourable origin of the work. In praise of its excellence, those especially are exhausted who have employed themselves in modern times in the restoration of the Egyptian chronology and history from her native monuments. But it appears to us, that these commendations arise far less from the thing itself, than from the certainly very natural and pardonable desire, in so doubtful an undertaking, to have at least some one firm hold, a more certain framework on which individual facts, as they appear, can rest, a test for the correctness of things which are of doubtful acceptance. Nevertheless, this favour, shown to *Manetho*, rests only on the king's names which are found. But if we here leave general assertions, and direct our attention to particulars, in order to see how far these encomiums have received confirmation from the latest discoveries, it will be perceived that they are not so important as might properly have been expected after such eulogies, even if we receive the data without question, from those who, with regard to them, are somewhat exposed to suspicion, since they start with the necessity of admitting an agreement between *Manetho* and the monuments.

Manetho begins with the rule of the gods and demi-gods. It is evident of itself, that the monuments here furnish no confirmation. But after such a beginning it is improbable from the nature of the

---

[1] See, e. g. Contr. Ap. 1, 23.

case, that he, as soon as he brings the first human kings upon the stage, will change forthwith from a writer of fiction or romance to a historian. Thus our very well grounded suspicion is found, on closer examination, to be confirmed in a remarkable manner. The most zealous friends of *Manetho* must acknowledge, that for this whole first fifteen dynasties, the monuments furnish almost entirely nothing, and that little can be adduced from them in confutation of the assumption, that *Manetho* has done as *Syncellus*[1] did, who from his own invention gave names to the kings of the twentieth dynasty, which were omitted by *Munetho*. *Wilkinson*[2] says: Whether any dependence can be placed on the names and number of the kings of those dynasties, is a matter of great doubt. The monuments indeed furnish no assistance in this portion of early history, except perhaps in so far as the names in the later dynasties of *Manetho* are similar to those on the monuments. *Rosellini*[3] says: "Shall the whole epoch which precedes the so called sixteenth dynasty be considered fabulous? I venture neither to affirm or deny it." This author then summons every thing in order to furnish at least *some* confirmation of *Manetho* from the monuments of this period. What he adduces is as follows: The name of the man who, according to *Manetho*, heads the succession of human rulers is found on the walls of the Ramesseion, in the representation of a religious train, in which the statues of the predecessor of the king are carried in procession by the priests. *Rosellini* thinks he has discovered the Suphis of *Manetho*, the Cheops of *Herodotus*, in a tomb in the pyramids. His inscription, according to this author, reads—Suten Oveb Sciuso; which he translates—il paro sacerdote o propheta Sciuso.[4] Likewise in the tombs of Geezeh, *Rosellini* affirms that he has found the name Sensciuf. This is said to be the second Suphis of *Manetho*, the Sensuphis or Sensaophis of *Eratosthenes*, which according to *Rosellini* must signify the brother of Suphis. Besides also there are three other king's names, but those which correspond are

---

[1] Page 91. [2] Vol. I. p. 18.
[3] Vol. I. 1. p. 111.
[4] Ros. p. 126 seq. Compare II. 1. p. 36. III. 1. p. 2 seq. The same name written Koufou has more recently been discovered upon the stones of the great pyramid at Memphis. Compare Lepsius in the Eclaircissemens sur le cercuil du roi Mycerinus traduits de l'Anglais et accompagnés de notes par Lenormant, Paris, 1839, p. 44 seq.

not found in the lists of *Manetho*.[1] The disconnected names of three kings then is all that the monuments in this period furnish for the confirmation of the lists of *Manetho*, or rather all they seem to furnish. It is true, *Rosellini* affirms that he has discovered a considerable number of other names of kings, which he from uncertain conjecture places in the fifteenth dynasty; but their names have no relationship to those of *Manetho*, and these supposed facts can therefore furnish no verification of *his* list.[2]

Rosellini[3] seeks to avert from his favourite the hazardous consequences which result from this silence of the monuments,—the " great void beyond the sixteenth dynasty, where only a few and disconnected fragments of earlier cultivation and civilization appear as little oäses in the desert,"—by the hypothesis that the Hycsos have destroyed all earlier monuments! Consequently the Hycsos alone must have accomplished what a whole succession of conquerors for thousands of years together, have not been able to do, to say nothing of the absurdity of the attempt to support another fable by that of the Hycsos. These Hycsos must always be such as to answer the purposes of *Rosellini*, a diligent scholar, and in his own province highly worthy of respect, but one who has, in historical criticism, too little discrimination. In their pretended *second* irruption having become civilized, they must have left untouched all the monuments which were erected by the monarchs of the eighteenth dynasty after their first expulsion![4]

The Tablet of Abydos also appears against the credibility of *Manetho* in the first fifteen dynasties. The first eleven dynasties of *Manetho* comprised 192 kings, the thirteenth alone sixty. In the Tablet of Abydos, on the contrary, the succession of kings which forms the eighteenth dynasty begins with number forty-one. *Rosellini* has here also a ready means of escape. He supposes

[1] Ros. Vol. I. 1. p. 132.
[2] Since the appearance of Rosellini's work, the name Menkare is supposed to have been deciphered upon a coffin discovered in the third pyramid of Memphis, and it is said to be the same as the Mencheres, who according to Manetho was the fourth king of the fourth Memphitic dynasty, and the Mycerinus of Herodotus, who according to him built this same pyramid. Compare the work of Lenormant, above referred to, p. 11, seq.
[3] I 1. p. 119; II. 1. p. 75.
[4] Ros. I. 1. p. 220.

that the Tablet refers merely to the Theban kings. But this is assumed merely from his regard to *Manetho*. The succession of his predecessors in authority over Egypt appears on this monument at the request of Remeses the Third.

Finally, if we consider *Manetho* as worthy of confidence in the first fifteen dynasties, we assume for the Egyptian kingdom a duration which is opposed to the probability, the analogy, and the chronology of the Pentateuch, which, judge of it as we will, is yet even more worthy of faith than a *Manetho*. According to *Manetho*, it is 4750 years from Menes until the Persian invasion, without reckoning the fourteenth dynasty.[1] The hypothesis, that the dynasties are contemporaneous, by which it was formerly sought, after the example of *Eusebius*, to reconcile *Manetho* with the Mosaic chronology, may now, since the researches of *Plath*, and especially of *Rosellini*,[2] be considered as entirely obsolete, although it is still asserted with a tone of so much confidence in historical writings, which are very much read. The sacred writings recognise everywhere only *one* king over all Egypt. Just so, not only *Herodotus*, *Diodorus*, and *Manetho* himself, but also, what is of more importance, the monuments, which indeed, by their magnitude and splendour, are witnesses against an origin from the petty kings of small territories. They bear upon them the title: Kings of the world, Lords of Upper and Lower Egypt. The names of the Pharaohs appear dispersed over all of Egypt, &c.

It is true, that in the later dynasties, the verdict is more favourable to *Manetho*. Several of his names here have received confirmation from the monuments. But if we descend to particular cases, it appears that here also there is very much wanting to a complete harmony between him and the monuments, even according to the statements of his friends, whom we must follow in that which respects the monuments. How great the differences are, is shown by the comparison of the statements of *Manetho* and the data obtained from the monuments, in reference to the eighteenth dynasty, in *Rosellini*.[3] *Manetho* has, for example, made out of the one Usirei or Menephtha I., the two Akencheres; to Armais, Armes or Armesses, corresponding to the Remeses of the inscriptions, he allows only four years, whilst the fourteenth year of his

---

[1] Wilk. Vol. I. p. 18.   [2] I. 1. p. 93, seq.   [3] Vol. I. 1. p. 286.

reign is represented on the monuments.[1] *Manetho* ascribes to the Great Remeses (III.), according to him Rammeses, a reign of one year and four months, while on the monuments his sixty-second year appears. If Sesostris is really, as *Champollion*, *Rosellini*, and others suppose, identical with this Remeses III., the error[2] of *Manetho*, who places Sesostris as early as the twelfth dynasty, is palpable. The monuments furnish no additional evidence for the whole account of Armais=Danaus of *Manetho*, and it is characteristic of *Rosellini's* want of skill in criticism, that he receives this account without argument, as true and original, and only examines it to designate the time of its occurrence,[3] although it is perfectly clear, that this tradition is as far from being an original Egyptian one, as that concerning Polybius and Proteus, with regard to which, however, even *Rosellini's* patience forsakes him, and he cannot avoid declaring,[4] that all the accounts concerning them have had their origin in the words of *Homer*.

With how little confidence one can rely even in those later times upon kings' lists of *Manetho*, such declarations as these show: Sethus was also called Egyptus, and from him Egypt received this name, an assertion which has a worthy counterpart in that of *Diodorus*: One of the immediate successors of Proteus was Nilus, from whom the river, which was before called Egyptus, took the name Nilus. The names of the kings of the twentieth

---

[1] Vol. I. 1. p. 255.

[2] *Wilkinson* obviates this difficulty, (Vol. 1. p. 63, 64): "Osirei was succeeded by his son, Remeses the Great, who bore the name of Amun-mai-Remeses, or Remeses-mi-amun, and was reputed to be the famous Sesostris of antiquity. The origin of the confusion regarding Sesostris may perhaps be explained. He is mentioned by Manetho in the twelfth dynasty, and Herodotus learned that he preceded the builders of the pyramids: I therefore suppose that Sesostris was an ancient king famed for his exploits, and the hero of early Egyptian history; but that after Remeses had surpassed them, and become the favourite of his country, the renown and name of the former monarch were transferred to the more conspicuous hero of a later age; and it is remarkable that when Germanicus went to Egypt, the Thebans did not mention Sesostris, but Rhamses, as the king who had performed the glorious actions ascribed in olden times to their great conqueror. Nothing, however, can justify the supposition that Sesostris, or, as Diodorus calls him, Sesoosis, is the Shishak of Scripture."

[3] Comp. I. 2. S. 1, seq.

[4] I. 2. p. 27.

dynasty are entirely omitted by *Manetho*, a circumstance which can by no means be explained, as *Rosellini*[1] has attempted to do, by supposing that these kings had accomplished nothing worthy of consideration, but by the fact that, even for this later time, his sources of information were defective.

But that which has been furnished from investigations upon the monuments, which is really in favour of *Manetho*, does not indeed compel us to place him in a proportionally early time, or to ascribe to him circumstances by which he was specially favoured in the use of sources of information. Even if he wrote in the beginning of the period of the Roman dominion, he could, out of the designations of Egyptian kings which were in circulation, easily obtain a certain number of the actual names of kings to which his whole real stock is finally reduced.

The question whether *Manetho* was an Egyptian or a Greek can scarcely be answered. The Egyptian and Anti-jewish interest which he exhibited, is not sufficient to prove his Egyptian origin. For many Greek writers appropriated to themselves Egyptian sympathies and antipathies; as, for example, *Apollonius Molo* was a Greek.[2] *Manetho's* ignorance of Egyptian religion, language, and geography, is just as little decisive against his Egyptian descent. There was in later times a multitude of subjects among this people who had entirely abandoned their nationality, with the exception only of their national arrogance and their antipathies; as, for example, Apion was an individual of such character, since he despised the Jews on account of circumcision and because they ate no swine's flesh, without thinking that this reproach could properly be made only by a Greek, not by an Egyptian, who thus, together with the Jews, contemned his own nation.[3] Now, from one of these classes of subjects must *Manetho* also have been. Yet he hardly lived in Egypt. Several of the errors attributed to him are of such a kind that they

---

[1] I. 2. p. 34.

[2] Josephus, c. Apion., says expressly: τῶν δὲ εἰς ἡμᾶς βλασφημιῶν ἤρξαντο μὲν Αἰγύπτιοι· βουλόμενοι δ᾽ ἐκείνοις τινὲς χαρίζεσθαι, παρατρέπειν ἐπεχείρησαν τὴν ἀλήθειαν. Similar descriptions are found in other places, Menander e. g. was a Greek from Ephesus, and yet he wrote Phoenician history with the spirit and interest of a Phoenician.

[3] Jos. c. Ap. 2. c. 13.

could scarcely have been made even by a Greek who lived in that country.

II. THE HYCSOS OF MANETHO.

In scarcely any inquiry has criticism taken so decided a retrogressive movement, as in that concerning the Hycsos of *Manetho*. The subject was considered by *Perizonius* as long ago as his time, at a right point of view, although it is acknowledged that he was wrong in a not unimportant particular, which will soon be pointed out. This author denied that the history of the Hycsos had its foundation originally in Egypt, and he explained it as a transformation of that which the books of Moses relate of Joseph and the exodus of Israelites, undertaken with a design to favour the Egyptians and injure the Jews.[1] In the footsteps of *Perizonius* trod *Thorlacius* in the little treatise, "De Hycsosorum Abari,"[2] which has been but little known, and which throughout bears the marks of a youthful attempt, but yet is written with a spirit of investigation and with talent for historical criticism. He brings the account of *Manetho* concerning the Hycsos in connection with the translation of the books of Moses into Greek,[3] and the consequent diffusion of the knowledge of the ancient crime and disgrace of the Egyptians, and he considers this account as an at-

[1] The result of his impartial and thorough inquiry, he gives on page 336, seq. of the Orig. Aegypt: Satis ni fallor liquere videtur, quando sacras cum hisce comparamus literas, Aegyptios, quia gloriosissimam non modo Josephi, sed et Mosis et Israelitarum ex Aegypto exeuntium historiam profiteri nolebant, finxisse falsam et vilem et deformem Judaicae gentis originem, suis ex terris, sed cum scabie et lepra repetendam. Verum autem Israelitarum in Aegypto agentium et inde exeuntium historiam variis multisque falsis circumstantiis ita contaminasse et adulterasse, ut agnosci vix posset, et sic ad alios eam homines tuto retulisse. Further, p. 339: Since Herodotus and Diodorus are entirely silent concerning the Hycsos, videtur sane Manetho historiam eorum suum ad arbitrium primus concinnasse, falsis et fabulosis circumstantiis adulteratam, ut ita Judaeorum antiquitatem et res ab eorum majoribus id Aegypto gestas—penitus obscuraret et extingueret.

[2] Copenhagen, 1794.   [3] Pp. 16 and 17.

tempt to throw the infamy of these things off from the Egyptians, and devolve it upon the Israelites.[1]

This view stood in so manifest opposition to the position which has been taken in modern times concerning *Manetho*, that it was necessary to abandon it. If, for example, we suppose with *Rosellini*,[2] that if *Manetho* were handed down to us unmutilated, Egyptian affairs, even those most uncertain from distance of time, would be as well known as those of Greece and Rome ; if we, in our blindness, go so far with him, relying upon the pretended witness of *Manetho* for himself, as to believe that this author has derived his facts from the authentic documents of historical science ; if we place to the account of the compiler all of that which, even in the list of the kings of *Manetho*, opposes this opinion ;[3] then we must naturally consider every thing which is in opposition to true history, so soon as the account of *Manetho* is applied to the Israelites, as proof that he could not have reference to them, we must go even so far as with *Rosellini*[4] to reproach the critical obtuseness of those who maintain the identity of the Jews and the Hycsos ! Truly this view may be considered as one which is commonly promulgated and believed, and we should not hope to obtain the renewal of a favourable hearing, if we did not believe, that by the foregoing inquiry concerning *Manetho*, we have given a powerful blow to the prejudice which has contributed to the rejection of the view held by us. We make only one additional remark, namely, that the current favourable opinion in regard to *Manetho*, even then also receives a check through his account of

---

[1] Hunc antiquum gentis pudorem Graecis saltem, Aegypti tunc dominis celare volentes auctores Aegyptiaci, narrandi rationes sic instituerunt, ut famosi istius et cum tanta Aegyptiorum ignominia, tantis cladibus conjuncti Israelitarum exitus narrationi Mosaicae indigenis parum honorificae, haberent quod opponerent. Ideoque falsa veris miscendo id unice egerunt, ut funesti eventus culpa omnis et opprobrium ab Aegyptiis ad Israelitas transferretur. Hoc consilium Manethoni, Chaeremoni et Lysimacho fuisse res ipsa loquitur, ut ad communem metam pergentes, quod fere mendaces solent, suam quisque viam sit ingressus. In the opinion of this author, the account of Manetho is, anilis Mosaicae de Israelitarum in Aeg. rebus narrationis larva et imago, qua afflictis subdole commentis, inauditam Aegyptiorum in Israelitas crudelitatem, quae in scriptis Mosaicis vivis coloribus depingitur, quodamodo tegere vel excusare Manetho volebat : hinc saevus Hycsosorum dominatus regesque sex in subsidium cusi.

[2] Vol. I. 1. p. 5.   [3] Compare Ros. I. 1. pp. 2 and 6.
[4] Vol. I. 1. p. 175.

the Hycsos, if any other people than the Israelites are understood by them. Applied to any nation which we can call to mind, the account comprises everywhere such palpable falsehoods, internal contradictions and improbabilities, as it has already been shown in part by *Josephus* and yet more thoroughly by *Perizonius* and *Thorlacius*—to whom we must refer, since we have no desire to enter on the discussion anew—that it is impossible to consider it as coming from a good historian. The admirers of *Manetho*, since they are ignorant of these circumstances, which are yet so perfectly evident, can scarcely be acquitted from a species of literary dishonesty occasioned by their blind predilection for him.

We will now collect the reasons which prove, that the Hycsos can be no other than the Israelites; that no older native sources are the foundation of the account of *Manetho*; that this account, on the contrary, is merely a transformation of the historical facts which have reference to the Jews, so as to favour the national vanity of the Egyptians.

1. The more ancient defenders of the reference to the Israelites have themselves, in regard to *one* important point, surpassed their antagonists. Namely, they have allowed that *Manetho* himself distinguished the shepherds from the Jews. The shepherds, relates *Manetho*, long *before* the time of the Jews, were expelled from Egypt. But the latter people having originated in Egypt, were, long after the shepherds, banished in consequence of a leprosy which polluted their bodies.[1] But the matter was not allowed to end here. It must be supposed that a report which originally had reference to the Jews, was in later times erroneously transferred to another people. But by this acknowledgment, one of their strongest supports was torn away. Is the contrary true, can it be shown that it did not occur to *Manetho* himself, that the Hycsos and the Israelites were a different people, then the friends of *Manetho* find themselves in a dilemma; they cannot defend without at the same time casting reproach upon him. If the Hycsos are the Israelites, he can lay no further claim to the reputation of a good historian, since he relates things of them which are not at all applicable to the Israelites. Are they any other nation, then he commits a gross mistake, in that he identified

them with the Israelites.[1] That *Manetho* did actually intend to designate the Israelites by the term Hycsos, it did not occur to *Josephus* to doubt. He was too thoroughly convinced that the whole point of the narrative lay in its application to the Jews, to consider it necessary to state expressly this reference.

The whole contest concerning the Hycsos owes its origin merely to the supposition of *Josephus*, that this reference would be perfectly understood from the thing itself. Could he have foreseen this contest, it would have been an easy matter for him to have prevented it, by adducing the direct proof that *Manetho* must have had reference to them, and to no other nation.—Let it not be said, in opposition to this, that the contents of the narrative itself disprove its application to the Jews. If *Manetho* understood the leprous persons to be the Jews, it is impossible that he should suppose that the Hycsos, who were different from them, were also the Jews. *Manetho's* view is evidently this: the Jews are composed of a twofold element—a barbarian (in reference to the origin, of which he is in doubt,) and an Egyptian. The foreigners, the Hycsos, go, after their first expulsion, to Palestine, and build Jerusalem. They return there, after their second expulsion, with the native Egyptians, the lepers. They were pursued, by Amenophis, even to the borders of Syria.

We leave it undecided whether the tradition of such a composition of the Jews, is founded on the passages of the Pentateuch, which designate under the names עֶרֶב, *Ereb*, rabble, and אֲסַפְסֻף, *Asaphsuph*, populace, an Egyptian multitude who accompanied the Israelites in their Exodus,[2] or whether the national vanity of the Egyptians availed itself originally of two methods of calumniating the original stock of the Israelites, and then *Manetho* later, or perhaps even the tradition itself joined together these things which at first existed independently, and in a manner exclusive of each other. The latter appears to us as the more probable supposition.

How little we can infer from the fact that the unclean persons

---

[1] Dr Hengstenberg forgets that the Hebrews were but a branch of the great Semitic race, and so far as any thing can be determined of the Hycsos, they appear to have been affiliated to the same stock. This distinction sufficiently refutes the dilemma on which this part of his argument is founded.   T.

[2] Compare Exod. xii. 38, and Num. xi. 4.

are the Jews of *Manetho*, that the Hycsos consequently are not Jews, is evident from the analogy of other writers who also allow that the Jews are made up of such a twofold element. A comparison of these writers is the more valuable, since we have already shown that the hypothesis that *Manetho* lived some hundred years earlier than they, is without foundation. While *Lysimachus* has only half of the falsehood, that concerning the lepers, but not that with regard to the Hycsos, *Chäremon* has the whole.[1] This author represents the Jews as composed of two elements, the 'impure people,' and the strangers, who are found on the borders of Egypt, and are called into their aid by the former. The nation formed by the combination of these two races, he designates expressly as Jews. Even he does not know how to characterize more definitely this foreign stock. The comparison with *Manetho* is also interesting, inasmuch as it shows how uncertain and changing the Egyptian traditions were, as from their origin it could not be otherwise. The main point, the attempt to bring disgrace upon the Jews, is common to both; but all, except some of the main features, is different. Even *Josephus* shows this, and also how unworthy of confidence the Egyptian tradition is, from the contradictions between *Chäremon* and *Manetho*.

Diodorus Siculus has recourse to Egyptian tradition concerning the origin of the Jews, in two passages. In Ecl. 34. 1.[2] he represents the friends of Antiochus Pius or Sidetes, as saying of the Jews: They are, even as to origin, contemptible; since they, on account of the leprosy, as hated of the gods, were expelled from all of Egypt. Here, as universally where the lepers are spoken of, the Jews are represented as native Egyptians. On the other hand, in the second passage in Ecl. 40. 1.[3] he relates: There was in Egypt, in ancient times, in consequence of the anger of the gods, a new disease visited upon the strangers, whose different worship had diminished the honours of the native gods. The latter, therefore, decreed to banish the strangers. The most distinguished and powerful of them banded together, and betook themselves to Greece, and some of the other neighbouring regions, under honoured leaders, of whom Danaus and Cadmus were the most conspicuous. But the great multitude of them proceeded to

[1] In Josephus, c. Ap. 1. 34, 32.
[2] T. 2. 5. 24. ed. Wesseling.
[3] T. 2. p. 542, seq.

the country now called Judea, which was then an unbroken waste. This colony was conducted by Moses, &c.—That which appears in *Manetho* and *Chäremon*, in connection, is seen here divided. In the one passage there is merely the one; in the other, the other element of the tradition. Now, is it probable that *Diodorus* separated that which was originally united, when perhaps he even intended to have the one expression completed by means of the other; or that *Manetho* and *Chäremon* united that which was originally separate? The looseness of connection and the artificialness of the separation, seem to us to favour the latter opinion.

2. From our view of the subject, the circumstance that *Herodotus* gives just as little information of the Hycsos as of the lepers, is easily explained, since certainly before the time of the Ptolemies, and (if our inquiry upon *Manetho* is well founded,) also before the time of the Roman dominion, no traces of these notices can be found.[1] The condition of their existence was the acquaintance with the declarations of the Pentateuch concerning the ancient relations of the Jews to the Egyptians, which at any rate could not have been until the period after Alexander. On the other hand, from the contrary view, the fact cannot be explained. The argument from the silence of the monuments, is of more weight, the more important the events concerned. Can it be supposed that *Herodotus*, in all his intercourse with the Egyptian priests, did not hear any thing of the dominion of the Hycsos, which extended through a succession of centuries, and especially not one word of their glorious expulsion, if these events were already known at that time, as they must have been if *Manetho* received his facts from native Egyptian sources?

3. Not the least trace is found in the whole Pentateuch of a foreign dominion over Egypt.[2] The credibility of the Pentateuch can-

---

[1] Herodotus derived his information from persons who were very anxious to conceal from him any thing that reflected discredit on their order or their nation. His silence proves nothing beyond the suppressions of his informants. It is not long since a History of England was published in which no mention was made of Magna Charta or the Revolution. T.

[2] We have already shown that the probability of a foreign and intrusive dynasty having been the persecutor of the Israelites, is established by the whole tenor of the Book of Exodus. T.

not be asserted without denying the reality of a government of the Hycsos. The proper name of the national ruler of Egypt, Pharaoh, meets us everywhere,—in the time of Abraham, Joseph, and Moses. The national hatred of the Egyptians to shepherds, presents itself before us in the period described in Genesis, and at the time of the Exodus. That which is adduced in support of this position, or indeed in proof that the Pentateuch bears witness to the existence of the Hycsos, according to the current opinion, is of little force. *Rosellini*[1] supposes that the Hycsos adopted the language of Egypt. By this, the fact is explained that the king bears the appellation of Pharaoh, and gives to Joseph a title of Egyptian etymology. We will not deny that such an adoption of the Egyptian language by the Hycsos is possible; but so long as their existence stands on so frail a foundation as it now does, it will always remain certain, that the universal prevalence of the national title of the king furnishes an argument against them.

Rosellini finds a positive proof for the existence of the Hycsos in Gen. xlvi. 31, seq. Joseph there gives direction to his brothers to make it understood by the king of Egypt that they are shepherds. With a native king this circumstance could not have been for their advantage, but, on the contrary, decidedly to their disadvantage. It must then be inferred from this passage, that the emigration of the family of Jacob took place under the dominion of the Hycsos, who, in *Rosellini's* opinion, were a tribe of Scythian nomades.[2] But the fact that they are shepherds is not

[1] Vol. I. 1. p. 183, seq.
[2] *Wilkinson* too supposes they were Scythians. "The Pastor race, called Hycsos or Shepherd Kings, appear to have been the first to follow the example of the early Asiatic invaders; and though the period and history of their conquest are involved in obscurity, it is evident that they entered Egypt from the side of Syria, and that they obtained for some years a firm footing in the country, possessing themselves of Lower Egypt, with a portion of the Thebaid, and perhaps advancing to Thebes itself. I at first supposed them to have come from Assyria; but on more mature consideration have been disposed, as already stated, to consider them a Scythian tribe, whose nomade habits accord more satisfactorily with the character of a pastor race, and whose frequent inroads at early periods into other countries show the power they possessed, as well as their love of invasion, which were continued till a late time, and afterwards imitated by their successors the Tartar hordes of Central Asia."—Sec. Ser. Vol. I. p. 2.

indeed intended to serve as a recommendation of the children of Israel to Pharaoh, but it is designed to cause him, understanding that they cannot dwell in the midst of his people, to appoint them a dwelling-place in the province of Goshen, which was especially adapted to the rearing of cattle. They are directed to say that they are shepherds, and have been from the beginning, so that they cannot think of a change in their occupation: that they may dwell in the land of Goshen. According to *Rosellini's* theory it must mean—in the land of Egypt. What the sons of Jacob are directed to tell Pharaoh was, according to this author's manner of understanding it, not sufficient to cause their residence specifically in the land of Goshen, and yet this only was brought into the account, not in general their abode in Egypt. But the passage not merely does not prove what, according to *Rosellini*, it is intended to prove; it proves the very opposite. That the Israelites were shepherds, is no reason, to a Hycsos-king, for a separate abode.[1]

Rosellini[2] derives a second positive proof from Exodus, chap. i. The appeal to the mentioning of the *new* king, in verse 8, is common to him with most of the defenders of the fable of the Hycsos. In his view, as he believes that he has proved that in the time of Joseph the Hycsos-kings ruled Egypt, Amenoph the First is naturally the new king. He even makes verse 10 subserve his purpose. "Who," he says,[3] "could the enemies be with whom the Israelites might unite and fight against the Egyptians, except the shepherds, who expelled but not destroyed, were always threatening to make an irruption upon the smiling valleys of the Delta." But the mentioning of a new king has no reference at all to a change from a foreign dominion to a national one, or the reverse. The reason why the king is called new is given in the phrase following: "who knew not Joseph." Disregard of the service of Joseph—only a forgetfulness of affection is spoken of —forms the point of distinction between the new king and the old. So long as Joseph's services were remembered, the Israelites were

---

[1] The hostility of the Egyptians both to "Hebrews" and "shepherds", is distinctly stated in the history of Joseph; and it has already been shown that Goshen was most probably granted to the Israelites on condition of their defending the frontier from the incursion of the Hycsos, and similar plundering tribes. T.

[2] Vol. I. 1. p. 292, seq.   [3] P. 294.

treated kindly. While the king yet lived who elevated Joseph to the first dignity in his kingdom, the house of Jacob received friendly treatment in this kingdom. That only in this sense a new king is spoken of, is evident from the circumstance that the old as well as the new king bore the name of Pharaoh. The same thing is confirmed by the view of the relation of the children of Israel to the Egyptians, which extends through the whole narrative. Were the dynasty under which Joseph's labours were performed, and the children of Israel received under favourable auspices into the land, really different from that under which the Israelites endured hard bondage, the guilt of the latter would have been far less than as it appears in the narrative—the reproach of unthankfulness, and the forgetting of former obligations, comes not upon them—their treatment of the Israelites appears to have far more reason for it, and the judgments of God in the same degree less called for. Verse 10 also is not in favour, but opposed to the existence of the Hycsos. When it is there said, " lest they multiply, and it come to pass that, when there falleth out any war, they join also to our enemies and fight against us, and so get them up out of the land," it is evident, that there was at that time only the general possibility of a war. The thought of a particular enemy was so far wanting that *Wilkinson* finds far more in this passage than it contains, when he infers from it that at that very time the Egyptians were engaged in a war with powerful enemies. But the general possibility of a war can easily be referred to if we appoint the Hycsos their proper place in the domain of fable. Egypt had at that very time in its immediate vicinity natural enemies, people whose miserable existence in the deserts and mountains must have awakened in them a desire for the spoil of the fruitful and cultivated valley of the Nile. Such were the Amalekites, the Edomites, and the Midianites.

4. From the monuments also, the Hycsos-fable has not received the least confirmation. *Rosellini*[1] is obliged to acknowledge that no trace of the pretended names of the Hycsos-kings appears there.[2] He indeed thinks he has discovered upon the

---

[1] Vol. I. 20, 21.   [2] Vol. I. 1. p. 183.
[3] The Egyptians, naturally enough, were unwilling to preserve any memorials of their national disgrace. There is a very popular History of Russia in which there is not a word said of the battle of Narva.   T.

monuments which belong to the eighteenth dynasty[1] the Hycsos themselves, as did *Champollion* before him, as appears from his letter to Blacas.[2] But that which is found on the monuments is nothing but the representation of a victorious campaign of the Egyptian against barbarian nations, such as are constantly repeated under other dynasties. Of the Hycsos in particular, there are no indications. On the contrary, where localities which can be identified are given, they always belong to foreign countries. No trace is any where found of an extensive civil war and victory, as that against the Hycsos must have been, and yet it can scarcely be supposed that all vestiges of such a one were obliterated; if it ever occurred, it can scarcely be imagined that the monuments of the Hycsos themselves should be annihilated even to their last remains. According to *Manetho* their unlimited dominion continued over all Egypt 511 years. Then followed a severe and protracted war. Finally under Alisphragmutosis even Avaris was besieged. This city was taken by his son Thummosis. It would seem that the Hycsos had time enough to leave behind them some traces of their existence, and the well known absence of such indications could only then be accounted for, from the assiduity of the next succeeding dynasties, in the destruction of their works, if their existence were certain from other sources.

5. The narration of *Manetho* concerning the Hycsos presents so many points of agreement with the account in the Pentateuch concerning the Israelites, and, on the other hand, where there are deviations, the causes can be so easily pointed out by a reference to the interest in favour of Egypt, that we cannot doubt their identity with the Hycsos.[3] First of all, the region from which they both come, and to which they both go, is the same. The Hycsos, as well as the Israelites, come to Egypt from the regions of the East, πρὸς ἀνατολήν. After their expulsion, they go through the desert to Syria, and found there a city which they call Jerusalem,—a circumstance which alone should be sufficient to make our opponents see that their course is a wrong one. Further, the manner of life is the same to both. In reference to the Hycsos, as well as the Israelites, it is especially prominent, that they are shepherds.

---

[1] Ros. I. 1. p. 175.   [2] S. 57.
[3] Few people would discover the least similarity between the main incidents of the two narratives.   T.

The first king of the Hycsos, whom they raised from among themselves to this honour, is called Salathis.[1] This not to be mistaken Semitish name, is alone sufficient argument against *Rosellini's* Scythians. It is evidently taken from Gen. xlii. 6, where it is said: "Joseph was the ruler, הַשַּׁלִּיט, over the land." Of this first king, referring to Gen. xlvii. 20—26, it is said, he made all Egypt tributary.[2] Then he founded Avaris, and was specially employed in measuring corn,[3]—a characteristic trait, in which an allusion to Joseph cannot be mistaken. The narrative of the oppression and cruel treatment of the Egyptians by Salathis and his successor has its point of digression in Gen. xlvii. 20: " And Joseph purchased the whole land of Egypt for Pharaoh; for the Egyptians sold each one his field, since the famine prevailed over them, and the whole land became Pharaoh's." The perversions of these facts are easily explained by the effort to transfer to the Egyptians, the historical circumstances which are given with reference to the Israelites, and consequently to remove the disgrace from the latter and devolve it upon the former. The reproach of unjust oppression and cruel abuse, which according to history belonged to the Egyptians, must be attached to the Israelites.

6. The view given by us also has analogy for its support. The Egyptians, from national vanity, loved very much to appropriate to themselves the accounts of other nations, with reference to facts which had any relation to Egypt;[4] and having transformed them so as to favour themselves, they were accustomed to pass off the borrowed treasure in its assumed mould, as originally Egyptian. If we seek first for other cases of such employment of Hebrew material, *Manetho* himself certainly furnishes them. The tradition which is found in him, and also elsewhere widely diffused,[5] concerning the leprosy of the Jews, was evidently founded on the minute Mosaic precepts in reference to this disease, in

---

[1] Ros. 1. 14: πέρας δὲ ἡ βασιλία ἵνα ἐξ αὐτῶν ἐποίησαν, ᾧ ὄνομα ἦν Σάλατις.

[2] Καὶ οὗτος ἐν τῇ Μέμφιδι κατεγίνετο, τήν τε ἄνω ἡ κάτω χώραν δασμολογῶν.

[3] Ἐνθάδε κατὰ θέρειαν ἤρχετο, τὰ μὲν σιτομετρῶν ἡ μισθοφορίαν παρεχόμενος κ. τ. λ.

[4] It would be a strange instance of national vanity to adopt a forged story of national disgrace; yet this is the theory which Dr Hengstenberg so eagerly advocates in this section. T.

[5] Compare Perizonius, p. 333 ff.

Lev. chapters xiii. and xiv.,—precepts which have at all times given abundant occasion for derision to evil-minded persons.[1] What *Manetho* relates further of the desire of Amunophis to see the gods, appears to be transferred from Moses to him, and copied from the well known narrative in the Pentateuch. When *Manetho* calls Moses, who according to him must have belonged to the Egyptian element of the Jews, a Heliopolite, (a proceeding characteristic of his whole course; national vanity is not satisfied with the humiliation of its opponents, it will besides claim for itself whatever is distinguished among them,) *Thorlacius*[2] seeks the first reason of this declaration from Gen. xli. 45, where Joseph is said to have married the daughter of the priest of Heliopolis. The confounding of Moses with Joseph implied here, is the less remarkable since *Chäremon* is in a direct road to the same thing when he makes them contemporaries, and asserts that the unclean persons were removed from Egypt under the guidance of both.[3]

Lysimachus relates of the unclean persons, that after they had been thrust out into the desert by the king, and night came on, they kindled fires and lights for the purpose of protection.[4] Any one sees at once, that this no other than the explanation of the Mosaic account of the pillar of cloud and fire, which is most in accordance with the laws of the natural world; the original Egyptian narrative is clothed in the fitting garb of one of Mosaic origin. It would be a strange mistaking of the facts in the case, to seek for any thing better in a writer who relates that the city founded by the unclean persons was first called Hierosyla, the city of temple-robbers and defilers of sanctuaries, but afterwards this name was changed to Hierosolyma,—words which betray to us the whole tendency of these writers, and show that we have to do

---

[1] How the tradition might arise from them will be easily understood, when that is compared which Sonnini, " Voyage dans la haute et basse Egypte," 3. p. 126, says in reference to the leprosy of houses and garments: Ces maladies des choses inanimées, qui servaient uniquement à former les Juifs aux détails de la propreté, ont disparu de l'Orient avec le peuple sale, pour lequel ils avaient été imaginées.

[2] l. c. p. 116.

[3] Ἡγεῖσθαι δ' αὐτῶν γραμματέας Μωϋσῆν τε ᾗ Ἰώσηπον, ᾗ τοῦτον ἱερογραμματέα. Αἰγύπτια δὲ αὐτοῖς ὀνόματα εἶναι, τῷ μὲν Μωϋσῇ Τισιθὲν, τῷ δὲ Ἰωσήπῳ Πετεσάφ.

[4] In Josephus c. Ap. I. 34: Νυκτὸς δ' ἐπιγενομένης πῦρ ᾗ λύχνους καίσαντας φυλάττειν ἑαυτούς.

not with historians but with polemists, and indeed those of the lowest sort. *Josephus* knows right well how to use such passages.[1] He never comes to a thorough procedure for a fundamental exposure of literary imposture, since it is for his interest that the exposure should not fully ensue. Pure love of truth lies far from him. He allows as authority whomever he can use, be he ever so worthless.

Apion relies for what he says of Moses upon the oldest Egyptians as his vouchers.[2] But it is only necessary to examine his narrative to be convinced, that even he received his facts only from Jewish accounts, which he perverted at his pleasure. Whence else than immediately or mediately, (the latter more probably in all the writers of this class,) from the Pentateuch does he derive his information, when he relates, for example, that Moses ascended the mountain between Egypt and Arabia, which is called Sinai, and remained concealed there forty days, and afterwards he descended thence and gave the law to the Jews.[3]

But not alone by the Egyptians was the original possession of the Israelites basely stolen, and after an easy transformation proudly exhibited to view by its new possessors, as if inherited from their ancestors; others also sought, in the abundance of the Jews, help for their own poverty. The Chaldean Berosus, for example, pretended that he obtained from the most ancient records of his nation, the history which he gave of the deluge, of the ark in which Noah was saved, of its resting on the highest point of the Armenian mountains, &c.[4] But since nothing of the kind is found in heathen records of the times before Alexander, at which time the Jews were still shut out from intercourse with the world; since, further, these notices coincide too nearly with the declarations of the sacred Scriptures to allow the possibility that they could have been derived from independent tradition, the assertion of *Berosus* in reference to his sources for the primitive age, (as

---

[1] He says, e. g. concerning the one under discussion, § 35 : ὁ δὲ γενναῖος ὑπὸ πολλῆς τοῦ λοιδορεῖν ἀκρασίας οἱ συνῆκεν, ὅτι ἱεροσυλεῖν οὐ κατὰ τὴν αὐτὴν φωνὴν Ἰουδαῖοι τοῖς Ἕλλησιν ὀνομάζομεν.

[2] Ὡς ἤκουσα παρὰ τῶν πρεσβυτέρων τῶν Αἰγυπτίων, c. Ap. 2. 2.

[3] Μωϋσῆν εἰν τὸ μεταξὺ τῆς Αἰγύπτου ἢ τῆς Ἀραβίας καλεῖται Σίναιον ἀναβάντα ἡμέραις τεσσαράκοντα κρυφθῆναι, κ.τ.λ. εἶναι τοῖς Ἰουδαίοις τοὺς νόμους.

[4] Josephus, contr. Ap. 1. 19.

respects later times he communicates also independent notices,) are to be taken as a bare pretence.

In this same category belongs also the account of *Dius*, which he pretends to have derived from ancient Phoenician sources, concerning the contest with problems between Hiram and Solomon,[1] where the fact at the foundation is evidently of Jewish origin, augmented with paltry additions which owe their existence to the national vanity of the Tyrians. Solomon, it is related, sent problems to Hiram, and received others from him, upon the condition that he who could not solve the problems proposed to him, should pay money to him who solved them. Hiram, failing to solve his problems, was obliged as penalty to pay a large sum. Finally, however, a man of Tyre, Abdemon, solved these problems and proposed others. Since Solomon could not solve the latter, he was obliged to pay back a large amount of money to Hiram.

The Jews, on their part, did not allow themselves to be found idle, and there was, between them and the Gentiles, an emulation in historical forgery, which must fill one who has first found the right position, with disgust at this whole species of literature, the remnant of which is handed down to us mostly by *Josephus*, especially in his books against Apion, and by Eusebius in his 'Preparatio Evangelica.' It is scarcely possible to be cautious enough here. Suspicion is the legitimate rule of the critic, and all accommodation is uncritical. Nothing was more frequent, than for the Jews to assume the garb of Gentiles, in order in this disguise to effectually weaken the calumniations of the Gentiles, to magnify the antiquity and greatness of their nation, from the apparent testimony of their enemies, and to confirm the credibility of their sacred books by pretended independent heathen tradition.[2]

How heathen fraud directly called forth the same thing among Jews, we will show by a single particularly striking example. *Artapanus*[3] relates that, according to the account of the Memphites, Moses, when he passed the Red Sea, waited for low water ; but it is entirely otherwise, according to the Heliopolites. They recognise the miraculous in the affair. Evidently the envy of the Egyptians had called forth the explanation of that which, on the

[1] Jos. c. Ap. 1. 17.
[2] The notices in Valckanaer, De Aristobulo Judaeo, p. 17 seq. may be compared.
[3] In Eusebius, IX. c. 27.

authority of the sacred books of the Jews, was current concerning the passage of the Red Sea, making it merely the result of the common laws of nature. Of this event, and the circumstances connected with it, the Egyptians (a people who have as little genius for history as the Indians) possessed no original, native information. This explanation, which accounts for the facts from natural phenomena, they gave not as such, but put it into the form of a parallel tradition of the Memphites, which was independent of the Jewish narrative. The masked Jew now opposes to the pretended authority of the Memphites, the equally assumed testimony of the Heliopolites.

We return after this digression. The Egyptians did not make use of Hebrew material alone. With equal impudence, and even earlier, they appropriated to themselves also that which belonged to the Greeks. *Heyne* expressly shows this, appealing, for an example, to the story of Proteus and Helen.[1] We will examine, a little more closely, the Egyptian narrative of Helen, in *Herodotus*,[2] since it furnishes for the account of *Manetho* concerning the Hycsos, according to our manner of understanding it, a very remarkable parallel. We premise that *Welker*[3] recognises nothing further in it than a transformation of material originally purely Greek, so as to gratify the national vanity of the Egyptians—a view which Bähr vainly opposes with the intention of bringing about a base accommodation. *Herodotus*, the good-natured admirer of Egyptian wisdom, asks his priests exactly how the matter stood with reference to Helen, implying that they must surely have the most certain knowledge upon the subject, and consequently provoking the deception itself; as indeed generally the credulity of the Greeks, and their childish admiration of Egyptian falsehood, has very much contributed to awaken the mere spirit of deception among this people. The priests now relate to him a long history, with the most characteristic circumstances, and much better devised than the Hycsos-fable of *Man-*

---

[1] L. c. pp. 108, 127 : Inoleveret Aegyptiis adeo illa interpretatio antiquitatis suae ex Graecis literis, ut sub Ptolemaeis et Romanis vix aliam ullam nossent. Pro exemplis sint narrationes de Proteo et de Helena, in quibus et hominum illorum vanitas, popularibus suis gloriam ex rebus Graecis comparantium et fabulas Graecas in cam fidei ...um, tum Herodoti his de rebus opinio apprimis intelligi n

[2] B. 2. 113—20. [3] Johan Jahr

etho. In the whole, the praise of the pretended Egyptian king Proteus, the magnifying of his wisdom and justice, is the 'punctum saliens.' In the Greek tradition, Egypt occupied but a subordinate place, here it is made prominent. The Egyptian king deprived the robber of his spoil. The Greeks go to Troy and take the city in vain. Menelaus first receives back his spouse from the hands of Proteus. Even here the Egyptians are not satisfied with self-praise; another's shadow must yield them light. Menelaus repays all favour and love with ingratitude. He steals away two Egyptian boys, and offers them in sacrifice. The whole, *Herodotus* allows to be imposed upon him, and supposes that *Homer* has deviated from the truth obtained among the Egyptians, since it was not suited to his poetical design!

We have before intimated that such stolen Greek goods are also found in *Manetho;* for example, the story of Armais=Danaus and Thuoris=Polybius.[1]

---

[1] It is not necessary to enter farther into the refutation of this strange theory propounded in this section, as its validity has been already examined in the preceding part of the volume. It may, however, be added, that Mr Cullemore has shown, from Egyptian chronology, that the dominion of the Hycsos is as well established as any other fact in ancient history. T.

www.ingramcontent.com/pod-product-compliance
Lightning Source LLC
Chambersburg PA
CBHW050901240426
43670CB00031B/2940